BERNARD INGHAM
EDITED BY IAIN DALE

THE SLOW DOWNFALL OF MARGARET THATCHER

THE DIARIES OF BERNARD INGHAM

Biteback Publishing

First published in Great Britain in 2019 by
Biteback Publishing Ltd
Westminster Tower
3 Albert Embankment
London SE1 7SP
Copyright © Bernard Ingham 2019

ISBN 978-1-78590-478-3

10 9 8 7 6 5 4 3 2 1

A CIP catalogue record for this book is available from the British Library.

Set in Adobe Caslon Pro and Didot

Printed and bound in Great Britain by
CPI Group (UK) Ltd, Croydon CR0 4YY

MIX
Paper from
responsible sources
FSC® C020471

To Nancy, my late wife, for making it all possible, and not forgetting the parliamentary lobby journalists, to give them their Sunday name, for adding spice.

CONTENTS

PRINCIPAL
CHARACTERS

ANNE ALLAN: Ingham's secretary

BRUCE ANDERSON: assistant editor, *Sunday Telegraph*

KENNETH BAKER: Education Secretary until July 1989, then chairman of the Conservative Party and Chancellor of the Duchy of Lancaster

MIKE BATES: No. 10 press officer

TONY BEVINS: political editor, *The Independent*

GEORGE BULL: former editor and editor-in-chief of *The Director* magazine; director of the Anglo-Japanese Economic Institute

ALASTAIR BURNET: ITN

SIR ROBIN BUTLER: Cabinet Secretary

PAUL CHANNON: Transport Secretary until July 1989

SARAH CHARMAN: No. 10 press officer

MICHAEL CHECKLAND: Director-General, BBC

KENNETH CLARKE: Health Secretary

DAVID ENGLISH: editor, *Daily Mail*

PAUL GRAY: economic affairs private secretary to the Prime Minister

GORDON GREIG: political editor, *Daily Mail*

EDWARD HEATH: former Conservative Prime Minister

MICHAEL HESELTINE: former Defence Secretary

BRIAN HITCHEN: editor, *Daily Star*

SIR GEOFFREY HOWE: Foreign Secretary until July 1989, then

Deputy Prime Minister, Leader of the House of Commons and Lord President of the Council

DOUGLAS HURD: Home Secretary until October 1989, then Foreign Secretary

PETER JENKINS: associate editor, *The Independent*

SIMON JENKINS: columnist, then editor of *The Times*

GEORGE JONES: political correspondent, *Daily Telegraph*

MICHAEL JONES: political editor, *Sunday Times*

SIR JOHN JUNOR: columnist, *Mail on Sunday*, and former long-time editor of the *Sunday Express*

TREVOR KAVANAGH: political editor, *The Sun*

TOM KING: Northern Ireland Secretary until July 1989, then Defence Secretary

NEIL KINNOCK: Leader of the Labour Party, Leader of the Opposition

NIGEL LAWSON: Chancellor of the Exchequer

MARK LENNOX-BOYD: parliamentary private secretary to the Prime Minister until July 1990

NICHOLAS LLOYD: editor, *Daily Express*

JOHN MACGREGOR: Agriculture Secretary until July 1989, then Education Secretary

MURDO MACLEAN: principal private secretary to the Chief Whip

JOHN MAJOR: Chief Secretary to the Treasury until July 1989, Foreign Secretary from July to October 1989, then Chancellor of the Exchequer

CHRIS MONCRIEFF: political editor, Press Association

PETER MORRISON: parliamentary private secretary to the Prime Minister from July 1990

COLIN MOYNIHAN: Sports minister

BRIAN MULRONEY: Prime Minister of Canada

ANNE NASH: head of the Information Officer Management Unit

DAVID NICHOLAS: editor, ITN

GUS O'DONNELL: press secretary to the Chancellor of the Exchequer

CECIL PARKINSON: Energy Secretary until July 1989, then Transport Secretary

CHRIS PATTEN: Minister for Overseas Development until July 1989, then Environment Secretary

TERRY PERKS: Ingham's deputy

PAUL POTTS: deputy editor, *Daily Express*

CHARLES POWELL: foreign affairs private secretary to the Prime Minister

CHARLES REISS: political editor, *Evening Standard*

TIM RENTON: Chief Whip from July 1989

NICHOLAS RIDLEY: Environment Secretary until July 1989, then Trade and Industry Secretary

MALCOLM RIFKIND: Scottish Secretary

GEORGE RUSSELL: chairman, Independent Broadcasting Authority

TONY SMITH: political editor, *Sunday Express*

NORMAN TEBBIT: former Cabinet minister and chairman of the Conservative Party

ANDREW TURNBULL: principal private secretary to the Prime Minister

DAVID WADDINGTON: Chief Whip until July 1989; Home Secretary from October 1989

JOHN WAKEHAM: Lord President of the Council until July 1989, then Energy Secretary

PETER WALKER: Welsh Secretary until May 1990 (having announced his intention to resign in March)

SIR ALAN WALTERS: chief economic adviser to the Prime Minister until October 1989

SIMON WALTERS: political correspondent, *The Sun*

(LORD) WILLIAM WHITELAW: former Deputy Leader of the Conservative Party and de facto Deputy Prime Minister

NIGEL WICKS: former principal private secretary to the Prime Minister

PEREGRINE WORSTHORNE: editor, *Sunday Telegraph*

LIST OF ACRONYMS

BMDF: British Management Data Foundation
BNFL: British Nuclear Fuels Ltd
CEGB: Central Electricity Generating Board
CHoGM: Commonwealth Heads of Government Meeting
COI: Central Office of Information
CPS: chief press secretary
CSCE: Commission on Security and Cooperation in Europe
DSS: Department of Social Security
EMS: European Monetary System
ERM: Exchange Rate Mechanism
FCO: Foreign and Commonwealth Office
FPA: Foreign Press Association
GATT: General Agreement on Tariffs and Trade
GIS: Government Information Service
IBA: Independent Broadcasting Authority
IOMU: Information Officer Management Unit
MAFF: Ministry of Agriculture, Fisheries and Food
MIO: Meeting of Information Officers
NASUWT: National Association of Schoolmasters Union of Women
    Teachers
NCB: National Coal Board
NUM: National Union of Mineworkers
NUT: National Union of Teachers
NPF: Newspaper Press Fund
PQ: Parliamentary Question
SNF: short-range nuclear forces

INTRODUCTION

THE LONG, SLOW ASSASSINATION

This book began to take shape after Charles Moore, Margaret Thatcher's authorised biographer, approached me in August 2017 for memories of her tenth anniversary in No. 10, which we celebrated in May 1989. At the age of eighty-five I needed to refresh my almost non-existent memory of this remarkable event, so I turned to notes I had kept at the time. These were not so much a diary as a record of my working day and what I, as the Prime Minister's chief press secretary, had to do. I began to see them as a historical document.

In fact, I kept notes daily from 1983, starting with Mrs Thatcher's visit to the Falklands six months after the recovery of the islands. I have resolved that if I survive the task of publishing this book, I shall transcribe them to provide a day-to-day record of the last eight years of her eleven-year tenure. This is always assuming I can read my handwriting, which often suffered at the end of a long day in No. 10.

The material is organised on a monthly basis – i.e. twenty-four chapters – broken down into weeks and then into a day-by-day insight into life in Mrs Thatcher's administrations. I have retailed sufficient record of home life to give you some idea of the life I led and have chosen to preserve the present tense of my notes to give the account greater immediacy.

To keep the text within reasonable compass, I should explain that invariably each weekday I got up at 6 a.m., drove into the office at 6.30, parking on Horse Guards Parade, and then started summarising the newspapers for the Prime Minister's more or less daily business meeting at 9 a.m. My secretary came in at 8 a.m. to type the three to four pages and produce half a dozen photocopies within the hour.

In the course of a normal working week, I or my deputy gave daily briefings to the lobby – political correspondents – at 11 a.m. and 4 p.m.; the Foreign Press Association (FPA) on Mondays; a European group on Tuesdays; the Association of American Correspondents just before lunch on Wednesdays; a group of UK provincial lobby journalists on Thursdays; and the Sunday lobby correspondents on Fridays. I also presided over a weekly meeting at 5 p.m. on Mondays of departmental heads of information, known as Meeting of Information Officers (MIO), to review the week gone by and prepare for the one ahead. Most weekdays I also had a lunch, generally with a journalist, and probably a dinner or an official reception. I tried to get home before the 9 p.m. BBC news and to bed by 11 p.m. unless I was at a dinner, a crisis was running or one of the first editions of the press contained an exclusive that left others catching up.

This was my basic workload, apart from reading mountains of government papers and trying to keep up with policy development and events and preparing a diary for as far ahead as possible for discussion with the PM on Fridays.

I imposed this agenda on myself when, soon after joining her staff in October 1979, I found that the PM did not read newspapers. I think she felt it was a waste of good reforming time. This presented a problem: how do you avoid your PM appearing to be out of touch on the floor of the House? My solution was to persuade the PM to read my digest of the day's press at her 9 a.m. business meeting. She used my press digest, supplemented by notes from radio and TV news and current affairs coverage, as the basis for her operations, especially on Tuesdays and Thursdays, when she took Prime

Minister's Questions (PMQs). The routine not only informed her but also her staff of her reactions to ideas and events. It was one of the most valuable things I did in her service.

In spite of an aching back whenever I sit too long at my computer, this book has given me great pleasure reliving old – and historic – times and reminded me how privileged I was to be in No. 10 in the 1980s and to have a wife who uncomplainingly put up with my long working days and frequent absences abroad. Fortunately, Mrs Thatcher saw weekends as being for families – except when she had to travel to summits, which all too often happened at weekends.

CHAPTER 1

JANUARY 1989: THE YEAR TAKES ITS TIME TO GET GOING

Politics, like the weather, are unseasonably mild until the last week of the month, when the PM goes over the top at a lobby party and causes ructions with Chancellor Nigel Lawson over Europe and economic issues. Normal service is also resumed with rows (real and manufactured) and leaks. I get a second job: head of the Government Information Service (GIS).

WEEK 1: 1–8 JANUARY

The year begins in a disarming way. A MORI poll gives the government a ten-point lead and Labour leader Neil Kinnock his lowest rating thus far.

I take the first four days off – that is, I do not go into the office until lunchtime on Thursday (5 January) to discover the usual logjam of paper awaiting digestion. At home – after reading at least eight newspapers a day from 7.30 a.m. – I spend my time gardening, painting and decorating, shopping and going for walks on the North Downs with my wife, watching TV and trying to summon up the determination to implement a New Year's resolution to slim. At fourteen and a half stone, I haven't been this heavy for more than twenty years. After dinner at a Chinese restaurant in Croydon and my 'last square meal' for the foreseeable future – a haggis from my Scottish secretary, Anne Allan – I go on short rations before returning to the office.

I feel very put out to find that my normal newsagent's is closed on New Year's Day. This means that I have to return home for some money to pay the open-all-hours Patels elsewhere in Purley for my comprehensive reading requirements. This reminds me that Mrs Thatcher has recently claimed that service in Britain is improving. I foolishly pass this on to the American correspondents, who laugh me to scorn. We Brits, they say, do not know the meaning of the words 'customer service'. (Heaven only knows what they would say now that the computer has eradicated the last vestiges of concern for the client.)

Not much disturbs the even tenor of our ways in this first entirely untypical week. The press give extensive coverage to a prime ministerial New Year interview on TV-am in which she counsels caution against revenge attacks for the blowing up of a Pan Am airliner above Lockerbie in the Scottish Borders on 21 December 1988 with the loss of 270 lives. Ironically, two days after her interview the US shoots down two Libyan MiGs over the Mediterranean on the very day of the Lockerbie memorial service.

Charles Powell, the PM's foreign affairs private secretary, rings to say that the government has conditionally agreed to attend a human rights conference in Moscow in 1991 if progress is maintained and human rights in the Soviet Union are statutorily reinforced. I curse myself the following day for not giving the story closer attention to bring out our requirement for the release of political prisoners, refuseniks and psychiatric ward inmates *and* the enshrinement of human rights in law.

My self-criticism takes a break when Iain Murray, a former No. 10 press officer from the Foreign and Commonwealth Office (FCO), returns to say hello. He is on leave from his posting to El Salvador, which he seems to be enjoying, even though he has five bodyguards and a machine gun on his roof. I tell him he was safer in No. 10, even if he was from the FCO, with which Mrs Thatcher has, shall we say, an awkward relationship.

On Thursday and Friday, I turn to the celebration of the PM's ten years in office, due on 4 May, first spending an hour with her vetting photos for inclusion in a commercial book and then writing a minute proposing a media programme to mark the anniversary. She accepts the broad outline of my suggestions. The first week ends with news of the death of Emperor Hirohito of Japan. Who, if anyone, will represent the Royal Family? And then, as I am thinking of going to bed, comes news of a British Midland aircraft crashing onto the M1 at Kegworth, near East Midlands Airport, killing forty-seven. Amazingly, seventy-nine survive. The PM will have to visit the scene tomorrow. Another thing sent to try Paul Channon, the Transport Secretary.

WEEK 2: 9–15 JANUARY

This is, as No. 10 weeks go, another gentle run-in for the Prime Minister, even though Parliament is back. She is not taxed at Prime Minister's Questions (PMQs) and would have had a relatively relaxed week but for the air crash and my arranging for her to give an interview to *Reader's Digest* at Chequers on a gloriously sunny Saturday. This goes well, as does the following lunch for the interviewers with the PM, and her guided tour of the house. My nose is kept to the grindstone and my main presentational preoccupations are:

1. Successfully pressing for an early announcement on which member of the Royal Family (the Duke of Edinburgh, it turns out) will go to Hirohito's funeral along with the Foreign Secretary;

2. Less successfully trying to clear a government line on a threatened takeover of the engineering giant GEC, which is beginning to take on distinct Westland undertones. Michael Heseltine is pressing for a referral to the Monopolies and Mergers Commission, while leading the bid is Sir John Cuckney, who piloted Westland into Sikorsky in 1986 after Heseltine walked out of Cabinet over his insistence that the Yeovil

firm should enter a non-existent European consortium.* I am charged at the PM's 9 a.m. business meeting with drafting a line to take, but the Department of Trade and Industry (DTI) has still not secured an agreed version of it by close of play. Incidentally, the Prime Minister shows a tender loving concern for me when the Lord President, John Wakeham, entirely reasonably suggests I should undertake the drafting. After all, I am in the business of communication. Mrs Thatcher bluntly asks, 'Why does he have to do all the work?' I begin to wonder before the week is over.

3. What we should say about Chancellor Nigel Lawson's unheralded trip to the USA to say farewell to his opposite number, Jim Baker, who is being made Secretary of State. I sometimes wonder whether ministers realise that the media are driven by conspiracy theory – what I call the John le Carré syndrome – when we spokesmen are left without authoritative briefing.

4. Lining up behind Paul Channon, who has been disgracefully blamed by the media for their jumping to conclusions and blaming the British Midland pilot for the crash twenty-four hours after they had hailed him a hero.

I am also under attack. *The Independent* elaborates on gossip in *The Guardian* about my ticking off ITV for putting up a cameraman to ask the PM a question at a 'mute' photo facility. Evidently, they do not know the meaning of 'mute'.

Then *The Scotsman* walks out of my lobby briefings, like *The Guardian* and *Independent* before it, because I refuse to end the tradition of No. 10 press secretaries briefing 'unattributably' instead of for direct quotation. In our parliamentary system, ministers are

---

* A Cabinet dispute over the future of Westland Helicopters had come to public attention in 1985–86, when Britain's last helicopter manufacturer was facing bankruptcy. Margaret Thatcher favoured a merger with the American company Sikorsky, while Defence Secretary Michael Heseltine pushed for a European consortium and eventually resigned over the issue. The public nature of the Westland affair, which featured a number of leaks to the press, was widely considered to breach the conventions of Cabinet government.

front men and press secretaries are preferably neither seen nor heard, though that is a bit difficult in this television age. *The Scotsman's* justification, like that of *The Guardian* and *The Independent*, is pure hypocrisy. They still continue to receive – even seek – unattributable briefings from ministers and officials. Michael Jones (*Sunday Times*) tells me that *The Guardian's* political correspondents wish to return to the lobby fold. Well, well!

In between all this I am offered the additional job of head of the GIS, or head of profession (information), as it is known. It comes at a meeting of a group considering the future of the Central Office of Information (COI), an organisation providing publicity services to government departments. Normally the head of the COI is head of profession, but the group proposes that the organisation should become an executive agency and its head downgraded (except when he or she becomes head of profession). I accept the charge, subject to the PM's approval and a satisfactory meeting with the Cabinet Secretary, Robin Butler, on my pay. I haven't a clue how I will cope with the extra workload, which, among other things, requires me to establish a man-management and training system for information officers.

WEEK 3: 16–22 JANUARY

This mild winter becomes a little colder but still refuses to warm up politically. The PM has untroubled passages through both PMQs sessions. Her 9 a.m. business meetings are identifying far more issues than ever emerge on the floor of the House. MPs even initially ignore reports of a meeting between William Waldegrave, Minister of State for the FCO, and Yasser Arafat during which Waldegrave is said to have predicted that Israel will be the loser if it fails to respond to PLO developments and described Yitzhak Shamir, the Israeli PM, as a reformed terrorist. We devise a line to dampen down the FCO's Arabist enthusiasm, but I feel I shall be lucky to get away without another No. 10/FCO row. Waldegrave subsequently has little trouble in answering a Private Notice

Question (PNQ) on the issue. Politics is becoming unreal. My administrative challenge is altogether too real. I seem to do very little else but attend meetings and write. This is how the week panned out:

Monday: Write briefs for the PM's meeting tomorrow with the Independent Broadcasting Authority (IBA) and for a video that the Department of Health (DoH) want the PM to make for the launch of its NHS review. I then wade through a host of questions posed by Christopher Ogden, the departing head of the *Time* bureau in London, for his book on the PM, clearing about two thirds of them.

Tuesday: Having worked for five years in the Department of Energy, I get involved in a discussion of the subject at the PM's business meeting, at the end of which she asks me if I am proposing to attend her next meeting on the current NHS review. I feel obliged to go. They seem to like my redraft of several paragraphs and then Tom King, Northern Ireland Secretary, suggests I should edit more of the text. I work on that before going with the PM to the IBA. An hour later I am back in another NHS review meeting, where my further redrafting gets a good reception.

Wednesday: By now I am running to keep up. I find that the Football Bill trying to make football grounds safe from hooligans gets a reasonably fair wind. (I have been deeply involved in this as a long-standing season-ticket holder at Crystal Palace and have found Colin Moynihan, Sports minister, a brave fighter.) The *Daily Mirror* wants a national identity card scheme as a panacea; the *Daily Telegraph* is half-hearted, *The Guardian* says it is 'unworkable' and, surprise, surprise, *The Independent* is beside itself with libertarian rage. I then talk to Paul Gray, the PM's economic affairs private secretary, and Romola Christopherson, the DoH's head of information, about a title for the NHS review. We favour 'Power to the Patient', with 'Putting Patients First' as first reserve. I then pay my first visit as head of the GIS to the Information Officer Management Unit (IOMU). Anne Nash and her team are impressive.

Thursday: John Major, Chief Secretary to the Treasury, pays his usual debriefing call on me after Cabinet and is amused by the *Evening Standard*, which is promoting Kenneth Baker, the Education Secretary, as the PM's heir apparent. Back to the NHS review. I seem to be the sub-editor of last resort, spending another generous hour on the document.

Friday: Shorthanded. Terry Perks, my deputy, is on a recce in Scotland for a prime ministerial visit and Simon Dugdale is with the PM in Basingstoke and later at a memorial service. I spend three hours on GIS work, including attending an IOMU training course ahead of the first reception in my room in No. 10 for information officers as part of my morale-boosting drive. It seems to achieve its objective and many of them are clearly delighted to be inside No. 10.

A relatively quiet weekend follows, though I spend a lot of time on reducing the usual pile of paper and writing a speech I have to make next month.

WEEK 4: 23–29 JANUARY

At last politics comes alive. The PM goes over the top at a lobby party with some vigorous briefing that brings trouble between the PM and Chancellor Nigel Lawson (a sign of things to come). And Peter Walker, Secretary of State for Wales, telephones in response to a *Daily Express* story to deny claims that he is in a resigning mood or has threatened to do so over his cherished plan for handing over all council houses to their tenants. (Retrospectively, another straw in the wind.)

The week begins with a telephone call to the PM from George Bush Sr, the new US President, on the day she unveils a statue to President Eisenhower in Grosvenor Square. The Anglo-US special relationship is cemented. In a ten-minute conversation, both declare their determination to work together. I spend a lot of time with the PM at the week-ahead and diary meetings, at her video recording of a foreword to the NHS review, and while clearing the answers to Christopher Ogden's file of questions for his book on the PM. In between, we hear reassuring news of John MacGregor, Agriculture Secretary, who is recovering after fainting and being taken to hospital while on EU business in Brussels. There are also reports of a major earthquake in Tajikistan. By way of light relief, a woman journalist at my Foreign Press Association briefing accuses me of being fat. This has everybody in stitches.

Tuesday: I manage to calm down the *Daily Mail*'s report of a row between the PM and the Chancellor, both of whom are exercised about the reportage. They both attended an evening lobby party at which the PM was very vigorous in her response to journalists' questions about a host of things. Indeed, we discover she went over the top on economic policy, the European Monetary System (EMS), Euromoney, mortgage tax relief and the alleged row between her and the Chancellor. She denies she ever talked about the EMS at the lobby party. The *Financial Times* says she did. The Sunday press seems likely to keep up the level of noise, since Michael Jones proposes to write, on the basis of her party remarks, that she would only meet the South African President, P. W. Botha, at the border of South Africa.

I take this 'row over the garden fence' with the Chancellor head-on, briefing on it unprompted at the lobby and at a lunch with David English (editor, *Daily Mail*), who has been stirring it up. 'Bunkum and balderdash' comes through in *The Times*. But matters are not helped by a speech by the Chancellor on EMS at Chatham House that causes the PM angst. Indeed, I note she is 'spitting mad'. Oh dear. On Friday, I have to cancel lunch with the *FT* in order to catch up with all the work and reduce my weekend reading to two briefcases. During the afternoon, Alastair Burnet (ITN) comes in to brief me about ITN developments, notably the likelihood that David Nicholas, with whom I have a good relationship, will be made chairman and editor-in-chief. George Russell, head of the IBA, tells me that he is rather taken with my idea that ITN should come under the IBA. I am astonished that he is taking this notion seriously and stress that it was only a throwaway thought. I must be more careful.

At last, the publication of the NHS review approaches (due on Monday 30 January). But Robin Cook, Labour shadow minister, interrupts my weekend with a pretty blatant leak of its contents. What is there left to say? When I get the document, it looks good, even if the title, 'Working for Patients', is less imaginative than we might have hoped. The lobby takes its usual interest in the possibility of a leak inquiry.

The PM does not think Robin Cook has done himself any good with his leak. Paul Gray and I suggest that she might dub him the 'Official Receiver of the Labour Party' and she asks me to keep it to myself until she has had a chance to use it in PMQs. In the House, Kinnock refuses to censure his side for receiving documents and says that the government is in no position to talk when the last minister to leak (Leon Brittan, DTI, in the Westland affair) was knighted and sent off to Brussels as European Community (EC) Commissioner.

We get news on 30 January that Mikhail Gorbachev is to visit the PM in April. Coverage comes with what is thought to be critical FCO activity over Gibraltar force levels and the impending expulsion of Soviet spies. The latter report causes such a prime ministerial eruption that I wonder whether the Foreign Secretary, Sir Geoffrey Howe, is long for this political world. I keep quiet about it. Otherwise I would have six months of misery.

All this in a week in which I decide to soldier on as chief press secretary (CPS) until the next election, due in 1992, when I shall be sixty, in spite of lucrative offers from outside the civil service. Am I mad? Not really. I believe you should do what you really enjoy doing. We do not doubt whether the PM will go on until 1992 in spite of the rumblings with the Treasury and FCO. I reach my decision after seeing Sir Robin Butler about my remuneration for doing two jobs. I get the impression that the system does not want to promote me to Grade 2 (deputy secretary), so I bid for 20 per cent of my existing salary while reckoning it might turn out to be 10 per cent.

I end the month briefing the Westminster branch of the Institute of British Management on my job. They seem to think I am a phenomenon coping with what a CPS has to do.

CHAPTER 2

FEBRUARY 1989: IS THIS WHERE THE PRIME MINISTER'S TROUBLES BEGIN?

Again politics remain as benign as the weather for most of the month. Journalists complain I am slipping because there is no news. And then an 11 per cent government lead in a MORI poll recorded early this month evaporates in a Harris poll into a narrow lead for Labour. Trouble almost inevitably ahead, given that the Tories become paranoid when behind. The PM is appalled by the number of criticisms of the government recorded in my press digests. We are also assailed by listeria hysteria – a follow-up to Edwina Currie's resignation two months ago as a junior Department of Health minister after shattering the egg market with a claim that most British egg production is infected with salmonella – and Iran puts a fatwa *on Salman Rushdie over his book* The Satanic Verses.

WEEK 5: 1–5 FEBRUARY

My friends say I look tired and Jean Caines, a former deputy in No. 10, asks me in a meeting if she is keeping me awake. Perhaps it is the anti-climax to the NHS review, which has had a good press. Only the *Mirror* and *Guardian* are against the proposed reforms or critical of most of them. I tell the PM when we go in to bat on writing her speech on Friday to the Newspaper Press Fund (NPF) in Glasgow that, if the *Mirror* and *Guardian* are against it, the government must be right. She thinks Kenneth Clarke, Health Secretary, has done 'an extremely good job' in presenting the review. Incidentally, she perked up yesterday with the news that Robert Maxwell, owner of the *Mirror*, is to retire from public life.

After two hours, we are, I think, almost there with the speech for the NPF lunch, allowing me to catch up with a backlog of telephone calls. Otherwise, I am determined to delegate today and my deputy, Terry Perks, takes both the lobby meetings and the weekly briefing of the American correspondents. The result is that I feel to be on top of things by 7 p.m. when I go home.

On Thursday, I put the Glasgow speech finally to bed – or so I think. Terry returns from briefing her about the mechanics of the visit to Glasgow to report that she now wonders whether she has got the right speech. Ye Gods! I can't spend any more time on it. In any case, I think it is a good speech that will throw a rather large brick into the pool of Scottish politics, where the constitutional conference involving opposition parties is falling apart.

I spend an hour after the PM's 9 a.m. business meeting revising the text. I then plunge into a series of meetings with the Chief Secretary for his post-Cabinet briefing and, among others, Robert Rhodes James MP, who is proposing to write a book about Denis Thatcher.

In between, I get a call from Cecil Parkinson, Energy Secretary, about Charles Reiss's front-page lead in the *Evening Standard* (*ES*) claiming that No. 10 knows the identity of the leaker of material about an alleged reshuffle of the government. I have to tell him that gossip has identified him as the hand behind a leak on creating room at the top. He categorically denies responsibility. Then Alan Clark, Trade minister, calls me worrying about another aspect of the reshuffle leak.

At last, Glasgow, on Friday. We are going through a lean period for the press, if you ignore Ted Heath's claim that the No. 10 press office is being used in a corrupt way. On the way to Northolt for the flight to Glasgow, the PM asks me whether she should write to Heath over his 'disgraceful' remark. I tell her not to waste her time. After all, Heath has already called me 'a menace to the constitution'. To which I retorted at the time, 'Well, he should know. He abolished Yorkshire in 1974 and that is a very unconstitutional thing to do.'

We drive through a wet Glasgow to the Holiday Inn, where an audience of 680 – a positive gathering of the clans – awaits after an endless round of photocalls. The PM's speech is astonishingly well received bearing in mind the number of opponents in the audience, including Gordon Brown MP and Jim Sillars MP. She throws down a challenge to the meaning of devolution and the concept of Scotland as a separate nation state within the EC. Her uncompromising message leads the news bulletins and raises the devolutionist/separatist argument to a new level.

Curiously, the speech gets little coverage in the London papers, but Jim Rodger, the indefatigable NPF organiser in Scotland, telephones on Saturday to say he has never known such publicity. 'Terrific,' he says. I send the PM a note on this and on a MORI poll giving the government an eleven-point lead. Incidentally, Rodger sent my secretary, Anne Allan, a beautiful bouquet yesterday because she could not get to the NPF event in her native Glasgow.

On a lovely Sunday, Bruce Anderson of the *Sunday Telegraph* questions in an article whether I should remain a civil servant or become a political appointee, but adds that 'as a man of impeccable integrity' I would not do anything that Donald Maitland, Heath's press secretary, would not have done. Quite. I go out to admire our wonderful display of snowdrops. Inside, I prepare a brief for the announcement next week of my second job, watch England Rugby Union draw 11–11 with Scotland and repeatedly play Elgar's haunting violin concerto.

WEEK 6: 6–12 FEBRUARY

The media lust after Edwina Currie's blood because she declines to give evidence before the Agriculture Select Committee. She says she has nothing to add to what the public already know. They claim she is going to write a book about it, whereas, in fact, she is planning a book on health issues and how to keep fit. I put over these points at the morning lobby and they are reinforced by her letter to the select committee. But at the end of the day on Monday, I fear that only half a tale is being told on TV and that the committee is being strengthened in its resolve to make her give evidence.

The PM, at her 9 a.m. meeting on Tuesday, feels the NHS review needs to be hammered home more. At noon, I see Alan Clark over his worries about being blamed for the reshuffle leak, which, among other imagined moves, would send Kenneth Baker to the Home Office. I tell him not to worry. I have advised the PM that he was only having a joke and she has not reacted adversely.

The newspapers are rather empty today, though Edwina Currie continues to cause concern. She only reluctantly goes along with Lord President John Wakeham's strategy of writing to the select committee to set out her stall, because she does not think it will work. It doesn't, so she writes another letter asking to be allowed to get on with her life. That only increases the pressure, so she agrees 'for friendship's sake' to meet the committee even if she has nothing to say. Collapse of strategy. The PM thinks she would have been better advised to stand on her rights and freedoms as an MP.

The Cabinet Secretary tells me that I am to be promoted to deputy secretary from 1 August. The promotion will give me not much more money but higher rank after eleven years as an under-secretary. I then plunge into a series of lobby meetings and one with the Lord President at the House on televising the Commons.

A quiet day on Wednesday. I duck the 4 p.m. lobby because Mrs Currie is giving evidence before the select committee and, as I thought, there is little interest in No. 10. She does not answer a single question against her will and generally underlines the futility of the exercise. I am afraid this select committee is not interested in getting to the bottom of the salmonella issue but to lay on a show in which it stars with Cruella. The following day's press raises my spirits. Mrs Currie is seen to have wiped the floor with the parliamentarians, who are treated with disdain, contempt etc. The PM is delighted because she believes Mrs Currie's summons raises serious questions about the liberty of an individual MP.

Some of the broadsheets are critical of the privatisation of water supply as a 'natural monopoly'. But food dominates the Cabinet, with no inclination by either the Ministry of Agriculture (MAFF) or the Department of Health to underplay the seriousness of the salmonella problem.

Departmental heads of information are summoned to a meeting with the Cabinet Secretary to announce my appointment as head of the GIS and of Mike Devereau as Director-General of the COI. Mine is not going to be an easy job. After another drinks party in my room for departmental information officers, my wife and I celebrate my promotion at the Savoy Grill with Geoffrey Tucker, a PR consultant and former director of publicity at Tory Central Office, and his wife.

To my relief, my promotion goes quietly, though *The Guardian* and *Independent* (who else?) attack it. *The Independent* toughens up its 'mocking' headline from earlier editions, according to the Cabinet Secretary, no doubt after organising the opposition.

Sarah Charman, press officer, says Chris Moncrieff, political editor of the news agency the Press Association (PA), rang last night in something of a panic, believing I was giving up the press secretary job. Michael Jones tells me he has taken *The Guardian* and *Independent* to task in an article for Sunday. Bill Deedes (*Daily Telegraph*) does a snide piece on Saturday about my appointment. I respond in military terms – from Col. Ingham, as he describes me, to General Deedes.

Back then to salmonella. The press is still going mad on food poisoning. I decide we really have to sort out this issue. I therefore write a brief for MAFF, the Department of Health and an internal group that has been charged with advising the government on microbiological issues. I tell the media that many people will be amazed that they have made it to fifty-seven (my age) in view of all the bugs they encounter along the way. My Saturday evening is disturbed by Jim Coe, MAFF head of information and another former deputy of mine in No. 10, to say that the PM is to approve legislation to make it a criminal offence to sell contaminated food. This is news to me.

Eggs and food are still on the media's menu on Sunday. My defence of Mrs Currie comes through in the press. I restore myself with a walk on the North Downs with my wife.

WEEK 7: 13–19 FEBRUARY

The week starts with an enjoyable and successful dinner with the BBC – Duke Hussey, chairman; Joel Barnett, deputy chairman; Michael Checkland, Director-General (DG); and John Birt, the next DG. Among other things, we defiantly ingest soft cheese. Before the PM leaves for a 10 p.m. vote in the Commons, she voices her objection in principle to a compulsory levy in the form of the BBC's licence fee. On the way to the House, she judges that the BBC has improved considerably under Duke Hussey.

I am getting testy about listeria hysteria. On Tuesday, I ask the media why they should expect anyone to be open with them when they distort and interpret what is said in briefings out of sight. The Labour Party, bereft of policy, is reduced to playing on alleged discrepancies arising not necessarily from what ministers are saying but what they are interpreted as saying. I try to stoke up the PM on this issue in her 9 a.m. meeting but she does not act as decisively as I would have hoped, perhaps because she is awaiting a report from the advisory group. I have to play a dead bat at the 11 a.m. lobby before a meeting with MAFF and the Department of Health to try to get some discipline into presentation. This is not easy with the *Daily Mail*, under the headline 'Foot in mouth disease', reporting alleged discrepancies between John MacGregor (MAFF) and Kenneth Clarke (Department of Health).

I try to secure a decisive line for the PM at PMQs this afternoon. The result is a 75-minute meeting with the Chief Medical Officer, ministers and other officials that thrashes out a three- to four-page comment.

Neil Kinnock, who has latterly reduced his questioning of the PM at PMQs to a few words, first elicits the fact that the PM had Cheshire cheese for lunch, delivered that very day by a Cheshire mayor. Then she reads out the agreed line. I have no difficulty at the subsequent lobby.

Before I go to the Civil Service College in Sunningdale to talk about government and media, I learn that Max Hastings (editor of the *Daily Telegraph*) is threatening to pull out of the lobby if he does not get his man on the PM's plane on a future trip and is trying to use Charles Powell to apply pressure. I warn Charles off.

I am out for the third night running on Wednesday as guest of Dan McGeachie of Conoco at the Institute of Petroleum dinner. This is becoming ridiculous. I am also eating like a horse. The day begins with a visit to TV-am, where I have a breakfast meeting with Bruce Gyngell, who seems to be a dynamic leader. I am impressed with their operation while retaining my worries about the glitter of TV. They tell me that government departments are not taking the channel seriously. I shall try to sort this out.

Lunch is with Jeffrey Archer in his flat and with such fellow guests as Adam Faith, the singer and, later, financial journalist; the film director Bryan Forbes; the Spanish Ambassador; the lawyer and Labour peer Lord Mishcon; and Lawrie McMenemy, a former manager of, among other clubs, Sunderland, who confesses to being bored with life, though not surely at an Archer lunch.

Between breakfast and lunch I am invited to the Cabinet Secretary's weekly meeting of Permanent Secretaries (heads of department) to enlist their support for my efforts to reorganise the GIS. A lot of them are sympathetic.

I stay at No. 10 overnight and, as usual with my routine broken, I feel a bit scruffy in the morning. The press is scruffy, too. The PM is appalled by the catalogue of niggles and complaints about the government as set out in my digest, which also records a Gallup poll that gives her only a 1.5-point lead – a very substantial drop in support, apparently because of distrust of the government's NHS policy. I also record some good news: unemployment is down below two million for the first time in eight years.

My preoccupation on Thursday is to get on top of pay review body reports and the Cabinet's debate on the economy. I am resolved not to let the *fatwa* against Salman Rushdie swamp us. I give a briefing at the FCO on the PM's summit next week with Chancellor Kohl in Frankfurt. At PMQs, Kinnock asks sharply how the government's anti-inflationary policies are proceeding. The PM says, 'They are proceeding,' which is rather a false start.

Next morning, I put on my 'Thank God It's Friday' tie and sally forth confidently. There is a hint in the press that the government is being too soft on the Iranians for threatening Rushdie's life. I urge the PM not to rise to Kinnock's bait and to use her next major speech to rebut the charge that the government is generally going too far, too fast. At lunchtime, I have a third drinks party for government information officers. They are not exactly young but clearly delighted to be invited to No. 10 and to meet each other. The Sunday lobby leaves me uneasy, given their propensity for going over the top. Will they lead on food poisoning, the forthcoming Budget or the economic background to the Budget?

At the weekend, Rushdie apologises for any offence *The Satanic Verses* may have caused, but Iran does not lift the *fatwa*, assuming anyone thought it would. The Sunday press comes as a relief in that they do no worse than say that inflation will get worse before it gets better. But the government is getting a bad press on Rushdie, though Peregrine Worsthorne (*Sunday Telegraph*) attacks intellectuals like Rushdie for portraying Britain as a police state and then being only too ready to be protected by it.

WEEK 8: 20–26 FEBRUARY

Off to Frankfurt for a summit with German Chancellor Helmut Kohl. No sooner is the PM in the VIP suite at Northolt than she is on the phone to the Foreign Secretary, telling him in no uncertain terms that he is being too soft with Iran over Rushdie and warning him he will be responsible for the staff of our Tehran Embassy if anything goes wrong. It is such a stiff lecture that she seeks re-assurance from us during the flight. The trouble is that Geoffrey Howe simply cannot handle the PM. He just sits there and takes it instead of winning her respect by having a spirited argument with her. Mind you, it is as well to have a good case.

After lunch at the Bundesbank, we go to the cathedral and then to Goethe's house, where she quotes Goethe to the curator: 'What-ever thy father bequeath thee, thou must earn it anew' – a rather quaint but accurate summary of the PM's emphasis on individu-al responsibility. On to the Paulskirche, site of the first German Parliament, followed by summit talks in the town hall. They dance around short-range nuclear forces (SNF). This is not a summit for shattering relations.

I am debriefed by the PM on her talks, sipping champagne, and then change for the opera before briefing the press – all in forty minutes.

We stay in Frankfurt overnight before we leave after breakfast for Belfast to an ecumenical memorial service for victims of IRA atrocities. Last year British soldiers were killed in Lisburn and Ballygawley. For security reasons, nobody knows the next stop is Northern Ireland.

The PM is worrying about my note last week about the belief that the government is doing too much, too fast, but we manage to concentrate her mind on the press conference with Kohl before she leaves Frankfurt. All goes well until she reads out to Kohl her line on SNF and defence.* Before the press conference, I urge her

---

* In disarmament talks, the Prime Minister's position was to maintain parity of nuclear and conventional weaponry, with arms to be modernised where necessary. She rejected 'zero options' on the grounds that nuclear weaponry could not be disinvented. Gorbachev had waged a successful effort to win over German opinion for a denuclearised Germany. Chan-cellor Kohl, while initially holding firm, was under pressure from his Foreign Minister, Hans-Dietrich Genscher, to weaken.

to read out that line in English. She gives a masterly performance while Kohl tears up bits of paper. She 'does a Boycott' (i.e. stone-walls) in the face of the *FT*'s hostile bowling. There is little coverage in the London tabloids the next day. The broadsheets see it as a successful failure – it did not resolve the SNF issue but was friendly.

Back in No. 10, I (and later Charles Powell) see a very attractive Austrian politician, Hannes Androsch, who wants to inform the UK what he is doing in central Europe to secure management expertise to ease the pain of any transition from Communism. On then to the Henley Management College to give them my well-worn routine on government and media.

At last, a threat of snow in this mild winter, Thursday bringing light coverings that soon melt in the sun. Today's press is so bitty that we have to put our thinking caps on at the PM's briefing for PMQs. I note that a curt prime ministerial response to Kinnock's short question puts him off. I envisage monosyllabic exchanges in future, which causes some hilarity.

Time has run away with me this week and my in-tray shows it. But I don't get much opportunity to attack it because of meetings with the Lord President on televising the House; a briefing on the Paris summit next week; and a meeting with the Chief Secretary after Cabinet before clearing the cover for a report on inner cities. I then host another party for government information officers.

Not much doing on Friday, which enables me to regain control by 8.30 p.m., when I leave for home – the earliest this week. But there is trouble on Saturday – a Harris poll puts Labour one point ahead (42–41), followed by Gallup placing the parties neck and neck (35–35). This should shake the Tories. Iran also looks to be going sour, with the Iranian Parliament threatening to break off relations with the UK over *The Satanic Verses*. They will have to be taught that the UK does not ban books – unless they are written, as *Spycatcher* was, by former secret service agents with a duty of confidentiality. We go for a brisk walk into a freezing wind across the old Croydon Airport.

Up at 5 a.m. on Monday (27 February) to be driven to Northolt for a
7.20 a.m. Andover flight to a summit with President François Mitterrand in Paris. I am soon installed in the Elysée Palace reading
the papers before a plenary at 12.15 p.m. There is hardly any story in
this apart from UK concerns about the French exclusion of Nissan
(UK) from the French market, except as part of the Japanese quota.
Instead, the media are still preoccupied with Rushdie, about whom
there is nothing new for the press conference.

I am back in No. 10 by 4.30 p.m. – this is really ridiculous –
to take the 5 p.m. MIO meeting. Having been driven from home to
Northolt, I decide to walk off some fat to Victoria to get the train
home. Next day, Trevor Kavanagh and Simon Walters (*The Sun*)
tell me I am slipping – no news. Consequently, the lobby goes on a
fishing expedition for morsels. It seems to take hours.

My wife and I end the month with an enjoyable dinner at Beotys
with Michael and Sheila Jones. He tells me that the *Sunday Times*
paid Willie Whitelaw £100,000 for his memoirs, which produced
next to nothing by way of indiscretion. I am not surprised by his
discretion. The only other noteworthy event of the day is the PM
being interviewed by a certain V. Korotik of *Ogoniok*, a Russian
magazine. Poor chap, he can scarcely get a word in. The PM has a
severe dose of verbal salmonella.

CHAPTER 3

MARCH 1989: 'WE ARE A GRANDMOTHER'

Celebrating the birth of their first grandchild, the PM famously tells the press: 'We are a grandmother.' The trouble this month – apart from a 13 per cent interest rate – is that for some reason she lacks concentration. I warn her later that a skittish press will latch on to any indiscretion or slip of the tongue to make fun of her. Consequently, for the second time in my life I ask a minister to be as dull as ditchwater for a change. The month ends with a lead in the polls and a tour of Africa – Morocco, Nigeria, Zimbabwe, Malawi and Namibia – with the PM hailed as 'The Great Rainmaker' in Marrakesh.

WEEK 9: 1–5 MARCH

The outstanding event of the week is news of the birth of the Thatchers' first grandchild. It will never be forgotten because the PM tells the media outside No. 10: 'We are a grandmother.' I do wish these grannies would not allow their delight to transpose the first-person singular into the Royal 'We'. It is very wearing on press secretaries.

The PM gives me a note about the details of the birth of Michael Thatcher at 9.30 on Friday morning. I give the news to the PA at 12.30 p.m. and inevitably it leads the bulletins, especially after the PM has used the Royal 'We'. I shall never live this down, since PMs are thought to be intensively rehearsed before they utter a word to the world.

I suppose it adds to the gaiety of the nation. It is badly in need of it with the interest rate static at 13 per cent as the PM tries to recover control of inflation after Chancellor Lawson's disastrous private enterprise ploy, behind both the PM's and the Cabinet's back, to contain it by shadowing the D-Mark at three D-Marks to the pound.

Otherwise, the week is grindingly busy but dull. The American correspondents turn out in force to quiz me over Salman Rushdie, listeria hysteria and the environment, notably about the ozone layer, which is reportedly thinning dangerously.

I lunch with the BBC (Michael Checkland and Margaret Douglas) on Wednesday. This enables me to reflect the government's concerns about reportage of the BSE inquiry findings, in which ministers felt the BBC set itself above the official inquiry; and the Thames TV programme *Death on the Rock*, broadcast seven weeks after three IRA members were shot dead last year in Gibraltar. The latter caused great concern in the government and the PM accused Lord Windlesham, a former Tory minister and vastly experienced in TV, of bias in his independent inquiry report. Both Checkland and Ms Douglas support Windlesham's report because of his integrity. Checkland gives me a tome: BBC guidance to staff. It will make interesting reading, always assuming I ever find the time.

I spend the afternoon seeing the Institution of Professional Civil Servants in my capacity as head of the GIS; taking the 4 p.m. lobby, at which Gordon Greig (*Daily Mail*) is at his outstandingly cheeky best after a good lunch; and briefing Peter Hannam (*Eastern Daily Press*).

Next day, the tabloids – notably the *Daily Star*, *Today* and *Daily Mail* – come down hard on the all-knowing and infallible Agriculture Select Committee for its report on salmonella in eggs. The *Daily Telegraph* makes the point that it is genuinely difficult for the government to time its interventions in these matters. I am busy rejecting on the basis of current knowledge front-page stories that next year the government is to ban the use of chlorofluorocarbons

(CFCs), which have been identified as damaging the ozone layer, in fridges, along with lead in petrol. I also have to knock down a *Guardian* crib from *Private Eye* that the PM has intervened to change the route of the Channel Tunnel rail link.

Cabinet decides to put more effort into communicating the virtues of the Water Privatisation Bill as an environmental measure. A day later comes Michael Thatcher's entry into the world. That evening, my wife and I go to the Festival Hall for Elgar and Mahler with Mr and Mrs Mick Newmarch (Prudential). Felicity Lott leads a spirited rendering of 'Happy Birthday' at the end for the conductor, Bernard Haitink.

And so to a Saturday break, if I am lucky. I am not. I am in some difficulty with the press allegation that the PM has criticised Environment ministers over their handling of the Water Privatisation Bill. On the evidence of her own words on TV, that is a reasonable assumption, but I surmise (correctly, thank heavens) from the ITN broadcast that she is criticising not ministers but the opposition and media for their distortion and misrepresentation.

Then the No. 10 press office rings to say there has been a rail crash just north of Purley, where I live. Two people have died and many are injured. The PM visits the injured in Mayday Hospital, Croydon, the next day following a European conference on the ozone layer in London. Chris Patten, former Tory Party chairman, agrees with me that it is an imposition to have to turn out on a Sunday to discuss the atmosphere, though it must be said that the issue causes great anguish among the opposition parties. They must be infuriated that the PM has taken a trick by attending a conference on it on a Sunday of all days.

WEEK 10: 6–12 MARCH

It is far too nice to be working. The press is full of the Purley rail crash and ritualistic leaders on the need for the culprits to be found and public confidence restored. All this becomes very pointed when there is another fatal rail crash in Glasgow on Monday.

The opposition and unions, and especially John Prescott (shadow Transport Secretary), blame the government for its alleged lack of funding for all and sundry.

Most of the coverage of the ozone conference is positive. Twenty participating countries have decided to sign the Montreal Protocol on the control of substances affecting the ozone layer and another eleven are thinking very seriously of doing so. At the end of a busy day with meetings with the PM and Lord President Wakeham, the FPA briefing, two lobbies and the usual Monday evening MIO, I have to write two minutes to the PM: one to try to stop the Central Statistical Office from being swallowed by the Treasury – it must be seen to be independent – and one for the concluding press conference on the ozone layer.

All would have gone well at the press conference the next day if Nicholas Ridley (Environment Secretary) had not corrected the PM on the UK's contribution to the UN Environment Programme. She makes a meal of it and feeds speculation that she is at loggerheads with him, which is anything but the truth. This carries over into PMQs when Kinnock asks her when she is going to sack Ridley. Instead of showing disdain, she goes on the offensive in defence of Ridley. Later she confesses she has had a bad PMQs – one of the worst for a long time.

The trouble is that for some reason she is wayward these days. She is simply not concentrating and we shall have to do something about it. I think the problem at PMQs is that she is a serious politician and Kinnock a jokey one. They simply do not mix. She has to find a way of putting him down. I have made umpteen suggestions – including, latterly, to stop using the Royal 'We'. The opposition see that as a new way of getting at her.

With some misgivings, I go to Manchester on Wednesday to speak at the North West Fuel Luncheon Club – a link with my days at the Department of Energy (1974–79). I have misgivings partly because the PM seems to want me to be involved in writing her speech for Newcastle on Thursday, and partly because of my travelling to Manchester by train. These crashes are inevitably at the back of your mind and my peace of mind is not improved when the 7.30 a.m. train leaves ten minutes late because of a fault, is diverted by way of Northampton, and then crawls through Cheshire, arriving at Manchester Piccadilly thirty minutes late. My patient son, John, a journalist working in the north, takes me to the Piccadilly Hotel for a chinwag before we go to Trafford Park for a hugely attended lunch.

In the afternoon, I see the COI staff in Manchester as head of the GIS and get back to No. 10 for 8.30 p.m. I am immediately whisked upstairs to help with the Newcastle speech for thirty minutes. My contribution is 'Howay the lads'. This causes trouble when I tell the press office next day. Simon Dugdale, who worked in the Newcastle COI office before moving to No. 10, says that Jimmy Carter used the phrase on a visit to the north-east with Jim Callaghan. We substitute 'Gan on, mi canny lad'. In the end, probably wisely, the PM uses neither at Gateshead that evening. And to think we civil servants spend our time on Geordie sayings.

Before she flies to Newcastle with Ridley and my deputy, we prepare her assiduously for the short, sharp Kinnock question at PMQs. So what does he do? He ignores the argument about toxic waste generated by a select committee report, goes bipartisan over the killing overnight of two soldiers in Northern Ireland and then asks whether the PM will put money into the Channel Tunnel rail link. No dice on the latter. PMQs are thus something of a non-event, but I note that she seems to have the support of Tory MPs. By Jove, we are getting jumpy!

Before PMQs, the PM gives a clear hint in Cabinet that she is thinking of going to the country in 1991, in the context of Queen's Speech strategy. The Cabinet settles the legislative programme – another heavy one – for the third session of this parliament.

Before the PM goes on to Liverpool from Newcastle, we hear that Birds Eye is to close its factory at Knowsley, Merseyside, with the loss of 1,000 jobs, because the workers – or more likely the unions – won't cooperate to raise productivity and reduce costs. I suggest down the line that the PM might say that this is more of a blow to Merseyside than to her, sorry though she is about the threat to jobs.

A very enjoyable lunch with David Nicholas (editor, ITN) at the Savoy. He wants to thank me for my help over the years and discuss my throwaway idea some months ago of the ITN coming under the wing of the IBA, which he favours.

The lobby for Sunday newspapers, like the general one at 11 a.m., is virtually bereft of questions. They don't even ask me about The Great Paris Cheese Mystery retailed in *The Spectator*. I am alleged to have said during the Paris press conference a fortnight ago that Camembert can kill you. I may have had such an irreverent thought, since I am fed up with listeria hysteria, but I have no recollection of uttering it audibly, even to those sitting next to me.

Saturday is crowded socially since I, Sarah Charman and my secretary are taking advantage of the perk of showing relatives and friends around No. 10. Over lunch at home after the No. 10 tour, my wife and I have a rare old reminisce around Halifax with Mr and Mrs Ian Gillis – he being head of information at the Department of Energy. All of us used to work in Halifax. In fact, Nancy and I met in court there. I should hasten to add that she, a policewoman, was the court usher and I a reporter.

Charles Powell rings me up on Sunday seeking my view on the Sunday press. It is bitty, fractious and uneasy about the government and the PM's performance – her use of the Royal 'We' etc. – and calling for a reshuffle. *The Observer* has a go at The Great Paris Cheese Mystery. My wife and I go for a wet and windy walk on Riddlesdown. My brother, Derek, a farmer, keeps me in touch with the real world: he has had four calves born this week.

WEEK 11: 13–19 MARCH

Paul Gray briefs me on the Budget. It is going to be a dull affair, but the Chancellor will get criticised for not raising the tax on alcohol and tobacco to keep down inflation. It will also build expectations of big tax cuts in the next two years. Some journalists have got the drift but no detail.

The PM meets Brian Mulroney, Prime Minister of Canada, and King Hussein of Jordan and then vice-chancellors of universities. I lunch with the perceptive Paul Barker, columnist and former editor of *New Society*, who followed me at Hebden Bridge Grammar School. Returning to No. 10 after the 4 p.m. lobby, I encounter Kenneth Baker, Education Secretary, who says that he and the PM have had a good meeting with vice-chancellors. My immediate reaction is to say, 'That sounds serious. How much has it cost?' He gives me a lecture that the PM cannot take on everyone. I point out that she has to take on every spendthrift every day of her life.

As forecast, Tuesday's Budget is boring, but Cabinet colleagues acknowledge that Chancellor Lawson has taken notice of their views.

Before all this, I find a way of telling the PM to be more careful about what she says, since the media will latch on to any indiscretion or infelicitous expression just as they did with 'We are a grandmother'. Her objective must be to starve them out by being as dull as ditchwater. This reminds me of my advice to the anti-EC Tony Benn around 1974–75 when he became chairman of the EC Energy Council. I said that the Brussels press would pounce on anything remotely anti-Brussels. He promised to 'bore for Britain'. And, by Jove, did he bore – mellifluously and surefootedly.

On Wednesday, the BBC disrupts my evening party for the Buckingham Palace press office. Earlier I had lunch with Martin Dowle and, I thought, Mike Baker (BBC), and made it clear that No. 10 knew nothing about a 22 per cent rise in water charges and objected to announcing such news in answer to a Parliamentary Question (PQ) at the last minute. Under questioning as to whom the PM was criticising when she said that water privatisation had not been well handled, I say the government – i.e. ministers generally. They could not leave presentation just to the parent department. She most certainly was not attacking Nick Ridley or Michael Howard, Minister of State at the Department of the Environment, who was doing a remarkable job processing the Bill through the Commons.

Imagine my surprise, with the Buckingham Palace party about to start, when the BBC 6 p.m. bulletin claims that the PM is to take charge of water privatisation and is critical of Michael Howard. It even flashes up my photo, implying that I am the informant. I work until 7.45 p.m. to try to sort this out with several talks with Ridley, a tough exchange with Michael Howard and some very rough talking to Dowle. I issue a 'bunkum and balderdash' response through the PA. I fear I do not have much time for my Buckingham Palace guests.

It turns out that I did not have lunch with Dowle and Baker but with Dowle and a Lance Price (who eventually became deputy to Alastair Campbell in No. 10).

The following day, the BBC claims at 6.35 a.m. that I rubbished Michael Howard, but curiously little of this comes through in the press. I give the PM a full written account of my lunch and copy it to the Chief Secretary and the Chief Whip. After reading it, the PM wonders why she pays the BBC two licence fees and thinks of getting rid of one of her TV sets. John Major detects that I did not sleep much last night because of all this and tells me not to worry about it. I fully expect it to be raised in PMQs, but, apart from references to aspects of water privatisation, only Paddy Ashdown comes close, asking the PM whether she regards something as 'bunkum and balderdash'.

Earlier in the week, the Cabinet Office informed me that I was still on the IRA's hunted list and should vary my route home. So I drive Sarah Charman to Putney and Beth Frier, my deputy's secretary, on to Croydon via Wimbledon. That should confuse 'em.

On Friday, I get steamed up about a *Mirror* front-page attack on Transport Secretary Paul Channon with a headline 'Sorry, you're dead. Warning lost in post'. I stoke up Tristan Garel-Jones, a senior whip, who gets an Early Day Motion tabled, which I dictate, calling for Robert Maxwell to apologise for his disgraceful journalism and his treatment of Channon. Gill Samuel, head of information at the Department of Transport, calls to say how much this is appreciated.

An extensive programme of meetings follows on the diary; the IOMU; another drinks party for government information officers; lunch with Frank Melville, Bill Tuohy and Don Cook (American correspondents) on the occasion of Cook's retirement; and the Sunday lobby.

On Saturday, the PM dominates the civilised – indeed, wonderful – discussion at dinner with my wife; Geoffrey and Margit Goodman, he being the political editor of the *Mirror*; Monty and Betty Meth, he the former industrial editor of the *Daily Mail*; and Mr and Mrs Richard Dixon, ITN. This hotbed of socialism does not so much as mention Neil Kinnock and is very good natured as I defend the government's line on the NHS, electricity privatisation and whether politicians get isolated from the people. I interpret the evening as their wondering when the PM will pack up and give us all a rest.

Nigel Lawson gets a reasonable Sunday press for his Budget and Peregrine Worsthorne claims that the editors of the *Sunday Times* and *Observer* have let the side down by cavorting with a remarkable lady, Pamella Bordes, otherwise known as Bordello. Poor old Paul Channon continues to get it in the neck over the Lockerbie disaster; a monstrous injustice.

WEEK 12: 20–26 MARCH

The press challenges Paul Channon to sue them for claiming he lied about his briefing last Wednesday that the authorities knew the Lockerbie bomber. I do not believe that, even if the authorities did know, he would ever say so. It turns out that he lunched with Julia Langdon (*Daily Mirror*), Geoffrey Parkhouse (*Glasgow Herald*), Ian Aitken (*Guardian*), Robin Oakley (*Times*) and Chris Buckland (*Daily Express*).

I advise Channon and Lord President Wakeham to take a tough line with the lobby. Its members have clearly broken the rules about unattributable briefing and must make it clear that the story is not correct. Parkhouse could do this as chairman of the lobby. I get exceedingly ratty at lobby briefings over the allegation. I have lunch with the regional lobby, brief the FPA, preside over MIO and, with Nancy, attend the PM's general reception.

On Tuesday, the *Mirror* accuses Channon of lying and the press is full of accounts of last Wednesday's lunch at the Garrick, where, to compound the abuse, discussions are supposed to be private. I report to the PM and Channon the lobby's attempt to keep the story going. The PM resolves to stand firm and to try to preserve the integrity of the lobby system, even if its members don't. As we meet, we learn that the Speaker has accepted a PNQ from Kinnock on the issue. Kinnock makes an awful mess of the occasion, leaving John Prescott with steam coming out of his ears, while Channon puts up a stout performance.

I then write a speech for the PM for the *Daily Star* awards lunch tomorrow. Paul Potts (deputy editor, *Daily Express*), acting as a go-between for Lord Stevens (chairman of United Newspapers), enquires whether I would like the editorship of the *Yorkshire Post*. Indeed, I would, but I cannot accept, having just become head of the GIS and having promised to stay as CPS until 1992, when I shall be sixty.

A busy morning on Wednesday, what with advising on the 'popular' version of a White Paper on the abolition of the National Dock Labour Scheme, briefing the lobby, meeting a Swiss editor and talking to Paul Channon. Then off to the Inn on the Park with the PM for the *Daily Star* awards lunch. I sit next to John Junor (columnist, *Mail on Sunday*, formerly long-time editor of the *Sunday Express*), who is pretty disagreeable about government policy, the PM's presentation and Channon, who, he says, should have resigned. Today's press acknowledges Channon did well in the House but its knife is so deep into him that I fear it is only a temporary reprieve.

The PM performs brilliantly distributing the awards, which come with generally inspiring stories of fortitude. But for the first time she momentarily breaks down in public when Brian Hitchen (editor, *Daily Star*) presents her with a Gold Star award and the audience rises to sing 'Land of Hope and Glory'. On the way back to No. 10, the PM says, somewhat reproachfully, that she wishes she had been given notice of her award. Indeed, but that would have spoiled it.

Dinner with Alastair Burnet and Sue Tinson (ITN). Get home 10.30 p.m.

Then off for three days in the north. My wife accompanies me to the office and waits until I have done the press digest. Still more trouble for Transport. Last night Geoffrey Holland, a former colleague at the Department of Employment (1968–73), rang me to say that the press are calling for a statement about a van carrying gelignite that has blown up in Peterborough, causing the death of a fireman. He explained that this is a matter for the Department of Transport and the Health and Safety Executive. I get to work on a reaction.

My gamble of doing a press digest for the PM pays off. The traffic has eased by the time we get on the road. It still takes a slow five hours to Halifax, where we visit Nancy's two sisters living in different parts of the area; my brother's farm at Triangle, near Halifax; and my son and his wife at their cosy canal-side cottage in Lymm, Cheshire. We eat well, walk a lot and are refreshed by the wild, windy weather. Wuthering Heights must be really wuthering, but we do not have time to go up and find out.

On Saturday, Michael Jones phones me to report a MORI poll giving the Tories a four-point lead (44–40). I phone this through to Chequers. We return home next day and I spend the rest of it preparing for next week's tour of Africa. Without enquiring of me, *The Observer* says wrongly that I am to be the next editor of the *Yorkshire Post*.

WEEK 13: 27 MARCH–2 APRIL

Morocco. Before we leave for Marrakesh, we learn that *The Guardian*'s average poll gives the Tories a three-point lead and that the PM's old handbag has fetched £2,000 for charity. There is also a persistent leak, probably from the Tory backbench 1922 Committee, that some of the proceeds of water privatisation will go to environmental and infrastructural improvements.

A 3-hour 15-minute flight takes us to Marrakesh, where it is pouring with rain which continues into the night. Paths at the swish Hotel La Mamounia are awash and our cars make bow waves. Ministers and officials at our lunch speak only French but we gather they are enthusiastic about the arrival of 'The Great Rainmaker'. 'She can come again,' they say. The PM has lunch with the King's womenfolk – the Crown Prince's mother, the King's No. 1 wife, three daughters and some cousins. The King sends a message that he will see the PM at 4.30 p.m. Later I discover that the press are claiming that the King kept a very prompt PM waiting for an hour. A ludicrous story. Next day I rebuke them over it on the plane's Tannoy. The atmosphere is frosty and the *Evening Standard*, according to No. 10 press office, is claiming that No. 10–media relations are at an all-time low. The travelling press treat me very warily when Paul Reynolds (BBC) tells them that I told him they are 'shits', as indeed I did. But however sore I feel about their behaviour, this must be the end of it.

We have magnificent views crossing the Sahara on Tuesday en route to Nigeria, where the PM meets President Ibrahim Babangida before a brief press conference at which he pays tribute to the PM's helpfulness. Then we are off to Zimbabwe, where we arrive at 10 p.m. to a warm welcome from President Robert Mugabe and his government. We get to our hotel at 1 a.m., only to find that our luggage has not arrived.

Rumours are beginning to circulate that we are going to Namibia, which is about to get independence. I have necessarily to play a straight bat on this until 9 a.m. on Saturday.

Wednesday is a military day in Zimbabwe. We fly by helicopter for an hour, roughly east, to Nyanga, about thirty miles from the Mozambique border. The military are very welcoming and take the party down to the meeting place, overlooking a tumbling river. President Mugabe is joined by Joaquim Chissano, President of Mozambique. The outcome is a perceived need to expose the Renamo* rebels in Mozambique as a brutal bunch of bandits. Back in Harare, our splendid High Commissioner, Ramsay Melluish, gives a reception and dinner at which I sit next to Zimbabwe's first President, Canaan Banana, who tells me he speaks ten languages.

Our second day in Zimbabwe is spent inspecting rural developments in the Mount Darwin area. In a village, amid the singing and dancing, I spot posters emblazoned 'Comrade Thatcher' and 'Lady Thatcher'. Oh dear, what will the press make of this? The PM donates on behalf of Britain a new classroom and footballs (Brazilian and bought in Harare because Lillywhites' supply had not turned up from London). She is given baskets of wood carvings after announcing funds for water supply improvements and the creation of a clothes washing area for the women. Gordon Greig says this is becoming an expensive visit. While the Minister of Agriculture waxes eloquent, three women of the village enact a ritual that ends with flagellation. And before the PM, too.

On then with gifts, including fearsome lances, we fly to Algy Cluff's gold mine at Bindura. The PM bangs a drum to launch the Freda Rebecca mine and sees gold cast in a bar. After an uneventful press conference back in Harare on Thursday, we fly to Malawi to a warm evening reception in Blantyre.

I try to keep awake at ninety-year-old President Hastings Banda's long welcoming banquet on Friday by retracing our eventful day in Malawi. We leave at 8.15 for a helicopter flight over mountains and crocodile-infested swamps in a valley recovering from devastating floods, to a Mozambique refugee camp. Some have just arrived,

---

* A guerrilla organisation that sought to overthrow the government of Mozambique.

looking vacant, shocked and all in, though not ill fed. What hope is there for them? Their despair is a moving experience. A huge crowd gathers at the centre of the camp and the biggest cheer comes not from offers of help but the PM's hope that they will soon find it possible to return to their homeland.

We visit a tractor rehabilitation factory and meet the Mayor of Blantyre in his medieval regalia – he is a wonderful speaker – and the PM is given the keys to the city. On then by helicopter to a tea estate and macadamia nut groves and finally back to Blantyre for the exchange of gifts. I get a yard-tall ashtray carved in wood. And so to the banquet.

Dr Banda does not start his panoramic view of the twentieth century until 11.18 p.m. precisely. I am told that Denis Thatcher wakes up at 11.45 to discover Dr Banda becalmed in 1964, whereupon he tugs the dress of Madam Cecelia Kadzamira, the power behind the throne, to say we have had enough. By some remarkable telepathy she conveys the message to Dr Banda, who winds up at 11.53. DT, as he is called, is invaluable on tour. We get to bed early on Saturday morning.

From Blantyre to Windhoek, Namibia. For security reasons, I tell the press our next stop is Windhoek only when we have taken off. Our departure from Blantyre began dangerously. Dr Banda, ninety, in his open-topped claret Rolls-Royce, stops quickly to have the hood put up, causing a squealing of brakes and much tyre-burning in the cavalcade. We have music, singing and dancing all the way to the plane.

Our journey takes us across the Kalahari Desert to a series of aircraft swaps in Namibia. The first flight takes us to a subdued Leopard Valley camp, where the British 30th Signals detachment in the UN Transition Assistance Group (formed in 1988 to lead Namibia to independence) has just lost two men. A young officer, Philippa Owens, attracts a great deal of attention in this dangerous male world. We lunch on bangers and mash in the camp before flying on to the deep pit in the Earth's surface that is the Rossing uranium mine. There, we learn what the company operating it is doing for the native workers in the mining town of Arandis. On then to Windhoek, an attractive back-of-beyond capital dazzling in the clear light.

The PM opens the British Liaison Office, unveiling a plaque, raising the flag and then lowering it to half-mast out of respect for the two soldiers killed. Her talks with, among others, Martti Ahtisaari, the new Finnish UN Special Representative, and the celebrated UN peacekeeper General Prem Chand take on a sense of crisis because of a bloody incursion from Angola that has left two policemen and thirty-eight of the invading SWAPO dead. I arrange for the PM to give a brief press conference to put across British support for the UN's authority.

Before we leave for home, the PM has one more engagement: forty-five minutes for talks with Pik Botha, the South African Foreign Minister, who is somewhat hysterical about the SWAPO incursion. He wants to break the UN peacekeeping agreement by sending in troops. The PM, accompanied by Robin Renwick, our Ambassador in South Africa, tells him bluntly he could bring the UN agreement crashing down if he does. South Africa should take no unilateral action without the consent of the UN.

As the discussion goes round in circles, I get agitated. The PM says in open meeting that she presumes I am worried about what the press will make of the length of the talks. I nod, whereupon she winds up the meeting rather quickly. The press think that the PM looks cross as the plane is leaving for home an hour late. I think this was a good day's work.

We land at Heathrow at 9 a.m. on Sunday. Nothing much seems to have happened while the PM has been away. I shift accumulated paper for an hour before going home. Charles Powell disturbs home life to say that Lord Young, Industry Secretary, is blaming me for leaking plans for a briefing for the PM this evening on Lonrho and the fallout from the battle for Harrods.* I ask the DTI to convey to him my anger at the suggestion.

The Sunday press gives the PM's tour a good show, some of it devoted to the crisis talks on the SWAPO incursion.

---

* In 1985, the Egyptian businessman Mohamed Al Fayed and his brothers bought the House of Fraser group, which included Harrods department store, for £615 million. A significant proportion of the shares were acquired from Roland 'Tiny' Rowland's Lonrho group, which had mounted a bitterly fought campaign for ownership. Rowland claimed the brothers had lied about their background and their wealth and pressured the Department of Trade and Industry to launch an inquiry. The resulting report, leaked by *The Observer* on 30 March, concluded that the brothers had indeed been dishonest about the wealth, but did not advocate further action.

CHAPTER 4

APRIL 1989: THE HILLSBOROUGH FOOTBALL TRAGEDY

Our African adventures are followed by a visit by Mikhail Gorbachev and a trip to Luxembourg for a Commission on Security and Cooperation in Europe (CSCE) conference.

Welsh Secretary Peter Walker manifests more Tory unrest with a speech before a by-election wanting less monetarism and more intervention.

Then, in the middle of the month, comes the cruel Hillsborough football disaster, which kills ninety-six spectators. The PM visits the scene next day. Paradoxically, this involves me deeply in saving the Football Spectators Bill to make grounds safer. Along with Charles Powell, I get a lot of flak over the Westland affair three years ago and from leaks and assorted conspiracy theories.

For a little light relief, the PM sweeps Downing Street to promote a cleaner Westminster – of litter, as distinct from conspiracy theories.

WEEK 14: 3–9 APRIL

On Monday it seems that the PM may well have saved Namibian independence. A UN investigation reports that it agrees with the South African contention that SWAPO crossed the Namibian border in force. I am tired and slow to face up to a visit by Mikhail Gorbachev this week. He is now in Cuba after his 'Shamrock and Sickle' summit in Ireland. Lord Young gives a powerful statement to the Lords on Lonrho/Harrods but is castigated in the course of the day by the PM for accusing me of leaking about the Sunday briefing.

Tuesday brings the coldest day of the winter so far. At a briefing on the Gorbachev visit I have a run-in with Hella Pick (*Guardian*), who brings to the occasion a whining objection that makes my hackles rise. To compound the problem, she comes in to see Charles Powell during the afternoon behind my back. Have people no shame? When I leave for home at 8 p.m., I am concerned to see the press office still working on media passes for the Gorbachev visit. Later, No. 10's security adviser agrees that Tom, Dick and Harry should not have to come into No. 10's entrance hall to collect their passes. We shall have to find a more secure way of distributing them.

On Wednesday, Gordon Greig resurrects the Westland affair of 1986, reporting that Leon Brittan, then Industry Secretary, has said in a ITV interview that Charles Powell and I gave our express approval for leaking the Solicitor General's letter to Michael Heseltine pointing out some 'material inaccuracies' in Heseltine's earlier letter. This is tommyrot. I told the DTI I did not like the idea of leaking the letter one little bit and when they said they wanted me to leak it, I replied, 'No. I won't do that. I have to keep the PM above this sort of thing.' I am afraid that the DTI has never been concerned about the facts in this case. I refuse to comment on Brittan's allegation. John Cole (BBC), my host at lunch at the Athenaeum, is embarrassed when a radio reporter turns up as we are leaving to quiz me about the affair.

Cabinet at 8.30 a.m. on Thursday before Gorbachev arrives at 10 a.m. He pauses en route to the PM's study to remark on the number of girls lining his way on the corridor. This is not surprising since two thirds of the staff are female. At 12.30, when Mrs Gorbachev and Eduard Shevardnadze, Soviet Foreign Minister, arrive for the signing of agreements, I get a quick run-down on the talks from Charles Powell and successively brief the lobby and the FPA on an interim basis. All this with a migraine – the first for years. I lunch at my desk after the PM and Gorbachev have spoken to the press in the street before going off to Westminster Abbey. I have a good chat with the PM at 2.50 p.m. and Charles gives me a good run-down on the Gorbachev visit at 3.30 before I brief the lobby and the FPA more substantially. I get a lot of paper shifted in the evening after the photocall at the dinner for the Gorbachevs. I brief the press on the dinner at 11 p.m. and then go home.

Next day, there is a good press for the Gorbachevs' visit. While Gorbachev and the PM are speaking at the Guildhall, I write an opening statement and brief for the PM's press conference later in the day. The PM returns very late – 4.20 p.m. – to No. 10. I then brief her hurriedly outside the Cabinet Room for what turns out to be a gentle press conference followed by six radio and TV interviews. I think the press office has passed the test. I get away at 9 p.m.

Grand National Day on Saturday, on which I lose £11 but our son backs the winner. I am somewhat delayed in my reading an excellent and extensive Gorbachev press because Charles rings to report that he had a message from Gorbachev in the middle of the night about a nuclear submarine going down south of Bear Island. Gorbachev had assured him that there is a negligible threat of an explosion or nuclear contamination. After arranging for the press office to send the story to the PA, I give my lawns their first mow of the year.

The next day, Peregrine Worsthorne does a vicious piece in the *Sunday Telegraph* about the government, No. 10, Charles and myself. And Robert Harris (*Sunday Times*) does his usual grossly inaccurate job on both Charles and me. [I once told Harris to stick to fiction. He took my advice and, dammit, he has made a fortune.] After gardening and a nap, I get myself more or less up to date with one eye on the Nottingham Forest–Luton Littlewoods Cup final.

WEEK 15: 10–16 APRIL

I learn early that the PM's plane was fired upon above Malawi last week from Mozambique by its army, who are very twitchy about Renamo. Intelligence indicates that they fired a shell with a range of 10,000 ft. Fortunately, we were then at 15,000 ft. I cannot share the news with the press. It shows you that we lead a dangerous life with Mrs Thatcher.

I am leading anything but a dangerous life today. The PM tells me outside the Cabinet Room that after the Worsthorne leader in the *Sunday Telegraph* yesterday she does not want to see either the *Daily* or the *Sunday Telegraph* again and does not propose to buy them or let the taxpayer do so on her behalf. The list of acceptable newspapers becomes ever shorter, but I must read the lot, however unacceptable, if only to monitor their criticisms.

I lunch with Peter Luff, a PR consultant, and General Mangham, of the Brewers' Society, at Selfridges and learn a great deal about the brewing industry. Only two journalists turn up for my FPA briefing. After MIO, I see a German civil servant who wants to know the secret of the PM's 'tight control' over her government – unlike, by implication, Chancellor Kohl's in Bonn. I stress the importance of her twice-weekly PMQs sessions in the House.

Ironically, this very evening, Peter Walker makes a speech challenging the government's reliance on monetarism and calling for more intervention. Not much sign of 'tight control' here. It is a moot point whether Walker has said anything new, but the media play it up and my three lobbies (one with the regionals) on Tuesday try hard to get me to react angrily and quotably. We have enough trouble round our necks at the moment, so, with immense restraint, I point out that Walker is carrying out government policy like his predecessor – a policy that has created the conditions in which Wales and other parts of the country are expanding.

At PMQs, Kinnock raises the Westland affair, perhaps taking his cue from Michael White (*Guardian*), who says we should be harried. Later, we learn that the issue may be reopened by a select committee. An excellent dinner at the Moroccan Embassy with officials from Zimbabwe, Malawi and the Sudan to mark the PM's tour.

I start the next day with nausea, for which I blame anti-malaria pills. Thank goodness, another gentle day. I am unfortunately getting a lot of press coverage and Charles Powell comes along to show me yesterday's Hansard recording some outrageous allegations – notably by Labour MPs Tam Dalyell and David Winnick – about both of us.

Later, I have meetings on televising the House and then, as head of the GIS, with senior officers at Scotland Yard on finding them a new director of public affairs because the present incumbent is moving on.

Peter Walker's behaviour at Cabinet on Thursday is watched with interest. Apparently outside the Cabinet Room, where ministers foregather, he concentrates on a conversation with Tony Newton (Chancellor of the Duchy of Lancaster), to the exclusion of all others. Then in Cabinet I am told he parks himself out of the PM's vision. There is no eye contact – only atmospherics – and he resists all temptation to say a few words. Some colleagues wonder what possessed him to make such a speech before a by-election on 4 May. After Cabinet, Chief Secretary John Major is pretty uptight about his behaviour.

Picture, if you can, the PM sweeping Downing Street and swilling away pigeon droppings. This burst of cleanliness on Friday is to publicise the campaign by Lady Porter, leader of Westminster Council, for a cleaner Westminster. The *Evening Standard* correctly reports that the PM waved to me as I watched her manual labour from behind the curtains in my office – the one with the bow front to the right of No. 10's black door. After a meeting with Anne Nash (IOMU) to prepare for the GIS's weekend conference in a fortnight, and lunch with Robin Esser (editor, *Sunday Express*) at the Café Royal, I learn that Scotland Yard want their next director of public affairs to be in-house. Somebody has leaked my visit to see the Commissioner, implying that No. 10 is seeking to put its own man in the job. More conspiracy theory producing absolute rubbish.

A lovely Saturday that turns to tragedy. While I am gardening, Nancy hears of the Hillsborough disaster over the wireless. From that moment, my time is consumed by the unfolding tragedy, during which an initial of five dead becomes ninety-three. (Eventually a total of ninety-six die at the Nottingham Forest *v* Liverpool Cup semi-final in Sheffield.) I soon receive my instructions for tomorrow: the PM flies by helicopter at 10 a.m. to the scene. Our son, John, rings up to say the Bradford *v* Ipswich match he was covering was much interrupted by the developing horror, and returning home to Cheshire he saw coaches on the M62 with many empty seats.

Before we leave for Hillsborough I have a big row with Charles Powell because of a paragraph in the *Sunday Telegraph* in which his friends exonerate him over the Westland affair and blame me. He is utterly embarrassed and I am very angry. But what really matters today is the PM's visit to Hillsborough.

We land on the police sports field nearby. The police are strangely silent, accepting that they opened a gate because of the crush outside the Leppings Lane end of the ground.

They (the police) gave the impression that a large number of Liverpool fans turned up late without tickets determined to get in. It then seems that the police panicked into opening a gate because they thought the fans might climb over the turnstiles. They went through a tunnel and in the process crushed spectators up against anti-hooligan metal nets.

The PM inspects the Leppings Lane end and gives the media good rations, announcing an inquiry and £500,000 to the appeal before the trauma of visits to two hospitals. It is a harrowing business looking at rows of lads in intensive care with no one knowing whether they will awaken or, if they do, whether they will be brain damaged. Football has a lot to answer for.

WEEK 16: 17–23 APRIL

The press gives massive coverage to the Hillsborough disaster and I am still haunted by the sight of rows of lads in intensive care. The police get it in the neck along with the management of football. I am left wondering how long it will be before allegations made by the police against drunken Liverpool fans will surface.

At 11.30 I am called to a meeting on the Football Spectators Bill.[*]

---

[*] Three months earlier, the Football Spectators Bill had begun making its way through Parliament. Motivated by a number of stadium disasters in which football fans had lost their lives, the legislation aimed to combat football hooliganism by using an ID card system to ban known perpetrators from attending matches.

Lots of Tories want to kill it and some ministers want to delay it, but not Colin Moynihan, Sports minister. Eventually, I write a note to the PM saying that she will be portrayed as acknowledging she was wrong all along if she agrees to drop or postpone it. She fights back and eventually I come up with a compromise based on all-seater stadia and all-member spectators. It does not quite carry the day in the Commons, but it is better than it might have been. Because of all this, I have to cancel a lunch and my FPA briefing to keep up with work. After the 4 p.m. lobby and MIO, I have a ninety-minute meeting on the weekend GIS conference planned for York. Then I have dinner with Gennadi Gerasimov, the Soviets' foreign affairs spokesman, and Deputy Foreign Secretary Vladimir Petrovsky. Gerasimov is wooden but I get on with Petrovsky like a house on fire. We talk about Stalingrad, which I once visited on holiday.

Off to Luxembourg on Tuesday after the PM opens the London Information Forum – a follow-up to the formation of the Commission on Security and Cooperation in Europe. I hope her tough passage on the abuse of freedom from a lack of respect for fact, fairness and balance discomfits the media, who get no change from her on the ban on IRA spokesmen. Petrovsky meets the PM immediately before her speech to invite her to Russia in June next year – and specifically to Kiev. I can't wait. I love Kiev.

In Luxembourg, we have an audience with the Grand Duke and bilateral talks at this CSCE celebration with Franz Vranitzky, the Austrian Chancellor; Javier Pérez de Cuéllar, UN Secretary General; and Nikolai Ryzhkov, the Soviet Prime Minister, who is visiting Western Europe for the first time. I give a press briefing at the Embassy and manage to brief the No. 10 press office before dinner with fellow spokesmen at a lovely castle in the countryside. A slightly Ruritanian day ends back in London; at 10.30 I decide to go home rather than stay at No. 10.

A troublesome day on Wednesday. The allegations against Liverpool supporters, which broke surface yesterday, dominate the press. It all deteriorates into an unseemly argument between the police in

Sheffield and Liverpool, and the South Yorkshire Chief Constable banning his men from discussing the incident. Home Secretary Douglas Hurd pleads for calm at a press gallery lunch. Tory backbenchers are in an emotional state about the Football Spectators Bill, and Lord President Wakeham, standing in for the PM at PMQs yesterday, could not damp them down. I argue that it would be better to get an enabling Bill through the House and construct a scheme to protect football crowds in the light of the Hillsborough Inquiry's findings.

I clear my lines with the PM on how to mark her tenth anniversary as premier next month before lunch with Robin Janvrin, the Queen's new press secretary.

What a week! The Football Spectators Bill again arises at 9.30 on Thursday, with Tory backbenchers' opposition to it continuing in a controversial, back-biting way. Irrationally, they seem to find something unseemly in trying to improve the safety of stadia after ninety-six deaths. It is clear before Cabinet that all the PM's colleagues would capitulate to the Bill's opposition apart from that doughty fighter Colin Moynihan. I am called upon yet again to 'steady the buffs', as Denis Thatcher puts it, and do so in pretty blunt terms. This has the desired effect of achieving a solution. The government will seek to pass legislation this session, with a couple of months' slippage, in the hope that a firm stand by the PM and ministers has some impact on Tory backbenchers. They are helped by Kinnock at PMQs by his being objectionable to the PM. This wins over her backbenchers. Colin Moynihan and I are sent out of the pre-Cabinet meeting to draft a speaking note, returning with it after Cabinet for another fifty minutes with her.

In the evening, I have another GIS drinks party – this time for deputy heads of departmental information divisions.

On Friday, I tell the PM that the press is a joy to read today. The tabloids take little interest in Hillsborough because the PM, ably abetted by Kinnock with his male chauvinist rudeness, has killed it. There is a hint in the broadsheets that the government has climbed down on the Football Spectators Bill. This is explicitly stated by *The Guardian*, which says 'the lady is for turning'. I tell her before a meeting on broadcasting that this is a small price for putting the issue to rest for a bit. Who would have thought the government would have ended the week in such a good state?

Murdo Maclean, the Chief Whip's principal private secretary, calls in to say that I singlehandedly saved the Football Spectators Bill. That is overstating it a bit, but I do not overestimate my popularity with ministers.

Press office then troops off for dinner to say farewell to Colleen Harris, our sparkling Guyanan press officer, who is moving on and upwards. (She later becomes Prince Charles's press secretary.)

On Saturday, my wife and I go as guests to Ascot for an entertaining but financially bleak day. I find that the press is full of alarmist stuff about Bonn's conversion to the 'Scrap SNF, don't modernise' line. We brief that what matters is the view of NATO members. An admirably firm US President, George Bush rings the PM late afternoon.

The Sunday press has calmed down over Hillsborough and treats the German retreat from SNF responsibly. I get rather a lot – too much – publicity, with *The Observer* describing me as 'the most influential Yorkshireman'. Whatever next? An *Observer* poll gives the Tories a three-point lead.

WEEK 17: 24–30 APRIL

BBC journalists are on strike so there is no *Today* programme on Monday. In No. 10 we bear this with fortitude bordering on equanimity. There are lots of foreign stories and at one stage we thought that we might add to them: two trips by the PM to Russia next year and in 1991. But our Moscow Embassy tells me they have not completed discussions on 1991. Nothing really seems to catch fire today.

Next day, we are preoccupied with the health of the NATO alliance, as a result of the German-engineered crisis over SNF – or, more properly, the crisis engineered by Hans-Dietrich Genscher, the

German Foreign Minister, who leads the minor liberal party, FDP, in a coalition. What an indictment of proportional representation! It is clear from my briefings that the PM's forthcoming visit to Deidesheim will, in the media's view, generate a severe handbagging for Chancellor Kohl. The man who ought to get it in the neck is Genscher.

In between all this, I get on top of my work, including the editing of a report by the Lord President on alcohol misuse. To No. 10's surprise, Kinnock leads on SNF at PMQs in a very simplistic way. He is becoming ever more eccentric. After all, the PM cannot lose on SNF. Is he thinking straight?

In the evening, I meet Peter Vey, director of communications at the Central Electricity Generating Board (CEGB), to bring me up to date on its privatisation. It seems to be going well, but at enormous expense.

Frost on Wednesday. I hope it does not damage our apple blossom. It is perhaps the right way to start Global Warming Day. The press have interpreted my press briefing yesterday to mean that the PM will go over Kohl's head to appeal to the German people in Ludwigshafen at the weekend. A Tube strike is threatened for 8 May.

At 9.30, I go to the PM's global warming seminar, which is handled well by the scientists. It seems that warming is taking place faster and more extensively than experienced historically and that doing nothing is not an option. What is fascinating is the inter-reaction of winds, waves, tides, the Gulf Stream, oceans, ice caps, forests and plankton. We have a fascinating day in good humour and some canvassing for funds for more research.

I brief in No. 12 Downing Street, the offices of the Chief Whip, with the Department of the Environment's chief scientist for thirty-five minutes and then rush over to the House for a meeting with the Lord President and the Chief Whip, David Waddington, on handling difficult select committees. Before I go, Professor Ian Fells of Newcastle University tells me that engineers have to take decisions while scientists do more research. He also offers me a visiting professorship at Newcastle on government/industry communications. I shall have to clear my lines with the Cabinet Secretary.

On Thursday, I am very pleased with the coverage of the global warming conference, bearing in mind that no conclusions were reached. What comes over very strongly is the nuclear power option. The PM asks me whether I led the press on this. I tell her that I did brief fully on this aspect of the discussion without pushing it. She seems content, even pleased.

Cabinet is concerned about the growing ambitions of the EC over its competence, and the PM signals her intention to have this further considered. Cabinet does not deal with entry into the EC's Exchange Rate Mechanism (ERM), which has surfaced in the press today. It is presented as a new effort by the FCO and Treasury to get us in it.

Then my wife and I, Anne Nash and Sarah Charman leave for York in my car for the first GIS weekend conference in the Chase Hotel beside the Knavesmire racecourse. Next day, Friday, brings a beautiful, frosty morning. All my ambitions would be realised if Westminster were transferred to York. At the various sessions during the day, I try to develop an esprit de corps and secure the introduction of an effective recruitment, training and career management system. In the afternoon, Brian Mower, a former deputy to me in No. 10 and now head of information at the Home Office, briefs us on the forthcoming explosion in broadcasting.

On Saturday, our conference is interrupted by two photo-journalists with flowers in their lapels pretending to be looking for a wedding. Very soon afterwards they are snapping away through the windows. When I go outside, one of them asks me what I am doing there. I tell him to bugger off; it has nothing to do with him. And that is the last we hear of them. In the afternoon we are given a conducted tour of the Jorvik Viking Centre by the director.

As we suspected, yesterday's disruptive duo came from the *Mail on Sunday* and their piece about us causes much mirth. I resolve to write to Stewart Steven, its awful editor, seeking an apology. I am satisfied that the conference has been valuable and cost-effective. It has reached a number of conclusions that Sarah Charman, secretary to it, will have to set out for the GIS membership. I drop Sarah at Doncaster railway station before we go off to see Nancy's two sisters and my brother and his family in Halifax and then over the M62 to spend some time with our son and his wife in Lymm.

CHAPTER 5

MAY 1989: DANGER: MEN AT WORK, STIRRING

The Tories begin the month with a poll lead of three points, but before it is over interest rates are hoisted to 14 per cent to bear down on inflation. Chancellor Nigel Lawson whinges on about who is responsible for inflation while Ted Heath attacks the PM for misleading the public over the EC – as if either had room to talk. I also note that both Lawson and Foreign Secretary Sir Geoffrey Howe have been stirring up trouble for weeks over entry into the ERM. This is not a happy government.

The PM gets the Freedom of the City of London, surprises everyone at a NATO summit, meets President Bush and expels fourteen Russian diplomats.

WEEK 18: 1–7 MAY

May Day bank holiday in Lymm. Not much in the press apart from a fatal shooting at Monkseaton on Tyneside, which I expect will bring another volley against shotguns. The *Mail on Sunday* nonsense about the GIS weekend in York does not seem to have carried through to the dailies. We go for a walk in the morning with John and Christine – otherwise known as birdwatching when you go out with John – and see a couple of great crested grebes. After lunch we have a fast drive down to Surrey and upon arriving home I ring No. 10 to send me a briefcase of reading and action papers to keep on top of the job.

On Tuesday, I concentrate on preparing for the PM's tenth

anniversary on Thursday. Her PMQs briefing gives me the opportunity to persuade her to turn all her venomous critics to her advantage: nothing demonstrates more conclusively the impact she has made than all this carping. She does more useful work at PMQs on the NHS, noting, in contrast to Labour, who she says cut everyone and everything, that this government has expanded it.

I am occupied by one briefing after another and a meeting with Alastair Burnet (ITN) and George Russell (IBA) before dinner with the top men at British Nuclear Fuels Ltd (BNFL) – Neville Chamberlain and Harold Bolter.

Wednesday is a memorable day for the PM. She sees her grandson, Michael, for the first time and joins him in a photocall during which Mark Thatcher is impossible. He tells the PA woman reporter not to touch his son and keeps on at me to ban close-ups of the infant. What is the point of a photocall if they cannot photo the latest Thatcher in close-up? In any case, you cannot prevent close-ups with modern camera technology. I do absolutely nothing to stop it.

Back then to the tenth anniversary. I have given Chris Moncrieff and Julie Cockroft (PA) an exclusive interview so that all news outlets will have the same basic material. Her dominant words of the experience of the past ten years are firmness, battle and tigress. The PM appears on a sunny doorstep at 8.30 a.m. and after five minutes Denis Thatcher, rather late, appears with her. At Cabinet, Sir Geoffrey Howe pays her a handsome tribute. All this is followed by six radio and TV interviews and attending the Aurum press launch of two books about her: *The Revival of Britain* (collected speeches) and *Ten Years in No. 10* in pictures. Before a party reception in her honour, I tell her the Tories have a three-point lead. Later the Cabinet gives her a dinner.

I feel rather triumphant about the day's press – front-page pictures of her with her grandson, and Chris Moncrieff's 'tiger in the tank' interview comes through strongly.

The next day, Friday, is extremely bitty. I get to the office late

(10.45 a.m.) because I have to take my car to be converted to un-leaded petrol and visit the dentist. I race around attending four meetings before a very successful lunch for the PM given by her senior staff over the past ten years. Andrew Turnbull, principal private secretary, pays due tribute to her on our behalf. Nancy joins me in the evening for dinner with Fernand and Helga Auberjonois – he being the European correspondent of the *Toledo Blade* in Ohio, with whom I have a strong rapport – and his proprietors, Mr and Mrs Block.

As predicted, I have appeared on *Spitting Image* as a ministerial compère. I look revolting, but I shall try to get the mask. [I never do.] I spend a lovely weekend making arrangements for Nancy's sister Kathleen's funeral, gardening and reducing my three briefcases of reading to a third of one. Most people who read a profile of me in the *Sunday Times* think it is OK. I feel that we in the press office have handled this difficult week well. Then I learn that the Germans are causing more trouble over SNF that seems likely to persist this month.

WEEK 19: 8–14 MAY

Back to work, with my three briefcases of work done sitting a foot high in my out-tray. A satisfying sight. Everybody ribs me about *Spitting Image*. I tell the PM that the most problematical development for her is Labour's claim to have ditched unilateralism. So far as I can see, that is not so. If I am right, it is up to Tory Central Office to rubbish it. The PM takes the point and makes arrangements accordingly.

SNF keeps coming back like a song and dominates Monday's press because the Americans have suggested that the PM will not take part in any negotiations. There are not going to be any negotiations, though the UK will probably have to fudge nuclear modernisation. I brief the BBC's journalists' course before lunch with George Bull (director of the Anglo-Japanese Economic Institute and former long-time editor of *The Director* magazine).

On Tuesday, the press presents Labour's defence policy as Kinnock battling through to victory. I fear this government is not made of real politicians; otherwise, they would have ensured that the unilateralist label still hangs around Labour's neck. The PM is commendably resolute over the Football Spectators Bill amid melting support. She emerges from a meeting determined to go ahead with it but to give a bit on the enabling nature of the legislation.

I manage to write an account of the recent GIS weekend in York for the GIS bulletin and to clear a summary for the PM of a select committee report on televising the Commons. Before going home, I brief an American journalist on the government's information system.

On Wednesday, Nancy and I go to Kathleen's funeral in Luddenden, Halifax. We leave home at 5 a.m. and are with Miriam, Nancy's other sister, for 9.15. We are later joined by John and Christine, and Raymond, Nancy's brother, and his wife Simone. At St Walburga's RC Church, Luddenden Foot, Father John Gott is a sympathetic priest and sums up Kathleen to a T. She is buried in Luddenden churchyard – a wonderfully peaceful, beautifully kept spot beside a flowing stream. We are home for 7.15 p.m.

The next day, the government is in the firing line over the production of a leaflet on the community charge (poll tax). It has been produced in the three different countries of the UK without liaison between them. We shall have to remedy this. Lord President Wakeham rings me seeking advice on an opposition debate next week on government publicity. After Cabinet, Chief Secretary Major, who is to be the main speaker in the debate, calls for a briefing. I set it out on paper before going off with Mike Bates, FCO press officer in No. 10, for dinner with the Polish community at their club in Exhibition Road, Kensington.

On Friday, I have to write a speech for the PM for the opening next week of the *Mail*'s new printing plant. She is occupied with speechwriting for her weekend in Scotland. Heaven only knows what the Sunday lobby will write about after my briefing. I hold my sixth drinks party for information officers. I judge the exercise to have been very successful in helping to create an esprit de corps and making them feel we (IOMU) are working to improve the GIS.

On Saturday, the PM opens the Torness nuclear power station in Scotland before a strong speech in Perth condemning Labour's alleged opportunism on defence. Otherwise, the press have a news-starved weekend, although Ted Heath bursts onto the scene with an attack on the PM for allegedly misleading the public on the EC. We maintain indifference. I devote the weekend to gardening, reading and watching football.

WEEK 20: 15-21 MAY

Off to Rotherhithe for the PM's opening of the *Mail*'s new printing plant. She is greeted by Lord Rothermere and his wife, Bubbles, who hogs the show. Painted like a tart, and wearing a short bell tent skirt showing an elastic band around her knee. Oh dear!

We wonder whether the bus and Tube strike will make the journey difficult, but the removal of buses has freed up the traffic. On the way, the PM is disinclined to say anything about the EC after Heath's accusation that she is misleading the public. I think this is because she does not want to be seen to be dancing to his tune. I tell her that it would be good for publicity for her to turn her attitude into a positive asset. Instead, much to editor David English's concern, she gives them something of an hors d'oeuvre for Wednesday's interview with his paper.

I have lunch with David Burnside, head of PR for British Airways, who is trying to buy the *Belfast Newsletter*. Most of the afternoon is spent briefing John Major for tomorrow's debate on government publicity. I think I am more worried about the debate when we finish than when we started. It turns out to be a damp squib.

At the PMQs briefing earlier, I urged the PM to push the Football Spectators Bill because of another outbreak of hooliganism at the weekend. Our main concern, however, is with Heath's behaviour and the Tories appearing to be split. I write a note for the PM for her interview with the *Daily Mail* tomorrow, putting a positive gloss on her approach to the EC.

After reading a pile of paper, I rush off to the United Newspapers' lunch, where I sit between Simon Jenkins (columnist), John Junor, and, at one remove, David Owen (SDP and former Labour Foreign Secretary) and Lord Shawcross (the eminent lawyer who as Hartley Shawcross led the British prosecution at the Nuremberg war crimes trial after World War II and was a Labour minister). (Lord) Woodrow Wyatt (*Times* columnist), who seems not to like me, probably because I have never taken him too seriously, makes fun of both me and David Owen. Gordon Linacre (United Newspapers) presses me to take the editorship of the *Yorkshire Post* but I tell him I can't because of my commitment to stay at No. 10 until 1992 and my recent appointment as head of the GIS.

On Wednesday, I begin to fear I have over-stoked the PM on the EC. She opens her interview with David English and Gordon Greig with twenty-five minutes of solid Thatcher positivism on the EC. Greig says it was like being run over by a tank. I resolve to tell interviewers in future to lead her in gently. Ask the crucial question first and you will lose most of your interview time. Her line gears me up for the two lobbies and the American correspondents, who seem to enjoy it enormously. The afternoon lobby applauds me – or at least Julia Langdon (*Mirror* political editor) does – to everyone's amusement. Later I give an interview to John Knight (*Sunday Mirror* political editor) for their magazine.

The *Daily Mail* does the PM proud on Thursday with four pages of the interview, leading with her nightmare about the EC – its being regulatory and corporatist. There is little follow-up from the lobby, who are preoccupied with a White Paper on roads and the first of two Lonrho judgments – this on whether Lord Young, Industry Secretary, was right (it is judged he was) to decline to publish the Monopolies and Mergers Commission's report on Harrods.

I then dash off some speech notes for my appearance at the Cook Society (Australia) lunch at the Royal Yacht Club attended by Colin Cowdrey; absorbing briefing on the fourteen Russians to be expelled tomorrow; and advising Colin Moynihan, Sports minister, on his tough speech to the Football Writers' Association about the state of the game. After lunch I brief first the *Los Angeles Times*, then Paul Potts of the *Daily Express*, and eventually attend a reception associated with the recent ozone conference in London.

On Friday, I discover that the press has given Kinnock's programme short shrift. Only the *Mirror* has anything approaching good to say about it, but qualifies it by saying it isn't perfect. *The Guardian* dismisses it as timid.

Before lunch with the High Master at St Paul's School, I tell its Junior Political Society about my job. It is very informal, but I conclude that it is perhaps as well that I never became a geography teacher, as intended, because its teachers seem to show far more patience than I have ever had.

In the evening, we say farewell to Simon Dugdale, a press officer who is moving upwards. It is sad to lose another real asset.

The weekend takes me to Glyndebourne as guests of BNFL with Harold and Sheila Bolter; the Gaffins, Neville and Jean, both former deputies of mine in No. 10; and Mr and Mrs David Fishlock, he being the energy editor of the *FT*. That morning, the Chancellor, predictably, rings No. 10 to complain about press reports of a row that broke last night over responsibility for inflation at 8 per cent. The PM admits she has not handled the issue well and asks me to calm things down. I try without success.

I am getting fed up with hypersensitive ministers – especially with the childish Chancellor, who, with Foreign Secretary Howe, has been stirring up the idea of the UK entering the ERM for weeks. I don't lift another finger to help. This has got to sort itself out. Little to worry about in the Sunday press except the nonsense that the PM rang the Chancellor in Spain instead of vice versa. I decide that perhaps least said, soonest mended.

On Sunday, news of the expulsion of fourteen Russian diplomats and their retaliation against the UK, including three journalists, breaks about 10 a.m. I sit out in the hot weather under a canopy from 11 a.m. to 5 p.m. reading, writing and sorting myself out. I get few calls from the press.

WEEK 21: 22–28 MAY

The main item of interest is the new campaign for freedom of information, on which Peter Hennessy (columnist and historian) and Des Wilson (political campaigner) wax eloquent in *The Independent* and *Guardian*. Sadly, no one asks me about this at the lobbies, so I cannot repeat the government's uncompromising line. In my view, while the system could be more open, I cannot see how there can ever be absolute freedom of information because of the need for secrecy on defence, security, trade, negotiations of various kinds and, not least, personal information. The idea that government can be conducted in a fish tank is frankly absurd.

Excitements during the day are few, so I read a lot and clear admin. I have evening drinks at the RAC Club with Woodrow Wyatt, who has a fairly objective view of the PM. The Chancellor is still whinging.

On Tuesday, the PM meets the Chancellor and, subject to events overnight, they decide to raise interest rates. Everything else pales into insignificance. The PM is preoccupied with speechwriting for the Tory women's conference tomorrow and her being given the Freedom of the City of London on Friday. I spend a lot of time briefing about the expulsion of Soviet diplomats and the USSR's retaliation against us, railing against the Soviets making us conform with their 215 ceiling in the UK, including Soviet citizens employed by our Embassy.

Just as I am ready to go off to a very entertaining dinner with Brian Hitchen, a newspaperman to his fingertips, comes news of a run on the pound. It is said this stems from remarks by the PM at PMQs. A Reuters reporter tells a press officer she thinks it is a rum story.

Next day, interest rates are hoisted one point to 14 per cent to demonstrate the government's determination to bear down on inflation by both tightening the screws and cutting off an escape route for industrialists, who are only too easily persuaded to give in to large wage claims.

I lunch with Lyndy Payne, director of an advertising data company, and have an equally enjoyable dinner with Nick Lloyd, editor of the *Daily Express*.

Thursday finds me bleary-eyed. It is too hot to sleep well. The Chancellor's private secretary rings me at 7.50 to say how upset he is about today's press. *The Independent* is trying to stir up more trouble between the PM and Chancellor apparently by embellishing a quote. I sympathise.

Kinnock gets involved in an extraordinary fracas with Jim Naughtie on the BBC's *World at One* programme. Far from giving the Labour leader an easy ride, Naughtie asks him to set out his alternatives to the government's policies. He does not like this and an argument ensues. After a break, it is resumed. We give a briefing on the NATO summit at the weekend before another drinks party for information officers.

The press is agog on Friday over Kinnock's loss of temper with Naughtie. To make matters worse for him, the *Evening Standard* acquires a transcript of the interview. This is meat and drink to the chattering classes.

My wife joins me at the office to travel with members of the staff to the Guildhall for the conferment of the Freedom of the City of London on the PM. We all queue up to be introduced (which is rather embarrassing, but they don't hiss). At the ensuing lunch in the Mansion House, Peter Rigby, chairman of the City's policy and resources committee, tells me about the perils of 'crack', which is apparently much more potent than cocaine. I shall have to report this to the PM.

The weekend is spent gardening, swotting up on NATO, reading, watching cricket on TV and sleeping. The Sunday press is full of gossip about a reshuffle and whether Cecil Parkinson will return to the Cabinet. I leave them to chatter on. In the evening, we fly to Brussels from Northolt and on to a briefing at the residence of our Ambassador to NATO, Michael Alexander, who was formerly the PM's foreign affairs private secretary. It is clear that the Americans have got nowhere on SNF with the Germans and there is little confidence around. My late-night briefing of the press is a somewhat tetchy affair.

Instead of enjoying the late May bank holiday Monday in the sun, we are closeted in NATO, starting with a breakfast briefing at the Embassy at 7 a.m. Our game plan is clear: stick with the Americans and secure tight constraints on any SNF negotiations, which we do not want.

The PM gives me a lot of work with the media by intervening early in the debate, but then the conference is remitted to officials. They report no progress at 4.15 p.m., so the buck passes to Foreign Ministers, who are still at it when I go to the Holiday Inn at 11.45 p.m. to brief the media. The media are pessimistic about an agreement. I then go to bed only to be awakened at some ungodly hour by the BBC and Associated Press to say all is agreed, but with a British reserve. I decide to call it a day and make no enquiries about the outcome.

After next to no sleep I am back at the Ambassador's residence for 7 a.m. to await the PM's appearance to read the draft agreement to her. Charles Powell and I divide. I argue that the draft fully protects the PM's position and that we can sell it. Charles lucidly rehearses how the PM will suffer if she signs up. I don't see how, taken in full context, she can reject partial reductions in SNF.

She decides to sign up and I am given a positive line to take. When I get to NATO headquarters, I track down the BBC, the PA and the *ES* so that our line is generally available. I cause a great stir in reporting that the PM accepts the text. It confounds all the briefing and stories up to then. It does not go entirely smoothly, because Hans-Dietrich Genscher, German Foreign Minister, feels that he has got something, too. As he would. Back to No. 10 for 3.30 p.m.

The month ends with President George Bush arriving for a meeting on 1 June with the PM. I am positively delighted with the tabloid coverage of NATO and the reasonableness of the *Daily Telegraph*, *Times* and *FT*. The *Mirror*, *Guardian* and *Independent* are predictably sour. Ted Heath gets a hammering for criticising the PM.

I brief the PM for her interview with the *Glasgow Herald*. It has not taken off by the time I have to leave to prepare myself for the American correspondents. They are peculiarly passive and give me every opportunity to put over our positive points about NATO and President Bush's visit.

The BBC gets up to no good by inventing or retailing gossip about the PM considering alternatives to higher interest rates which seem calculated to raise them even higher. Ironically, I then spend ninety minutes with Biddy Baxter (BBC), preparing for a seminar with them. My daughter-in-law, Christine, arrives at No. 10 – she is on business in London – just before Prince Sultan of Saudi Arabia calls on the PM.

CHAPTER 6

JUNE 1989:
OPEN WARFARE

Before the PM leaves for the Madrid EC summit, the Foreign Secretary and Chancellor threaten to resign if she does not name a date for entry into the ERM. She does not name a date and they do not resign.

The press has a severe dose of reshuffleitis, about which the PM is not disposed to be rushed. She is in remarkably good spirits after losing thirteen seats in the Euro elections – a self-inflicted Tory setback – following some confusing polls. Sir Alan Walters, her economic adviser, is seen as undermining Chancellor Lawson.

Amid all this internecine warfare, she cements the 'special relationship' with President Bush and advances Anglo-Australian relations in a good meeting with Prime Minister Bob Hawke and four of his ministers.

Altogether a trying month in which I am too often on the defensive.

WEEK 22: 1–4 JUNE

The big question of the day is whether we are the best friends of the USA. This juvenile question stems from the wetness of West Germany over SNF defence. They are now in the position of debtor: the banker only wants to know the debtor, never the creditor. It takes me more than hour to drive in and get to grips with this because of the Tube strike clogging the roads.

The PM has an excellent summit with President Bush, marred only by a nasty piece by C4 about our alleged loss of pole position in transatlantic relations. Certainly, Bush teases on his way in by talking about having the 'gloves off'. Yet there could have been no better beginning to the new Anglo-American relationship under this new President than his visit to No. 10 and the successful NATO conference. The PM is very excited about the talks and I am satisfied she means it because I sit in on the plenary session with Marlin Fitzwater, the President's press secretary and an old friend who also served President Ronald Reagan. This fires me up for my briefing with the Sunday lobby, which my press officers say was my 'passionate best'.

All this and another drinks party – the seventh – for information officers who turn out to be the most intelligent of the lot so far. I don't know what these occasions do for information officers, but they certainly encourage me.

After an hour with the Sunday lobby, I go over to the House to honour my native Hebden Bridge Brass Band, in which my brother and I used to play second cornet. It is holding a festival on the terrace over which Donald Thompson, the constituency MP, presides. He introduces me over the loudspeaker to the audience. I am delighted to be seen to be supporting home industries.

My good run continues at the weekend. Crystal Palace win promotion. My next-door neighbour and I were season-ticket holders for years (and my son still is), though I always want to know how my boyhood clubs – Halifax Town and Burnley – have done. Not a single telephone call on Saturday apart from John, elated about Crystal Palace, and my brother, who says he is starting haymaking with his new baler.

Sunday is a momentous day for foreign news – Chinese troops shooting hundreds of students in Beijing in what becomes known as the Tiananmen Square massacre; Ayatollah Khomeini, first Supreme Ruler of Iran, dies; and hundreds are killed when a gas pipeline blows up a train in the Urals. There will not be much room for anything else in the Sunday papers.

My hand in the Sundays after my 'passionate' briefing on Friday is not well defined, although *The Observer* reflects my tough line on vested interests standing in the way of NHS reforms. Otherwise, the weekend is spent, as usual, gardening, reading, walking – this time we go to Reigate Hill – watching sport and sleeping.

WEEK 23: 5–11 JUNE

As expected, Monday's press is full of foreign disasters. I find it difficult to exclude myself from a drafting session for a party political broadcast on Europe, though I only listen. Then John Knight and Terry O'Neill get to work on the PM for the *Sunday Mirror*. As O'Neill snaps away, I'm afraid we keep General Altenburg, retiring chairman of NATO's Military Committee, waiting to see her. Lunch with Trevor Kavanagh, who is a good and perceptive host.

We are into the final lap before the parliamentary recess tomorrow. I try to damp down more speculation about a reshuffle but I cannot responsibly rule out July in view of the PM's remarks at an earlier meeting on the weeks immediately ahead. In the evening, Chris Ogden from *Time* magazine pops in to talk about Denis Thatcher. He has been very observant in his short time in this country.

On Tuesday, I am not fully engaged. I am letting too much go. I sometimes feel that all I want to do now is to complete my ten years in No. 10 in October and then wrap up. It could be the anti-climax after the success of the NATO summit and George Bush's visit last week.

Our main concern today is what to do with Hong Kong folk in an emergency. Charles Powell is curiously subdued and even his fertile brain is not sure of the way forward. The PM wants to push for more democratisation of Hong Kong before we have to hand over to China in 1997 and secure a more liberal regime for the admission of Hong Kong people with British dependency passports (BDP). She does not think we can take 3.5 million (more than the whole New Commonwealth immigration since World War II) but wants to admit more talented people.

On to Wednesday, when the PM is on the Euro hustings. The

morning lobby scarcely knows what to ask and the American cor-respondents are desultory. Lunch with John Junor. He wants me to ring him each week with ideas. He says he would like to retire but is afraid of ending up doing nothing. I doubt that would occur.

On Thursday, the Governor of Hong Kong, Sir David Wilson, has talks with the Foreign Secretary and then the PM. At the end of the day, we are looking for some 100,000 places for Crown servants and managers, but that, as the PM points out, does not include entrepreneurs. She makes it clear that we cannot admit all 3.5 million with BDPs but is urgently examining the scope within the immigration rules and the British Nationality Act for greater flexibility. We have a long way to go with this saga.

At the start of the PM's business meeting, I am drawn into a dis-cussion on televising the Commons. The PM accepts Chief Whip Waddington's recommendation that the payroll vote – i.e. members of the government and their parliamentary aides – should support Lord President Wakeham's proposal for tight restrictions. Having taken part as the PM's official representative in cross-party talks, I am sure she is right.

During the afternoon, George Jones (*Daily Telegraph*) tells me a Gallup poll puts the Tories seven points behind Labour, though only one point on an average of polls. A much larger sample for last month has the two parties neck and neck. I never trust Gallup – it throws up some quirky results from time to time – but I have no doubt Labour is ahead. It would be astonishing if they weren't, given all the unpopular things the government is doing.

On Friday, the PM is depressed about Gallup. She keeps me talking for fifteen minutes outside the Cabinet Room and does not seem to have much idea what to do about it. I suggest a bigger effort to get over the value of NHS reforms, which – the level of mortgage interest apart – is, I am sure, the most contentious issue.

For the second time in eighteen hours, I find myself in my ca-pacity as head of the GIS talking to information officers – on an induction course after last night's very successful gathering for senior information officers. Lunch with Hans-Ingvar Johnsson, the intelligent representative of Stockholm's *Dagens Nyheter*.

General Wojciech Jaruzelski, the Polish leader, is at Chequers on Saturday. My deputy, Terry Perks, covers it, but it attracts little publicity on Sunday. I write a minute to the Cabinet Secretary because I am worried about some aspects of the briefing for his appearance before the Treasury Select Committee on the government information machine next week. I hope he is robust about my role. My wife and I lunch with Ken Dodd and his wife – he a former colleague in Halifax and on *The Guardian*.

WEEK 24: 12–18 JUNE

We start a new week asking what game Chancellor Lawson is playing. I talk to Paul Gray, the PM's economics private secretary, about it. Does he want the sack or does he think he is unsackable? We conclude he is building up to another attempt to persuade the PM of the inevitability of going into the ERM after 1990, when, he seems to tell a select committee, the PM's excuses for staying out will be seen to have run out.

All this does not make for an easy day, with the dollar surging strongly, overheated retail sales figures and fevered speculation (fortunately unfounded) in the *Daily Express* about Friday's retail price index figures. We all assemble in the PM's study at 9 a.m. to tell her we need a period of silence from the Chancellor since when he appears in public he cannot resist being clever. Yet he takes the 9.30 a.m. party press conference on the Euro elections!

Lunch with a Nordic group of diplomats at the Norwegian Hus. I never feel right gastronomically for the rest of the day – all that fish. I then spend seventy-five minutes with the Cabinet Secretary going over his evidence to the select committee on Wednesday.

On Tuesday, I reach the conclusion that the Chancellor should be sacked. His vanity, his impossible sensitivity and his utter neglect of the country's wider interests require him to be replaced by Nicholas Ridley – a 'dry' whose appearance would signal a tough, uncompromising approach to inflation. And to teach the Foreign Secretary a thing or two I would have him swapped with Home Secretary Hurd. This outburst of candour with my official colleagues follows another difficult day on the exchanges, interest rates at 14 per cent, a falling pound and a lot of gossip about the differences between the PM and the Chancellor, whose sole attribute at the moment is to talk his way into people's confidence about his ability – without delivering.

Gorbachev shows his wooing of West Germany. Gennadi Gerasimov, Soviet foreign affairs spokesman, shamelessly tries to auction favours in Europe on TV. Ugh. Like the PM, I think I am getting too principled for this corrupt world. Perhaps we need a dose of Neil Kinnock to teach people what's what.

President Reagan calls on the PM for dinner, at which Richard Todd, his compatriot in the film *The Hasty Heart*, is a guest.

A wide variety of leads on a humid and oppressive Wednesday. Gorby-mania and Chancelloritis dominate, plus a great deal of evidence that the press think that the West Germans have gone over the top towards Gorbachev. They are also in their perpetual state of excitement over PM *v* Lawson, whom she so firmly backed in PMQs yesterday. Then, in between meetings with the BBC, ITN and Border TV, I get a call from Philip Stephens (*FT*), who blows the gaff on what the PM said yesterday in talks with the Treasury. On top of this, Peter Jenkins (*The Independent*) tells me of a Treasury–FCO effort to get the PM to declare herself for early entry into the ERM at the forthcoming Madrid Euro summit. He adds that this is to be complemented by a joint FCO–Treasury paper proposing such a course. Tempers in No. 10 are not very good.

Lunch with the PA, but I have to leave before John Smith (later Kinnock's successor as Labour leader) speaks. Anne Nash tells me she has got the increase in staff she sought at the IOMU. Now we should be able to make progress in developing a recruitment, training and career management system for the GIS.

A hot, sunny day on Thursday should get the electors out in the two by-elections and the European elections. We shall see whether they are neck and neck or whether the Tories, as the PM told her election press conference, are coming up on the rails.

There is little to excite us in the press except for an *FT* leak of the PM's confidential talks two days ago with the Chancellor over what she should say in PMQs. The *FT* plays it fairly responsibly. *The Indy* claims that Sir Alan Walters has been undermining the Chancellor at City lunches. Walters tells me his hosts are feeding *The Guardian* that he didn't do so. The predators of the press ring up Walters and he is less than forthright with me as to who he is talking to.

I am getting fed up with this childish nonsense – so fed up that I simply put up the shutters to the lobby. The PM also manages to put them up against Kinnock at PMQs. He ends up branded as the man who spends his time talking sterling down. This becomes one of the better episodes in the Tory backbenchers' undistinguished record latterly for supporting the PM at PMQs.

After inspecting the new IOMU HQ, I brief Polish journalists on General Jaruzelski's visit before an early dinner with George Bull and a Japanese diplomat.

We awake on another brilliant day – what a summer! – to news that, as expected, Labour has retained Vauxhall and Glasgow Central. A BBC exit poll in the Euro elections – the votes to be counted on Sunday – predicts a crushing win for Labour.

Lunch with Nicholas Wapshott (*The Observer*), from whom I learn more about the foibles of his editor, Donald Trelford, than he does from me about the government. Jack Warden (*Daily Express*) delivers a transcript of Robin Butler's remarks to the select committee on Wednesday paying me a handsome tribute.

Sarah Charman, doing a recce for the economic summit in Paris, reports that it is all a bit of a shambles over there. And, to end another trying day, Beth Frier, Terry's secretary, says she is going on promotion as an information officer to the Home Office. Good for her. They are getting a conscientious person.

Saturday's press is not at all bad considering the by-election defeats and the Euro election polls. I get a lot of work done outside in the shade at home before we go to the Royal Opera House for *Der Rosenkavalier* with Mr and Mrs James Poole, he of Barclays, followed by a late dinner at Rules. We get to bed at 2 a.m.

There is a tendency in the Sunday press to blame the PM for her trials with the Chancellor. When I ring her at Chequers, she is re-markably cheerful in spite of Heath's renewed venom, a widespread Tory inclination to blame her for the expected Euro elections de-bacle, and evidence of more Howe/Lawson disloyalty. I make the point that no one sees this as a victory for Labour, rather a Tory-in-duced setback. It is also notable that the Greens cannot command a good word from any serious commentator. I argue, in briefing the press, that the government is suffering from mid-term blues. It will, I say, continue to pursue policies in the national interest and the PM will not be rushed into a reshuffle. A defensive Sunday ends with a lovely alfresco birthday party for me – three days early – at the Brighton home of Mike Bates.

WEEK 25: 19–25 JUNE

The press and BBC make the most of the Tories' loss of thirteen seats in the Euro elections, but there is no feeling of doom and disaster. I think this reflects three things:

1. The European Parliament does not count for much;
2. This is a mid-term election, which is emphasised by the Greens getting nearly 15 per cent of the vote, even though they are unilateralist; and
3. The self-destructive nature of the Tory Party at present from Heath to Lawson.

If the government can get on top of inflation, thereby cutting the cost of mortgages, things will look better. The CBI's trends survey and petrol price cutting are encouraging. The PM makes clear that it is business as usual and that she will not be hustled into a reshuffle. I play a very relaxed game with the media at the two lobbies, though it is more difficult at 4 p.m. since Felipe González, the Spanish PM, has made his last call in the round of Euro leaders before the Madrid Euro Council next week.

After his call, No. 10 has a meeting on European monetary co-operation. I play the hardliner I am, trying to make sure the PM understands the consequences of trimming, though there is a tactical consideration as to whether to give a bit now to avoid worse at the Paris Council in December.

On Tuesday, I stay at No. 10 because of the impending bus, rail and Tube strike. Our attention is focused today on PMQs – the first after the Euro elections. To my astonishment, Kinnock waltzes off to the Socialist International in Stockholm, leaving Roy Hattersley to try to discomfit the PM. He does not succeed because, as one of the few Labour frontbenchers with ministerial experience, he presents a target. Indeed, the PM calls him the ex-minister for high prices. I seek to dismiss all gossip about a reshuffle by being extremely sarcastic and may have succeeded for the moment.

In the evening, after a lively regionals' lobby, I see the Solanki family, of Asian Trader fame, who want the PM to present their prizes in December. And then off to dinner at Beotys with Paul Gray and Sarah Charman. I read the first editions of Wednesday's newspapers before going to bed around 1 a.m.

I am very fragile on my birthday (Wednesday 21st) after last night's excesses, but I get lots of cards, letters and cream cakes from the press office and friends. It is also Australia Day in No. 10. Bob Hawke, the Australian PM, comes in with three of his ministers for a historic bilateral intended to initiate building a new, modern relationship. The morning's talks seem to go well, so I take the initiative and arrange for them to speak to the media in the street at 12.45, just in time for the news bulletins.

After lunch at the Goring Hotel with John Collins (ex-BP) and Dick Morris (Brown and Root engineering company), who are active in North Sea oil and gas production, I nearly fall asleep briefing a South African spokesman who seeks to impress upon me how things are changing in South Africa as the old guard (P. W. Botha) gives way to F. W. de Klerk's new generation. Press office organises lifts between us so that we can get home.

Off to Royal Ascot as a guest on Thursday. I lose £19 because, Nancy says, I will persist in backing outsiders in the hope of a big win. Nothing much doing at No. 10 apart from an Anglo-Australian dinner.

Friday puts me in a tricky situation – a briefing about the Madrid summit with John Kerr, of the FCO (later an Ambassador to the EC, now Lord Kerr). It is tricky because we have no idea how it will turn out.* I think we get away with it but only time will tell. The PM sees successively de Klerk; Lydia Dunn, senior member of the Hong Kong executive committee; and Mr and Mrs Andrei Sakharov, the Soviet dissidents and he a Nobel laureate. She then gives a farewell lunch for Andy Bearpark, her private secretary for parliamentary affairs, and for some reason – perhaps my longevity in No. 10 – I sit next to her.

In the evening we say farewell to Beth Frier, who is going to the Home Office press operation.

On Saturday, my family celebrates my birthday with dinner at the nearby Selsdon Park Hotel after a fire alarm that calls out five fire engines. It is a false alarm. On Sunday, John and Christine sun themselves on the terrace reading the newspapers, with a Harris poll in *The Observer* giving Labour a fourteen-point lead. I don't believe it. Then, having arranged for Sarah Charman to cover the PM's departure from No. 10 for Madrid, I am driven direct to Heathrow at noon.

The atmosphere on the plane is distinctly frosty, with the PM and Foreign Secretary working in different sections of the VC10. In fact, you could cut it with a knife. I have never experienced anything like it. I soon discover why. I am told that before the PM left

---

* The Madrid summit was due to discuss President of the European Commission Jacques Delors's three-stage plan for European economic and monetary union.

No. 10, Howe and Lawson formed up in the PM's study to tell her that, if she does not set a date for entry into the ERM in Madrid, they will resign. I would have sacked both on the spot, but the PM has doubts about the wisdom of ditching both her Chancellor and her Foreign Secretary in one fell swoop.

The iciness continues when we land, and the PM declines to go to an evening party at the British Embassy, which is hard on the Ambassador. Charles Powell and I decide we had better not go either. We dine with the PM at 10 p.m. She is worn with anxiety about the summit. We go over her speaking note and this enables me to brief the press firmly on her position after a meeting with Ruud Lubbers, the Dutch PM, who is disposed to be helpful on EMU. I have some hope of a good media tomorrow after my attempt to keep the temperature down, though nowhere near as low as it was on the plane.

WEEK 26: 26–30 JUNE

The big day at the summit. We enter it in reasonably good order but in a highly secretive mood. The Treasury and FCO are denied sight of the PM's speaking note until after she has spoken. After a Continental breakfast with the PM, we leave at 9.15 for the Congress Palace. I give the media a chance to check in with me at 10 a.m. ahead of the PM speaking just before lunch. Having collected her annotated notes from the meeting room, I brief the media extensively.

It seems clear that, with Peter Jenkins in unusual attendance, the media have been set up by Howe/Lawson. To my surprise, I get few questions except, as usual, from John Palmer (*The Guardian*). Under pressure, I admit that the PM has never been as positive about the ERM but note that she has not named a date for UK entry. I have to work hard on this during the afternoon but by the evening I think I have tempered the media's negativism.

On Tuesday, I am up at 6.45 a.m. to get hold of a draft communiqué produced by the Spanish presidency overnight. It is astonishingly good. The UK delegation to Brussels, FCO and Treasury meet separately on the detail. The PM, still bruised by the leaking and pressure put on her, breakfasts alone. We all agree there is no point in quibbling on detail. Having run a social charter into the buffers, she needs to break the links in Jacques Delors's staged programme of EC development and ensure that any intergovernmental conference to prepare treaty changes comes after, for once, proper study.

My 10 a.m. appearance before the media causes confusion when I see merit in the overnight draft, subject to clarification. Our briefings are crowded and the PM's press conference exceptionally so, with photographers fighting among themselves for advantage. After the usual six radio and TV interviews, I am en route for another night in No. 10 because of tomorrow's rail strike.

Up at 6.30 on Wednesday to discover the press office hard at work because of the rail strike. They are superbly motivated. I am blessed among press secretaries with my support. The tabloids make excellent reading on the Euro summit while the broadsheets are superior, hesitant and qualified. There is also promise of a better week for the PM – we could do with one – with her backbenchers behind her because of the effect of the rail and Tube strikes on opinion and the drubbing Kinnock is getting from some transport unions (NUR and TGWU). It is all EC and strikes at the lobbies and Hong Kong and the EC with the American correspondents.

Over lunch on my desk I write a brief and speech for the PM's opening of the Express Group's new office at the end of Blackfriars Bridge. We get cars to take us home, mine dropping off Terry's new secretary in Wandsworth and Sarah Charman in Putney. I get home at 9.30 with a pile of presents.

The main effort on Thursday is to win the argument in Parliament on the EC. All the major parties are split on it – and, not least, the Tories. The PM seems to have achieved the impossible by uniting all sides with her new positive approach to the EMU – on her own terms. Mr Speaker, after PMQs, allows a whole hour for questions on the PM's statement about the summit. She is magnificently commanding, knowing her subject and being her own person. This does not alter the fact that we need a new EC strategy and I tell the PM so in a very candid minute on the forthcoming reshuffle.

Immediately after the Commons grilling, we go to Ludgate House, the new HQ of the Express Group. The PM spends a little too much time on Lord Beaverbrook, long since gone, but she makes her peace with Jean Rook, the self-styled First Lady of Fleet Street, in her office overlooking the Thames. I reflect what a difference working in newspapers is today compared with my time. It is like living in a four-star hotel compared with the hovels I inhabited.

The month ends with the railwaymen coming under heavy pressure from Transport Secretary Paul Channon and behind the scenes myself on the PM's behalf. I repeat that there is no question, as decided by the Cabinet yesterday, of giving way.

The PM takes my stage management for the *Sunday Express* interview with Robin Esser (editor) and Tony Smith (political editor). She is tremendously upbeat about the economy and Europe. She even says 'I am a passionate European,' which causes my substantial eyebrows to soar. Tony Smith says he has never heard her expound so convincingly on the environment.

I feel sorry for Robin Esser, who might be out of a job next week in view of remarks to me by Lord Stevens, chairman of United Newspapers, last night. I got the impression he wanted to stop the Esser interview. I ignored his request. It is not for me to get involved in a newspaper's politics.

Lunch with Alastair Campbell (political editor, *Today*; later Tony Blair's press secretary), who is one of the nicer Labour people, though I do not expect him to write much good about the PM. At the Sunday lobby, I take the opportunity to correct nonsense in the *Daily Mail* and *Scotsman* that I was inviting bids for British Rail when I asked rhetorically, 'Who would buy the railways?'

CHAPTER 7

JULY 1989: MY MONTH IN THE DOGHOUSE

The government is in the doghouse, lagging anything from seven to thirteen points behind Labour in the polls. First Brian Mulroney, the Canadian PM, is upset because I am (wrongly) alleged to have said his recent visit to the PM was a PR exercise. Then the Evening Standard leads with a cock-and-bull story about Nicholas Ridley, then Environment Secretary, being hauled into No. 10 for a handbagging when in fact he was briefing the PM on the community charge. And then comes Sir Geoffrey Howe, now no longer Foreign Secretary in the much heralded reshuffle but nominally Deputy Prime Minister. His camp accuses me of rubbishing his DPM job by explaining it was in the gift of the PM, with no constitutional underpinning, and then explaining how Willie Whitelaw did it. I tell a sympathetic PM that I am Krakatoan on the Richter scale – as I once told the press, in jest, that she herself was at an EC summit.

It is quite a month with all this and a war of attrition over rail strikes, a highly stylised economic summit in Paris, which for once goes the PM's way, more rumblings about the economy and responsibility for UK inflation, and the discovery that No. 10 is importing mahogany from the Brazilian rainforest for renovations.

We start the month with Labour ahead ten points, according to MORI. The Sunday press is preoccupied with what to do about rail strikes and I discover that the Department of Transport is to open the Royal Parks for cars. This is not good enough. No. 10 press office must be told about such developments.

The Observer's first edition claims that No. 10 has confirmed that Peter Brooke is being considered for the Northern Ireland Cabinet post, as he is. We haven't. I have said I had heard gossip to that effect. The turnout for a demonstration against the Foreign Secretary in Hong Kong is much smaller than expected.

Otherwise, it is a typical weekend: gardening; watching sport – this time Australia walloping England 30–12 in a Rugby Union Test; having naps, to which I am increasingly prone; walking – this time we go to Banstead Woods, which seems to be full of dogs being taken on their constitutionals; and reading.

WEEK 27: 3–9 JULY

On Monday, the PM is at the Royal Show at Stoneleigh, so we have a quiet time after a terrible scare about a further rise in interest rates to 15 per cent because of over-heating, but very good credit and sales figures followed by abysmally low house-building returns. Curiously, sterling strengthens. Crisis over. I am told that Treasury forecasts demonstrate just how much control over the economy the Chancellor has thrown away. Fool. What an appalling gambler he is.

The press is fascinated by what the PM is going to do to strikers. I have to tell them I don't know, but that the government's main concern is the ability of transport workers to disrupt the middle of the week with minimum effect on themselves. Lunch with Neville Gaffin, my first deputy in No. 10 and now in PR, where he seems to be doing very well. After a very long briefing with the FPA and a lobby, Nick Guthrie (BBC) briefs MIO on the relaunch of *Breakfast Time*.

On Tuesday, I have yet again to stay at No. 10 because of the rail strike. The press's entire effort today is to get me to admit that the government will intervene. I hold them at bay while the Army puts down aluminium roads in the Royal Parks. Whether this will keep the traffic moving is not clear. The truth is that we are in a war of attrition – as is clear after a meeting of ministers, chaired by the PM, where they have a wide-ranging discussion, apart from legislation or rail privatisation. These are longer-term issues. After a lobby and a meeting with the British Management Data Foundation, I work until 9.45 p.m. and then go up to Leicester Square for supper.

I feel fragile on Wednesday because of Big Ben and the clock on Horse Guards Parade chiming out the hour and its quarters. How on earth the PM puts up with it in her top-floor flat is beyond me. Last night, she considered a reshuffle with Chief Whip Waddington, Andrew Turnbull, her principal private secretary, and Mark Lennox-Boyd, her parliamentary private secretary (PPS). I get an extensive and confidential run-down. We live in exciting and on the whole sensible times, assuming the chess board is moved as planned.

I clear briefs for Nigel Wicks (our economic summit Sherpa and former principal private secretary to the PM) for our media briefing tomorrow and then prepare for tomorrow's evening seminar with the BBC. I go with the PM to the Design Centre and on to a tall sail training ship for the disabled, tied up in the Thames, which she very much enjoys.

On Thursday evening, the GIS has a great success at a BBC seminar after a poor start. The opening contributor to the presentation has some disobliging things to say about the service, which dismays both myself and a large turnout of departmental heads of information. The BBC asks us to react, but I suggest it would be better to hear the full presentation. We on the GIS side then try to be constructive and a lot of good comes out of it, partly because we recognise our catalogue of problems and limitations: not much trust in broadcasters, time pressures, ministers' inclinations, proliferation of the media, parliamentary restrictions on disclosure of information before it has been given it; and the urgency of events with calls for comment. By the end I felt we had done a good job and the BBC seemed inclined to have another seminar focusing on radio.

Earlier, I gave a media briefing with Sherpa Wicks on the forth-coming G7 economic summit in Paris, which is not a very exciting prospect. PMQs were not exactly exciting either – rowdy but not very illuminating.

On Friday, I work on the backlog somewhat frantically before I meet Anne Nash. Things seem to be going quite well and we commission work on a GIS logo. My eighth party for information officers follows in my room, which is stifling in the heat, even with the windows open. The Sunday lobby is notable for my drawing attention to the appalling hypocrisy of the liberal establishment over Hong Kong. They wouldn't lift a finger to help the Falklanders in 1982, I said, but now want us to admit 3.5 million from Hong Kong. This does not add up. Surely the liberal establishment can't want them, because they are Thatcherites to a man and woman.

Nancy joins me for dinner with our friends the Rev. and Mrs Lou Springsteen, from New Jersey, at the Reform, whose menu does us proud. Home for 11.15 p.m., whacked.

Saturday brings a Labour lead – thirteen points – in a Gallup poll. This is three points up on the month on a sample of 9,000. I tell myself this is not a time to be rattled. This is easier said than done when Michael Jones tells me No. 10 is importing mahogany from the Brazilian rainforest for renovations. It is just one damn thing after another. Then Mike Bates and I try to track down my secretary, Anne Allan, to tell her that her father has had a stroke in Scotland.

The Sunday press does not make good reading for the government, what with the Hong Kong numbers problem, some sympathy for rail strikers, and imported mahogany – the last coming as a complete surprise; we had not been told about it until the day before, and then by Michael Jones rather than No. 10. I can feel a row coming on. I calm myself, buying rock plants with Nancy at Woldingham and then a walk on Reigate Hill. Our son, John, tells me he is going to an Edwardian evening at Dunham Massey in Cheshire in his cricket whites. He sounds like Bertie Wooster.

WEEK 28: 10–16 JULY

My secretary, Anne, comes in on Monday in spite of her father's stroke, which has put him in hospital. She faces a heavy out-tray after my Stakhanovite efforts at the weekend to clear a backlog. In the course of the day, Business in the Community seeks my advice on recruiting a new chief press officer, I am offered a job by Diana Rasbach, a PR consultant, in Yorkshire and I have lunch with the PA, a lively FPA briefing, a nondescript lobby and a brief MIO meeting.

On Tuesday, I have trouble with the Canadians. Their press fall upon me when I go outside during the afternoon, to move my car to Horse Guards Parade, because of a news agency story in Canada that quotes me as saying that Prime Minister Brian Mulroney's recent visit to see the PM was only a PR trip. Mulroney is said to be very concerned. I do what I can to calm it down by denying I ever said such a thing. The British press is very light, notwithstanding Labour's commanding lead in the polls. And this is July, when Parliament usually becomes bomb-happy with the approach of the long recess! Indeed, in the afternoon, Simon Walters complains that nothing much is doing.

To everyone's astonishment, what with the buzz about rail strikes, the public spending review and an approaching reshuffle, at PMQs Kinnock asks questions about energy conservation – the policy for which I was responsible before I went to No. 10. He is very unpredictable.

We spend an enjoyable evening in the Banqueting Hall celebrating the award of a knighthood to David Nicholas in *This is Your Life* manner. After this, I go to a late Chinese meal with press officers staying in town because of the rail strike. Bed at 12.45.

On Wednesday, I find that Mulroney has gone over the top about my alleged remarks by writing to the PM. She responds with an on-the-record statement repudiating the allegation against me. We eventually issue the statement at Mulroney's prompting, to mitigate the damage he claims he has suffered. Mike Bates has a terrible time trying to find the Canadian media. We wonder whether most of them have cleared off to Paris with their sensitive PM.

I have so much to do before tomorrow's summit that I have to cancel lunch with Jean Caines, my former deputy. I must sort out the papers for the summit and then take the 4 p.m. lobby on public expenditure. I foresee a very tough review. I drive two of the staff home via Wimbledon.

Off to Paris on Thursday for a stylised ceremony to mark the bicentennial of the French Revolution. We immediately discover a cock-up in the issue of No. 10 media passes which has my team and I turned away from the press village associated with Le Sommet de L'Arche, as it is called. We adjourn to the Embassy for lunch with our Ambassador, Sir Ewen Fergusson, and his wife, who are holding open house.

I give media briefings at 1.15 and 5.30 before we attend another mannered opening – of L'Opéra Bastille on the site of the old prison. The PM has to wait for what seems hours to get away because, since we are Royaume-Uni for the purposes of the summit list, she is thirty-second in the pecking order. We have dinner at the Embassy, feeling happier having learned that some IRA suspects have been arrested, one with a Bastille address on him.

Before t'battle commences on Friday we witness the Bicentennial Parade at La Place de la Concorde. The huge convoy proves too much for the stewards, so Andrew Turnbull and I get out of the car and sort out our own viewpoint. The horseflesh is interesting but the military less so, except for the Alpinists with their curious berets, a detachment of the French Foreign Legion with one gnarled veteran menacingly holding an axe, and the fly-past.

I brief the media at 3.15 after a quick visit to the Louvre and its magnificent conference hall under a hot pyramid. On then to the Sofitel, where our team are staying, to give the media details of the PM's economic contribution. I find myself having to knock down some imagined slights by the French to the PM. Dinner at the Embassy.

We start Saturday with the PM walking from the British to

the US Embassy to meet President Bush. I have a good chat with Marlin Fitzwater, the President's press secretary. Now that summit passes have been sorted out, I go to L'Arche to find the media are obsessed with slights and snubs and other non-stories instead of showing some interest in such serious issues as the environment and drugs, on which I brief extensively. I am afraid I have all the sexy stuff to impart and the FCO spokesmen lean pickings, though one of the main stories from the morning session is food aid for Poland. In the evening, I wait upon a session on the environment and brief Sarah Charman down the line for the press's benefit.

I am home on Sunday for 7.45 p.m. after a successful but tiring event in which virtually everything went the PM's way. President Mitterrand also made overtures to the PM to sort out their relationship and suggests he visit No. 10 for a quiet chat in the autumn. I awaken to find to my delight that we have a communiqué which gives us not a single problem. The PM goes through it for an hour under Sherpa Wicks's tutelage and pronounces herself well satisfied. This must be a record. The summit then proceeds at such an alarming pace that by 11.30 I am briefing the PM for her press conference as we await delivery of the opening statement I have drafted for her.

Then everybody gathers at L'Arche for the solemn reading of the summary of the summit's package of decisions, which takes nearly an hour. The PM is rather insensitive about the cause of UK inflation – failure to conduct sound policies – in the Chancellor's presence at her press conference. Nonetheless, it all goes rather well and she disposes with good humour the nonsense about French slights etc. I am delighted with how our press team – Anne Allan, Sarah Charman and Martin Smith (COI) – have worked.

The press on the summit is, like the weather, mixed. The *Sunday Express* and *Sunday Telegraph* are good to excellent; the *Mail on Sunday*, *Observer* and *Sunday Times* are generally awful, though my hand at the summit is put in better light in the *News of the World*.

WEEK 29: 17–23 JULY

By the time I get to sleep in No. 10, utterly exhausted, the National Union of Railwaymen (NUR) have announced that they have rejected British Rail's offer even though it has been accepted by the TSSA and ASLEF.

Presents from the summit pour in all day – a lovely paperweight and briefcase for me. I have my rearranged joint birthday lunch with Jean Caines, at which it is clear the GIS has got reshuffleitis. I have to advise her not to go with Nicholas Ridley to the DTI, where speculation puts his destination. My view, dinned into me earlier in my GIS career, is that heads of information should not follow their ministers around. It looks as if the reshuffle might drift beyond next Monday because of the PM's weekend – at Glyndebourne on Saturday and receiving the Sultan of Oman on Sunday.

The PM's main task today is to try to get the opposition and Kinnock at PMQs either to fail to repudiate or to back NUR strikes. She wins hands down. I fear the current Labour Party is congenitally incapable of condemning a strike.

I slept badly last night because workmen began at 4 a.m. unloading and setting up anti-terrorist and crowd-control barriers on Horse Guards Parade, with much shouting. I wonder whether they are trying to disturb the PM. In the evening, my wife and I are entertained by Alan and Judi Britten, of Mobil, to the Bolshoi at the Coliseum. It is great to see the extra dimension brought to ballet by the Bolshoi. I last saw them in Moscow with the PM and Mr Gorbachev two years ago. It is also a welcome break, even though I have not had much sleep for a week.

On Wednesday, there is an unholy row, as there often is, over procedure rather than the substance of policy, because Nicholas Ridley fails to get exemplification tables of help for local authorities (LAs) under the community charge proposals to the Commons in time. Before this, I deploy to the lobby my version of Paul Gray's simplification of government help for LAs. Political correspondents seem impressed.

American correspondents, like the Europeans yesterday, are thin on the ground for my weekly briefing. The PM entertains Sheikh Fayad of the UAE before I go, as head of the GIS, to the COI for a presentation of their proposed launch in 1991 as an executive agency. I then have an hour with regional directors of the COI, who seem well pleased with the way the GIS is going, though there are concerns about staffing.

On Thursday, the PM's concern is how to cope with her disgracefully wet backbenchers, who are indulging in a bout of bear-baiting with Nicholas Ridley after yesterday's cock-up. The Chief Whip calls to discuss what she should say to the 1922 Committee this evening. Then, after we have identified what we think Kinnock will go on at PMQs, Ridley himself comes in to go through the facts of the community charge with her.

At the end of it all, I have a spat with the PM. She wants to tie my hands with the lobby so that she can have a clear run on the community charge at PMQs. I point out that I cannot avoid explaining that Ridley came in to brief her because the media were on watch outside No. 10. I confirm to the lobby that she spent nearly an hour with him.

Imagine my astonishment – and cold fury – when Charles Reiss leads the *Evening Standard* with Ridley being hauled to No. 10 for a king-size carpeting. I give Reiss a king-size bawling-out – the biggest I have so far ever given to a journalist – write a letter to his editor and then go on the record saying the story is plain, unadulterated mischief-making, which ITN reads out in full. Mr Reiss, the No. 10 press office decides, will be frozen out for a time.

My wife and I set off to drive to Harrogate on Friday at 5 a.m. and arrive at the Old Swan Hotel at 9.30. After a look round Harrogate, I drive down to Leeds for a lunch with Yorkshire Water with Sir Giles Shaw, Tory MP for Pudsey, in the chair. They are concerned about 'K' – the factor over and above inflation by which water authorities will be allowed to raise prices to make good investment that, they say, has been neglected by local authorities for a century. Back to the Old Swan for a nap and dinner.

On Saturday, we go to Ilkley, sporting white roses, via the Cow and Calf Rocks, to open a watercolourists and miniaturists exhibition in the Winter Gardens. I meet many old faces: Donald Crossley, the Mytholmroyd artist with whom I went to school; Rodney Brooke, a leading local government official who was on a course with me in 1978; David Illingworth, a former journalist colleague in Halifax, and Denis Flack, a *Bradford Telegraph and Argus* photographer.

I was somewhat shocked at the end of it to be told it was the custom for an opener to buy a picture. This was news to me – and I had been briefed for the occasion. In any case, I only buy Donald Crossley paintings. The week ends with us back home and NOP giving Labour a lead of seven points. I have to go into No. 10 to be briefed by Andrew Turnbull on tomorrow's reshuffle. I spend the whole of a wonderful summer afternoon under a canopy reading myself in and writing a brief on the reshuffle for the press office. Sarah Charman goes to No. 10 at 5 p.m. to cover any early reshuffle activity with ministers, but none materialises.

WEEK 30: 24–30 JULY

Monday is reshuffle day. It dominates the news and is notable for the number of false media prognostications. It means I have to cancel my lunch with Monty Meth, former industrial editor of the *Daily Mail*, and his friends to mark his retirement. This is a blow. My memories of the day are:

1. Sir Geoffrey Howe standing on his dignity by demanding to be Deputy PM in recompense for his demotion from Foreign Secretary to Lord President of the Council.
2. John Major nervous as a kitten going in to see the PM and coming out dazed by the speed of his rise to Foreign Secretary.
3. The switch of John Wakeham, with whom I have worked closely for much of the 1980s, from Lord President to the Department of Energy.
4. The sad ending of the political careers of John Moore

86

(Department of Social Security), who is replaced by Tony Newton, and Paul Channon (Transport).

5. Nicholas Ridley (from Environment to DTI), Chris Patten (from Overseas Development to Environment) and John Selwyn Gummer (to Ministry of Agriculture) all going out to answer the media's question 'Are you happy' and saying, 'We are always happy.'

6. The last-minute failure of our photocopying machine just before I go over to the House formally to announce the changes, with a press notice, to the lobby. Technology. Grrr.

After this hectic day, the press office goes out for a fish-and-chip supper.

Tuesday brings a good media reception for the reshuffle, but the morning lobby gives early warning of trouble. This stems from John Cole (BBC) clearly having been briefed by someone close to Howe on what passed between him and the PM when they met yesterday. By lunchtime, we are hearing that Howe was offered the job of Home Secretary. This became hot news at the 4 p.m. lobby when the point was put directly to me. I initially discounted it, but a telephone call to Andrew Turnbull confirmed this may have been the case. I resolve to put up the shutters and stick rigidly to it.

Then another problem hits us: the nature of the Deputy PM's job. I told the lobby that the role of DPM was in the PM's gift and had no statutory underpinning and then described how Lord Whitelaw had done it. This is interpreted as my 'writing down' Howe's role before he has even started.

I go off to dinner with Walter Marshall, John Baker and Peter Vey (CEGB), who give me a rather frightening account of their relations with the Department of Energy and their inability to talk to Cecil Parkinson, who has now given way to John Wakeham as Energy Secretary. I promise to inform Wakeham about this.

By Wednesday, all the gilt has come off the reshuffle's gingerbread with the disclosure that Howe was offered the Home Office.

It is seen as having caused disgruntlement among the PM's top three ministers, Howe, Lawson and Hurd.

Chief Whip Waddington wanders in about 9.30 a.m. to say he has been to see Howe, who is complaining bitterly about my alleged downgrading of the post of Deputy PM. I explode and he agrees that it pales into insignificance against the leaking of the offer to Howe of the Home Office. Andrew Turnbull then calls in to say he has been in touch with Hurd's private secretary about the disclosure and that he is satisfied with our explanation. I then get together a form of words which I clear with the PM at 10.30 for the lobby.

The attacks on me then start from David Howell, whom I served when he was a useless Energy Secretary in 1979, Patrick Cormack MP and Peter Jenkins, who is becoming an FCO stooge. The 6 p.m. BBC news runs a mishmash of error and innuendo which causes me to lodge a strong protest that brings forward an apology at the end. We find it impossible to find anyone of substance at the BBC – Checkland, Birt, Cole etc. I write a tough minute to Lord President Howe asking if it is wise for him to hold his office's usual lobby tomorrow and letting him know I am utterly fed up with the allegations against me. I should have added that it only strengthens my resolve to soldier on, because I later discovered that long before this he had sent a two-page letter to the PM demanding I be sacked, apparently for giving out the PM's line instead of his.

The extent of the dishonour of the media and politicians is there for all to see in Thursday's press. I don't bother to read it until bedtime, when I take the view you cannot get much lower than Tony Bevins and Peter Jenkins (both of *The Independent*), the BBC and some MPs. But the idea that I rubbished Howe's position as Deputy PM when in fact I described the job done by Lord Whitelaw is in circulation now. My briefing clearly did not live up to the job description touted about by Howe's allies. It is another scar to show my grandchildren.

The first meeting of the new Cabinet is uneventful apart from the PM saying that she now thinks she has her election Cabinet in place. This predictably makes the afternoon news. Nigel Lawson no doubt thinks is he now cemented in as Chancellor. I meet Howe before his first lobby as Lord President. Mike Bates, who witnessed it, said he made John Wakeham sound entertaining. He certainly did not impart much either of knowledge or of information.

I let the media know the PM intends to go abroad for her holiday, and she and Denis are solicitous about me after a garden party at No. 10. I tell them I am Krakatoan on the Richter scale. In truth, I think this week has been a disgrace to journalism and honest politics.

On Friday, the press – or part of it – improves, and Bruce Anderson, guided by Charles Powell, makes the point that I could have done no other than brief as I did. George Gale in the *Daily Mail* shows some sympathy but thinks I should not have been so 'brutal'. Charles Moore in the *Daily Express* has little sympathy for Howe. Murdo Maclean pops in for a drink to say that a lot of people are on my side.

There is little left to say at the 11 a.m. lobby because the press office has done such a good job in preventing any announcements of substance on the last day of the parliament before recess. Such last-minute announcements always cause trouble because our conspiracy-ridden media think the government is trying to bury bad news. At least we have stopped up one source of it this traumatic week.

I come across Chief Whip Waddington packing up in Speaker's Court. He had earlier called me to say he has given Tony Bevins the mother and father of all tellings-off for his maltreatment of me. *The Guardian* says I have been hauled before him as Chief Whip. He authorises me to say he rang to check his understanding of what I had been saying about the DPM's job. Another good party for the GIS at lunchtime; a quiet Sunday lobby; a nap; then home early.

On Saturday, I collect my son and his wife, back from a holiday in Italy, from the airport and they leave for home after a meal. Before I get down to some serious gardening, I learn that the *Sunday Times* is to assert (wrongly) that Cecil Parkinson was first choice for Foreign Secretary in the reshuffle and the *Obs* is to quote Lord Whitelaw as rubbishing it. This sounds like Lord Whitelaw.

The Sunday press is mixed. *Sunday Express* and *Sunday Telegraph* good; *MoS*, *Obs* and *Sunday Times* pretty awful, though to be fair my role in the reshuffle is put in a better light in the *NoW*, *Obs* and *Sunday Times*. At last, the real villain of the piece – Howe – is beginning to be identified. We track down Lord Whitelaw, who issues a statement rejecting the *Observer* story.

My objective on Monday (31 July) is to tidy up both for No. 10 and the GIS before I go on holiday and to write a paper for the PM on presentation. The main news story is the alleged killing of a US colonel in a reprisal for the Israeli kidnapping of a Hezbollah leader in Lebanon. This brings a threat to Terry Waite, the prominent British Christian held there.

CHAPTER 8

AUGUST 1989:
HOLIDAY AT LAST

After three days of domesticated bliss, we set out on a 2,600-mile super fly-drive to the Wild West from Denver, Colorado, and then back again, via Wyoming, Idaho, Utah and Arizona. It is a wonderful release, with hardly a thought of UK politics, taking us to Cheyenne, Fort Laramie, Cody, Yellowstone National Park, Jackson Hole, Salt Lake City, the north rim of the Grand Canyon and the Mesa Verde.

Back home, my doctor tells me I am fit enough to continue as chief press secretary.

WEEK 31: 1–6 AUGUST

I finish my presentation paper for the PM. It is very frank but develops into an action programme. Sir John Junor entertains me to lunch at the Howard Hotel and is preoccupied with my veracity. Apparently the story is about that I was the source of an article in May or June that Howe and Lawson were to be sacked. I spend a lot of time killing the notion. (There is a difference between what I personally think and what I say in briefing. I have always made it clear that my views are of no account; I speak on behalf of the PM.)

Dinner with David Illingworth (PR consultant) and Mike Lomax (Pilkington), who wants to thank me for my help recently over energy conservation. David broaches the idea of my joining his firm (Paul Whitaker Associates) in Yorkshire in a consultative capacity.

On Wednesday, I have lunch with Julia Langdon, who has just left the *Mirror*, and Geoffrey Parkhouse (*Glasgow Herald*). I get lots of stories about Robert Maxwell's larger-than-lifeness at the Mirror Group and the vindictiveness of Joe Haines, a *Daily Mirror* writer who was Harold Wilson's press secretary. Parkhouse is a curious man: alternately naive (or is this a ploy?) and then showing considerable judgement. He is certainly a natural journalist.

I meet the GIS executive (Mike Devereau, COI; Brian Mower, Home Office; and Anne Nash, IOMU) to put everything to rights before I go away. A thorough session follows with No. 10 press officers to make sure they know what is required and are protected while my deputy and I are on holiday. We then all troop off to the *Sunday Correspondent* with a good turnout of departmental heads of information to meet their editorial team.

Next day, Chris Buckland (*Daily Express*) does a friendly piece about me and Ronald Butt (*The Times*) a disgraceful one, accusing me of rubbishing Howe. I write him a stiff note after letting Stewart Purvis (ITN) have it between the eyes for refusing to honour pooling arrangements at the Imperial War Museum yesterday. I go into No. 10 later, solely because I have discovered that the Garden Room Girls (secretaries) annually hold an auction of presents to the PM. I buy a bowl given by General Yazov, the first Russian Defence Minister to visit a NATO European council. Then I clear the decks and go on holiday at 6.15.

On Friday night, Sir David and Lady Nicholas treat Nancy and I to seats at *Anything Goes* at the Prince Edward Theatre – a brilliantly vivacious show watched by the Queen Mother on her eighty-ninth birthday. She gets a standing ovation as she takes her seat, and Bernard Cribbins and Elaine Paige lead a chorus of 'Happy Birthday' at the end.

On Saturday, the papers are remarkably docile about the Lord Chief Justice's report on the Hillsborough football disaster. I make the point to the PM that his report does not tally with the impression given by the police. The Sunday press leaves me asking, 'Why don't they go on holiday, too?' We go for another walk in the lanes at Chipstead, gathering blackberries and gleanings from harvested cornfields for floral displays. I finish Stella Gibbons's *Cold Comfort Farm* – a rollicking weekend read.

WEEK 32: 7–13 AUGUST

I prefer this domestic life – mostly gardening – to work, though the humidity is not conducive to hard work. *The Guardian*, feeding its obsession, has a fatuous leader about me. Otherwise, there does not seem to be much doing. Then, after three days of domestication, we set off for America on Thursday, on what turns out to be a fly-drive to beat them all. It does, however, have a bad start. Instead of TWA taking off for St Louis at 1.45 p.m., we do not leave until 4.15 p.m. because, we are told, they need to board extra passengers after delay to another flight. But then we see the ground staff sticking long rods and screwdrivers up the fourth engine to try to open a valve. We doubt whether we shall be able to catch our flight to Denver, Colorado, especially as it takes us seventy-five minutes to clear immigration and customs. My experience suggests it is always harder to get into the USA than to break into the Kremlin. After a fraught time in St Louis, never knowing where we stand, we suddenly fly first class to Denver at 10.20 p.m. After picking up our hire car at the airport – and getting a fellow traveller to show me how to operate the American-built Ford Taurus – we get to the downtown Holiday Inn at 12.10 a.m. This is not the sort of experience I need as a change from life in No. 10's fast lane.

Not having slept a wink, or so it seems, we spend the next day looking around the mile-high (5,000 ft) Denver, after I have got Hertz to show me where the spare tyre and jack are kept in the car. We go to the 16th Street Mall – a pedestrian precinct created by the restoration of a whole area of the city, with a horse-drawn buggy service on tap. It reminds me of Calgary.

Then on Saturday the big adventure begins with a run through ranch land to Cheyenne, Wyoming (which I have always wanted to visit), via Estes, a bowl in the Rockies. In Cheyenne, we visit the railway station, where cattle and grain are being loaded onto long trains drawn by three or four huge locomotives. Then to St Mary's Cathedral for mass.

On Sunday, it is sunshine all the way across the Wild West. Our first stop is at Fort Laramie, a tribute to the pioneers where the staff go about in period dress, the ladies in bustles. We then follow roughly the Bridger and Oregon trails along the North Platte River through Casper, Powder River, Hell's Half Acre, Shoshoni and Wind River Canyon into Thermopolis on the river Bighorn. This is a delightful town with large, round hot springs – hence Thermopolis. The day's drive at an average of 5,000 ft reminds me of looking down the Pennine Chain from the summit of Boulsworth (1,700 ft) near Hebden Bridge, with sage brush substituting for cotton grass and heather, and dry, multicoloured soil for sodden peat. This is a truly magnificent country of contrasts, from Wind River Canyon to the endless prairie.

WEEK 33: 14–20 AUGUST

Whatever is happening in Northern Ireland on the twentieth anniversary of the deployment of troops, we have a fascinating morning in Thermopolis, looking around the extensive sulphur springs and then at a buffalo herd in a park. The route to Cody takes us through near desert, via Meeteetse with its wooden sidewalks and an old-fashioned general store. It used to be a thriving frontier town, according to Wyoming State notices. We look in on its tiny museum before driving through dusty, cattle country to our log cabin in the Buffalo Bill Village.

In the afternoon, with thunder and lightning over the Rockies, we spend a good three hours in the Buffalo Bill Historical Centre, with its fascinating Whitney Western Art Museum. And in the centre's canteen we come across a certain Christopher Hunn, whom I last met in Paris. He is now with British Information Services in New York. You are safe nowhere these days.

On Tuesday, a Holy Day, we go to church with a lovely view of Shoshone Canyon splitting the Rattlesnake Mountains and then set out, fortified by pancakes, for Yellowstone. We go through Shoshone National Forest, apparently the first in America to be designated as such, and on through magnificent views at anything from 7,000 to 9,000 ft. The features of the day are:

1.   Vast tracts of blackened forest from last year's fires;
2.   Some magnificent falls in the Yellowstone River through Yellowstone Canyon;
3.   Geysers, mudholes and thermal springs, with Old Faithful spouting to its full height at 3.30 p.m.;
4.   Twice crossing the Continental Divide on our way to our log cabin in Grant Village overlooking Yellowstone Lake.

After clam chowder and steak for dinner, we go to a lecture in an amphitheatre under a full moon.

Wednesday is not our day. After breakfast with a view of geysers, we drive south for magnificent views of the Grand Tetons, which formed the backdrop to the film *Shane*. In spite of keeping our eyes peeled for animals crossing the road, we have a damaging encounter with an elk. It rushes out of the forest across the road into me, stoving in the driving door, buckling the front wing, cracking the windscreen and leaving a tuft of its coat in the smashed side mirror. Japanese tourists rush to see if we are all right and the car is driveable, as the elk, giving me looks that could kill, wanders back into the woods.

I report the accident to the Forest Ranger station. They take a statement and photograph the car damage without seeming unduly concerned. Hertz's representative is even less disturbed when he finds I can still lock the car door. 'Nothing unusual,' he says. 'We lose about a dozen windscreens a week, mostly from rocks.' So, on we drive to Jackson Hole to buy presents of Native American art in the Wagon Wheel Village, where we stay overnight in a 'superior' log cabin.

On Thursday, we follow the Mormon Trail to Salt Lake City across three mountain ranges in Wyoming, Idaho and Utah through lush farmland and desert – the Tetons through Snake River Canyon; the Salt River Pass; and the Wasatch Mountains forming the eastern wall of the Salt Lake Valley to Salt Lake City. We sit in the Mormon Tabernacle listening to its choir rehearse. This is very relaxing.

Next day, we explore Salt Lake City and are promptly snaffled by a matron for a thirty-minute lecture about the Mormons from their discovery of the Americas from Jerusalem in 500BC via the Pacific to the discovery of their ancient tablets in New England in the early nineteenth century. All this is news to us. We get a wonderful view of the city from the twenty-sixth floor of the Mormon administrative building, before visiting the Capitol and the museum, run by the Daughters of Utah Pioneers. Then we have a run out to the Salt Lake itself on the road to Reno – one of the least distinguished stretches of water I have ever seen.

On Saturday, we are away at 7.30 a.m. after breakfast before the sun is really up, into lonesome Utah to the Big Rock Candy Mountain, which is a bit of a fraud. The lemonade springs seem to have dried up. Then on to Bryce Canyon, with its breathtakingly vast array of vermilion and yellow rock and sand minarets or organ pipes formed by the weather wearing away soft rock. A notice quotes a settler saying, 'It's a helluva place to lose a cow.' We are further awed by the towering cliffs and slabs of rock in Zion National Park in the south of Utah.

On Sunday we are unable to find a church either in Utah or Arizona. We leave the Driftwood Lodge at 8 a.m. for a trip up Zion Canyon through a mile-long tunnel and along the Chequerboard Mesa before turning off south into Arizona. We then learn what the wilderness is all about in climbing to 8,000 ft through magnificent pine forests and mountain meadows en route to the north rim of the Grand Canyon. We spend an hour staring deep down into the canyon and at the vistas before reluctantly leaving through

Marble Canyon, over the Colorado River to Lake Powell, formed by damming up the Colorado. We watch the Shanghai-type traffic on the lake over supper in the rather plush Wahweap Bay resort.

WEEK 34: 21-27 AUGUST

Today (Monday), we cover 315 miles after yesterday's 276 miles. Most of the time the country is well worth seeing – a Navajo reservation; Monument Valley, which is not as impressive as in cowboy films because of their clever camera angles but still a spectacle not to be missed; and then a second day of endless vistas of wilderness, desert, sagebrush, ranch lands, mesas and Native American villages. Lunch in Mexican Hat, then on through a Texaco oilfield with its nodding donkeys, past the Ute Mountain reservation to the Mesa Verde – a great tableland, with its cliff dwellings where an ancient people lived from 500 to 1,300BC, when, it is thought, famine or disease drove them out. Our dinner at our hotel on the plateau is rabbit and South of the Border salad. Before us is a massive thunderstorm 100 miles away over New Mexico, according to the head waiter. Between the flashes of lightning, we get a perfect view of the Milky Way.

We leave at 7 a.m. on Tuesday into a blinding sun for Colorado Springs. Initially, it is a worrying drive because deer are roaming freely. Nonetheless, we make good time to Durango, where steam engines are stoking up for the famous run to the Silverton mines. Then over Wolf Creek Pass (10,860 ft); through 'Little Switzerland' (it looks like it); over the infant Rio Grande and Arkansas Rivers, with tourists white-water rafting down the latter, on either side of Salida; through some of the finest – and richest – ranching country we have seen, judging by the size of the herds; to Cañon City, which seems to amount to little more than a penitentiary. Finally, we get to Colorado Springs, where our hotel is at the foot of Pikes Peak (14,115 ft).

Next day, before running to Denver Airport, we decide it must be Pikes Peak or bust, as the settlers travelling west are reputed to have said. You can actually drive to the summit – a four-hour round trip – but we go by the cog railway. There are lots of ground squirrels and marmots to be seen as we rise to look east 100 miles in beautiful weather to the plains of Kansas. At 3 p.m. we leave for the Stapleton Plaza on the edge of Denver Airport. Embarrassed, I return our damaged car to Hertz who, to my amazement, quickly process the handover. I suppose my accident insurance waiver helps.

On Thursday, we discover that TWA, that model of timekeeping, has put the departure time for St Louis back by more than an hour. We find the outlandish dress of so many travellers helps to pass the time. We fly from St Louis at 9 p.m. and are back home on Friday for lunch after travelling 12,500 miles, including driving more than 2,600 miles. It has been very dry while we have been away, but it is raining now. I ring No. 10 to ask them to send down what turns out to be four briefcases of paper, which confirm it has been a desultory period for news, apart from a terrible accident on the Thames, poor trade figures and the unrest in Poland.

The weekend is lazy, if you ignore demolishing the pile of reading matter. I feel out of condition gardening – the penalty of a fortnight at the wheel. I have four more days of peaceful domestication before I return to what Nancy calls the grindstone. I find the BBC has come up with the idea of marking the fiftieth anniversary of the outbreak of WWII this coming Sunday by Sue Lawley reading the 1939 news in the run-up to the declaration on 3 September, which was also a Sunday.

WEEK 35: 28 AUGUST–3 SEPTEMBER

On Tuesday, I have my annual check-up to see if I am fit to continue in No. 10. Everything seems to be OK, subject to a blood test.

As a final fling, we go on Thursday in glorious weather to the coast, parking the car in Southsea and walking to Portsmouth for lunch. We go to see the historic ships, *Warrior* and HMS *Victory*. As luck would have it, all three of our aircraft carriers are in port. I buy a pewter ship's bell for Nancy in a shop where the saleswoman recognises me. The penalty of appearing on TV.

While the PM is at Chequers, I get off to a flying start with getting up to date because of my reading at the weekend. I work in the press office because my own room is being decorated and cleaned. My agenda includes preparing for the No. 10 press office's expedition to my native Hebden Bridge to mark my ten years in No. 10.

A restful weekend. While blackberrying on Sunday at Chipstead, my thoughts are on 3 September 1939, when my grandfather and I learned of the impending declaration of war by Neville Chamberlain from a fellow walker near Weasel Hall. We hurried home to listen to the PM's broadcast on the wireless.

Our son, John, finishes his doctoral thesis before he takes up a job in the north with the *Daily Express*.

CHAPTER 9

SEPTEMBER 1989: ALL SYSTEMS GO

It's all systems go – but politics are curiously quiescent, apart from wor-ries about the problem Sir Geoffrey Howe presents as Lord President and Deputy PM. I am heavily engaged on GIS work, with visits to Birmingham, Bristol, Cardiff and Newcastle upon Tyne regional offices of the COI. Labour's lead narrows during the month from ten to three points. Energy Secretary John Wakeham announces the privatisation of the electricity industry. And the PM has a successful visit to Japan via talks in Moscow with Mr Gorbachev and a memorable meeting with local and regional politicians and the KGB in Bratsk, Siberia.

WEEK 36: 4–10 SEPTEMBER

What a start to a new political year on Monday! I have lunch and dinner at the Savoy Grill – lunch with Alastair Burnet and Sue Tinson, who are determined to get ITN off to a flying commercial start, and then dinner with Kenneth Harris (*The Ob-server*), who thanks me for my help with his paperback on the PM and picks my brains formidably.

Another Neville Chamberlain, chief executive of BNFL, calls seeking to escape the constraints of public ownership and build BNFL into a private company generating international business. I write a brief for the PM's interview with the *Daily Express* tomor-row and the PM responds positively to my minute on litter.

I suspect that Nick Lloyd's interview will focus on another

outbreak of football hooliganism on a ferry to Sweden, where to-morrow night England play Sweden in the World Cup. I get a briefing together on this for the PM and in doing so talk to Colin Moynihan, Sports minister. He is thinking of appealing to the FA after the Sweden game to call off England's friendly with hooligan-ridden Holland in December.

I don't think Nick Lloyd got much out of his interview with the PM. It went on too long, partly because she is not yet focused after her holiday. The rest of the day is spent organising and briefing. I arrange for Brian Walden (London Weekend Television) to inter-view the PM next month and brief Geoffrey Smith (*The Times*), who subjects me to a searching inquiry about the Reagan–Thatcher relationship. In between, I have lunch with George Bull, partly to prepare myself for the forthcoming visit to Japan. We announce that the PM will be calling in on Mr Gorbachev on 23 September on the flight home from the summit.

Nick Lloyd leads the *Express* with the UK's approach to the Allies to give more aid to Poland in what proves to be the run-up to independence from the Soviet yoke. I think I can also claim to have got the PM some good publicity through her speech to the Inter-Parliamentary Union on drugs, Eastern Europe and the en-vironment. She then goes off to Scotland with my deputy, Terry Perks, knowing *The Sun* is alleging sexual activities by a prominent Tory academic. Not good timing.

I turn to GIS business, spending a jolly ninety minutes with the COI staff at their new London HQ. Later, I have a wrap-up meet-ing with Anne Nash before she goes on holiday. Things seem to be progressing favourably in the GIS. This is followed by a useful meeting with Brian Mower (Home Office) on handling emergen-cies. I also see Terry Wogan's producer and promise to try to get the PM on his show.

Wednesday's lunch is with Marc Schuster (Babcock), who wants the PM to address the Institution of Production Engineers and visit Babcock's Renfrew factory. I am no sooner back in the office than I learn that England football fans have been causing mayhem in Stockholm. It is absolutely sickening.

Thursday is given over to GIS business, with a visit to Birmingham and the National Exhibition Centre. COI morale is low, partly because of the loss of their regional director and partly because of uncertainty arising from the plan to make the COI an executive agency. My meeting is followed by a fast COI-conducted tour of the NEC and Arena. A worthwhile day.

On Friday, we have a very good meeting of the media honours committee. It gives me an insight into how candidates are viewed within their own organisations. A gentle afternoon before Nancy and then the Alis – Mohsin and Dolores from Washington, DC – come to No. 10 before dinner at the Reform. Mohsin was a fighter pilot over Burma during WWII and then the long-standing diplomatic editor of Reuters before he retired to Washington to work part-time for *The Times*. He took John under his wing when he was on a Fulbright scholarship to Georgetown University, Washington, and introduced him to journalism in the White House, State Department and Pentagon. Is it any wonder he became a journalist? We have a very entertaining evening. Dolores loves being shown around the historic club, and trencherman Mohsin is in seventh heaven with an enormous mixed grill.

Another relaxing weekend. We have drinks on Saturday with John and Christine at Gatwick en route for their holiday in Portugal, then a walk on the Downs and tea on Sunday on the terrace with our next-door neighbours, Ken and Margaret Bromley. The Sunday press is full of our all-action PM, most of it the product of invention apart from her halting an intrusive sex survey, allegedly designed to help the AIDS education campaign.

WEEK 37: 11–17 SEPTEMBER

Up with the larks at 5.30 a.m. on Monday to get a flight from Heathrow to Newcastle upon Tyne to join the Prime Minister. We follow roughly Hadrian's Wall to Border TV, via Carlisle Airport to pick up the PM. The airport is rather run-down and needs to decide its future. The PM has a good TV interview on the community charge, Scottish politics and the environment from a farming point of view.

She then has lunch with Cumbria Newspapers and presents their export awards. She ad libs her way through the issued text of her talk, much to the press's consternation, but she does include a passage on the need to keep interest rates high to squeeze out inflation. This gets extensive play on the news bulletins. We are back in London by 5 p.m. I discover that Calder High School, one of the first comprehensives, which replaced my Hebden Bridge Grammar School, has invited me to speak at its fortieth anniversary dinner.

Another 5.30 a.m. call on Tuesday, this time because the PM is off to Northern Ireland. I am in the office for 6.30 reading the newspapers. We have an excellent breakfast on board the HS125 to Aldergrove, arriving at 8.45 a.m. There, we transfer to a draughty helicopter, which leaks oil onto Charles Powell's suit. Our first call is a Londonderry industrial estate, where we are welcomed by the mayor. We have a look at several industrial units in the former Courtaulds factory before being shown Du Pont's Kevlar, a very tough fibre.

From Derry, we helicopter south to the most mortared outpost in Northern Ireland. It boosts the garrison's morale and so does her visit to the Worcester and Sherwood Foresters and their families in Omagh. In response to the BBC and others, she admires the bravery of the Ulster Defence Regiment (UDR), which is under sustained criticism, and expresses her confidence in it. She then does one of those tiresome walkabouts in Carryduff, less fraught than is usual in Northern Ireland, where the media think they own ministers, and especially Prime Ministers. We then fly to spend a fascinating hour with the Northern Ireland Forensic Science Service on detection through fibres, DNA, footprints and traces of explosives. A reception follows at Hillsborough, site of NI government. We are back in London for 9 p.m.

The press on Wednesday gives good coverage to the visit and mostly leads with her support for the UDR – remarks which, it is said, have upset Dublin. I brief a group of Malaysians on what I do and can't do, bringing out the dividing line between government and party. After a talk with Paul Potts, I have a riotous lunch at the Garrick with Don Cook, Bill Tuohy and Frank Melville (American correspondents). I take the opportunity to thank the actor Michael Hordern for all the pleasure he has given us over the years. He was with Dominic Harrod and (Lord) Jock Bruce-Gardyne, who shows wonderful spirit in spite of his brain tumour.

Later, I am called upon to write a paper on what the PM should include in her Blackpool conference speech from a government point of view. John Whittingdale, the PM's political secretary, calls in the next day (Thursday) to say it proved very useful at a meeting later on the speech.

The Guardian reports a ten-point lead for Labour – a lead which does not dismay Foreign Secretary Major, calling in to brief me on Cabinet. We discuss how he should handle the media and the behaviour of his predecessor and how Lord President Howe presents a problem for the government. By coincidence, I am called to see Howe in his role as Leader of the Commons on televising the House. I lunch with Victor Garland, formerly Australian High Commissioner and now with the Prudential. Then I brief Lyndy Payne and five other women in the communications business on the PM and government. In the evening we have another drinks party for information officers.

Friday finds me in Newcastle upon Tyne for the second time in a week. My role as head of the GIS takes me there to meet the COI staff as well as speaking at a lunch held by Shepherd's, the York building firm. The COI give me an extensive tour of Newcastle, Upper Tyneside, the site of the garden festival, Gateshead's Metro Centre and the magnificent flower displays in Blaydon and Ryton en route to Wylam for the Shepherd's lunch. I find that the COI staff, like those in Birmingham, are worried about the future of the

COI as an executive agency. They hope it will allow them to compete for public sector business. At the lunch, I give the audience my assessment of the PM's contribution to international affairs.

By teatime and the football results on Saturday, I have virtually cleared the decks for next week's visit to Japan – and a restful Sunday. The *Sunday Correspondent* launches itself on the market without much distinction. I fear it will not last because it will find it difficult to compete with established newspapers, even though I think *The Observer* has gone to pot.

The latest Harris poll gives Labour an eight-point lead and the press give Paddy Ashdown reasonable marks for his performance at the SLD conference. We go mushroom picking in Chipstead – rather warm work in the humid weather.

WEEK 38: 18–24 SEPTEMBER

To Japan via Moscow. But first, the press digest. I record Bryan Gould, a member of Labour's shadow Cabinet, making a gaffe by promising renationalisation; increasing evidence of the left-wingery of the Greens; the resignation of a doctor from the British Medical Association because he thinks the BMA campaign against NHS reforms is frightening patients; and an industrial feature which, promisingly for the government, finds that most people are optimistic about the 1990s. And on that happy note we fly from Heathrow at 12.30 p.m. We enter Soviet airspace over Lithuania and fly over Riga into a wet Moscow.

The PM is received at a six-course supper (caviar, salad, soup, cold meats, prawns and savoury sweets, with vodka, wine or fizzy water) by Yevgeny Primakov, Speaker of the Supreme Soviet of the Soviet Union, who is apparently called 'Harrier' after the aircraft – he rises straight and fast. It is an entirely enjoyable experience. The PM savages him over Afghanistan when he says the Mujahideen are being supplied by the USA. He is also hilarious about televising the Supreme Soviet because it has been used to raise people's expectations when they should be damped down or, at least, extended in time.

I get little sleep on the overnight flight, crossing the Urals and Siberia, and when we come to, we find ourselves over the endless plain of eastern Russia, with some snow on the top of the hills. Tokyo is awash under the twenty-second typhoon to hit it this year. We are driven to the Embassy for lunch with the Ambassador, Sir John Whitehead, and Lady Whitehead.

The PM feels worn out and has a break before a trip to the University of Tokyo for a presentation by a meteorologist, a chemist and an engineer on their work in combating global warming. They produce a graph showing how France, Canada and Sweden have cut their CO_2 emissions through nuclear power. On then to the Mitsui Bank to see BT and Reuters' equipment in use on the trading floor.

As we are to find during the whole of this tour, the PM is mobbed by girls who are beginning to flex their muscles in the cause of equality. They are so enthusiastic at the British Council reception that she has to leave early. I find that someone has leaked Primakov's mischievous throwaway line about the PM addressing the Supreme Soviet. I can't wait to see them wince. The day closes with my having a lively discussion with the editors of two Tokyo newspapers.

I sleep even less on Tuesday night than on the flight the night before. This is not the best start to a trip south by bullet train on Wednesday to the lower slopes of Mount Fuji to visit a high-tech industrial estate. The train is clean, smooth and affords excellent viewing but does not seem as fast as I imagined the bullet train would be. The countryside is at its best now that the typhoon has passed over and it is interesting to see how every bit of available land is given over to growing food.

The translating computer causes great fun in welcoming the PM's party with its poor fist at English. I fall foul of their technology when in the loo I press the wrong button and get sprayed by the built-in bidet all down my front. Very embarrassing. I dry out on the journey back.

In Tokyo, the PM delivers a call to arms against protectionism before a high-powered audience, urging the nations of the world to open up their markets. She then calls on a Laura Ashley store en route to talks with Toshiki Kaifu, the Japanese PM, at the Akasaka Palace, where we are quartered. I have a decanter of Scotch whisky in my room. The two PMs have a somewhat ludicrous discussion on TV before Mr Kaifu comes good, announcing two more places for British firms on the Tokyo stock exchange. To round off the day, he entertains the PM and her party to an eventful dinner in the palace's annexe, at a sunken table which tests the PM's ingenuity in taking her seat with decorum. Charles Powell, famished after a busy day, starts to cook his beef on his personal stove – we all have one. Unfortunately, the fat catches fire and his geisha girl, as we call our individual waiters, somewhat exasperatedly comes to the rescue. We get the message. It is their job to do the cooking.

On Thursday, the No. 10 press office tells me that the visit is getting good coverage. They also report Mr Gorbachev's reshuffle to strengthen his hand and Ford bidding for 15 per cent of Jaguar. Topically, Jaguar pull off a coup by getting the boss of Sony to buy one of their cars – and the keys presented to him by the PM. More joy follows at the British primary school within the Shibuya Girls' High School, where the welcoming banner spells 'Openening' on the stage. The British Council gives us the smoothest presentation I can remember – far too smooth for me. I browse through their library and find it records correctly that I was sent a letter bomb in 1987.

The PM has a private lunch with the Emperor and his family and clearly enjoys it enormously. An inconsequential hour-long press conference follows – if you ignore the PM's truly warm and admiring encomium to Mr Gorbachev. A bit over the top in style if not in content. Talks successively with Ministry of International Trade and Industry and the staff of the British Embassy follow before a ludicrous bilateral with US Vice-President Dan Quayle, in a tiny room where all kinds of conservatives meeting from across the world, including Argentina, lurk to accost the PM.

After nearly a week without proper sleep, on Friday I am roused at 5.30 a.m. to torrential rain, which means our helicopter trip to the Commonwealth War Cemetery at Yokohama is out of the question. Instead, we go by road and, as predicted by the Embassy, the police handle the journey brilliantly. It is fine by the time we get to the beautifully kept cemetery for a brief but moving ceremony, not-withstanding some out-of-tune bugling by Gurkhas from Seoul.

I work in my room over a sandwich lunch before we leave for the airport at 3.20 p.m. En route there is a false alarm: namely, that the travelling press are caught up in a jam and could delay our de-parture. We take off at 4 p.m. for Bratsk on the Angara River in Siberia. During the flight, we hear of an IRA atrocity at Deal, Kent, which causes a lot of teleprinter traffic on board.

Bratsk is a delight in a provincial, frontier way. The PM is met by local and regional party representatives, plus the KGB in shiny black coats and pork pie hats. The PM keeps the conversation going with them for ninety minutes during refuelling over a very curious coffee. Next door, the travelling press are treated to vodka at £1 a shot. I expect they will sleep during the six hours to Moscow, where we arrive just after midnight local time. I am quartered in the Spartan Rossiya Hotel.

I get to bed at 2.45 a.m. and am up at 7.30 on Saturday for an 8 a.m. start at the Embassy across the river. After the PM leaves for the Kremlin, I walk around Red Square among the tourists. At 1 p.m., Ambassador Rodric Braithwaite takes me to the Kremlin, where we are given a thirty-minute tour before the PM emerges from her talks with Mr Gorbachev. It has clearly been a good meeting and, after being given a quick debrief, I am able to provide the British media with a good run-down at the Embassy. During a successful press conference, she follows my advice to apply her formidable will in support of Mr Gorbachev. She also has some lively words for the large crowd gathered outside the Embassy, as well as to Soviet TV. We brief the US chargé d'affaires on the Gorbachev meeting before leaving at 7 p.m. Back in No. 10 by 8.30 London time after a

13,500-mile trip. I get home, burdened with a backlog of paper, for 10.30 p.m., completely bushed.

After eight hours' sleep, I have a gentle Saturday and find the Sunday press quite complimentary about the trip, with Michael Jones leading the way in the *Sunday Times*. The trip went far better than I expected. It may also have been rewarding for the PM: the latest opinion poll cuts Labour's lead to three points. I plough through the week's press and magazines sitting on the terrace in balmy weather until the midges get at me at 6.30 p.m. The press office tells me that a visit to Deal tomorrow is being arranged for the PM.

WEEK 39: 25 SEPTEMBER–1 OCTOBER

I write a brief for the PM's eighth consecutive visit to the Newspaper Press Fund's annual lunch on Wednesday, before becoming embroiled in GIS management issues. I have lunch with Marshall Stewart, ex-BBC and now in PR, who is puzzling out how to prepare for the next TV licence auction. What criteria, I ask, is the Independent Television Commission working out to aid its judgement?

I see Lord Whitelaw coming from a meeting with the PM. His concern is to get the Tory Party behind its government, and for Health Secretary Kenneth Clarke, Health minister David Mellor and junior Education minister Robert Jackson to be less abrasive. Sarah Charman goes with the PM to Deal in the aftermath of the IRA bombing and then to the *Good Housekeeping* dinner.

On Tuesday, I drive on a GIS pastoral visit to Bristol and Cardiff. At the Pithay, the rather decrepit home of the regional COI in Bristol, they seem pleased to see me and hear first-hand of my thinking about the development of the GIS. In Cardiff, the Welsh Information Office give me an excellent lunch in the ministerial flat and show me the 1930s decor in the boardroom of their listed building. They seem rather pleased with their professional performance and I have no doubt that they are very good at the mechanics of our trade.

Wednesday is a day of relative relaxation. Jim Craig, Ulster TV, comes in to see me at noon. We have a good chat about Ulster's view of the White Paper on broadcasting and their fears about losing C4 revenues and so wiping out their profit and consequently limiting their bid when the franchise comes up for renewal. Ulster TV thinks it has done pretty well by a divided community.

I have lunch in the rather pretentious Mark's Club in Mayfair with John Banks (Young & Rubicam), who wants to present their new VALS – values and lifestyle research – to the PM. It might be difficult to persuade her because of the friction in Tory Central Office during the 1987 general election. On then to a meeting with the lobby and press gallery officers about the inadequate availability of confidential private revises (CFRs) – documents issued under embargo – and press notices. I take the opportunity to register a complaint about the leakage of issued CFRs to commercial companies.

An inconclusive meeting follows on the leaking of one of my minutes. So what's new? I then help the PM to revise her speech to tonight's NPF reception, attended by the former Australian PM Malcolm Fraser, in Australia House. In a talk with her afterwards, she discloses her worries about the Lord President, Geoffrey Howe.

The next day, I fear Japan, and too much drink in my worn-out condition, catches up with me. The day begins with breakfast at the Horseguards Hotel with Dan Pedersen of *Newsweek*, who is very interested in how the UK government works. Afterwards, I spend three precious, blessed hours reading Cabinet papers and generally shifting paper before lunch with Ian McIntyre, ex-BBC author and now *Times* associate editor. He wants to interview the PM, but I doubt whether that will be possible before the party conference.

Cabinet discusses the launch of a televised House in November, on what seems likely to be the day of the Queen's Speech. They take my point about the need to use plain words – *Fowler's English Usage* should be compulsory reading – and to watch their demeanour, given that they are performing on a vast public stage instead of to a largely politicised audience. At a special meeting of MIO in the afternoon, we discuss the issue and set ourselves a lot of urgent work, given that the fateful day is only six weeks away.

On Friday, John Wakeham is able to announce a timetable for electricity privatisation. He has clearly done a good job of rescuing it from Cecil Parkinson's neglect. After compiling the digest, I then have a couple of hours to get a straight edge before Dick Foxton, a friend from South Africa, calls in to bring me up to date with developments in the republic and to discuss cricket. The *Sunday Express* then interviews me about my ten years in No. 10.

I then go to the City of London school near St Paul's to talk to pupils about my job. It appears to be a very well-run establishment, though the pupils seem wooden in response to my attempts to be humorous. I brief the Sunday lobby somewhat inconsequentially before writing a series of minutes to the PM on her engagements, visits and requests for interviews. Brian Hitchen gives me a friendly warning that he will lead the *Daily Star* with an exposé of the insecurity of footpaths on the Chequers estate. Sarah Charman returns from what seems to have been a rather fraught day with the PM in Nottingham.

On Saturday, we are guests of Paul Fox (BBC), along with Peter Sissons (C4) and George Russell (IBA), at Ascot. Nancy goes home weighed down with winnings. I lose £10. While there, I see Eric Varley, ex-Labour Energy Secretary, and his wife, Marjorie, guests of Morgan Grenfell. He tells me he is now out of work following the takeover of Coalite, of which he was chairman, and would like a job, as an ex-mineworker, with the National Coal Board (NCB). I promise to let John Wakeham know.

Sunday 1 October marks my tenth anniversary as the PM's press secretary. What a momentous decade! Various polls put Labour five to twelve points ahead. The Sunday press focuses on an attack by the Archbishop of Canterbury, Robert Runcie, on the 'Pharisee tendency' in Britain, whatever that means – unless he wants to drive the Iron Lady out of the temple. I keep the PM out of it. We don't want a Thatcher–Runcie row on the eve of the Labour Party conference. This starts with Kinnock siding with Runcie, who is visiting the Pope in Rome.

The *Sunday Times* is quite helpful on this and Peregrine Worsthorne has an excellent leader in the *Sunday Telegraph* on the PM's international stature. What is fascinating about the latest opinion polls, even with the Labour Party in conference, is that few if any newspapers feel able to predict a Labour victory. Instead, they are at best cautious and often quite gloomy about Kinnock's chances.

CHAPTER 10

OCTOBER 1989: CRISIS IN GOVERNMENT

Government is in a febrile state after I celebrate my ten years in No. 10. Chancellor Nigel Lawson resigns and is soon followed by Sir Alan Walters, the PM's economic adviser. Lawson proposes to announce his resignation to the PM's maximum disadvantage – just before she an-swers the first PMQs of the new session and her statement on a fractious Commonwealth Heads of Government Meeting (CHoGM) in Kuala Lumpur. He is persuaded to delay it for an hour. Walters earlier strongly opposed a rise in interest rates to 15 per cent, saying the economy is tight enough and rejecting a preoccupation with the level of the pound. But Lawson's resignation comes after the FT *mischievously published an article written eighteen months ago and before Walters returned to the PM's service. Both Michael Heseltine and Sir Geoffrey Howe let it be known they will not challenge the PM's leadership. Famous last words?*

The PM and Foreign Secretary John Major are on the defensive at CHoGM on South African sanctions and the environment amid talk of a global stock exchange meltdown. Their decision to publish their own communiqué because the official one does not spell out their reservations causes outrage, notably among the Commonwealth press buffs. They do not practise the freedom of speech they preach.

WEEK 40: 2–8 OCTOBER

On Monday, the *FT* does a pretty fair piece about me, and lots of people tell me they think the publicity about my decade in

No. 10 has been good. Anne complains about my weekend industry, which comes back into the in-tray beautifully typed.

At the PM's 9 a.m. meeting, everyone seems to think the government had a bad press yesterday because so many were trying to talk it into raising interest rates again. The PM follows this with a ninety-minute talk with Brian Walden, the former Labour MP and *Weekend World* presenter, about her future prospects. He thinks she has a real fight on her hands over the NHS, the community charge and rallying the women's vote.

I then go off to lunch with Lord Stevens, chairman of United Newspapers, who says he is trying to find ways of protecting the Express Group from takeover, with Conrad Black, the *Telegraph's* owner, apparently chief predator. During the afternoon, I brief journalists from Soweto, South Africa, on my job.

On Tuesday, I have lunch with Professor Graham Ashworth, chairman of the Keep Britain Tidy group. Our views have much in common. Later, the press office holds a party for me to mark my ten years. The PM, Robin Butler, Nigel Wicks and the entire press office I inherited from the Callaghan regime: Andy Wood (Northern Ireland Office), Charles Anson (who will later become the Queen's press secretary) and Jan Luke (COI). Most of the press office staff over my ten years turn up. Even Iain Murray (FCO, El Salvador) and Gordon Shepherd (now with an environmental organisation in Geneva) get there. The PM pays me a handsome tribute – my sense of humour, capacity to cope and power over the media. The last is something of a Thatcher overstatement. In return, I count my good fortune in working for her, admire her guts and commend to her the teams of press officers who have worked for her during my time. A 'reight good do', as they say in Hebden Bridge.

I go to bed on Wednesday knowing that interest rates will rise tomorrow by 1 per cent to 15 per cent. What a pity. But with the Bundesbank raising its rate, the government has little alternative, given that it is determined to drive down inflation and not let employers off the hook by refusing to allow the exchange rate to decline significantly. Professor Sir Alan Walters is very put out by this decision. He thinks the economy is too tight already and that we are facing a recession next year. He rejects completely the preoccupation with the level of sterling – indeed, the entire strategy and tactics. 'What happens if the pound continues to fall?' he asks when he pops into my room. To my layman's mind, he seems to have a point. But Paul Gray, the PM's economics private secretary, is worried about how emotional Walters has become. Everyone is wondering whether he will spill the beans over dinner with someone.

Earlier in the day, the government struggled without great success to sort out the transitional arrangements for the community charge. The PM also made an awful fist of her lunch with American correspondents. Her mind simply was not on it. Altogether, I spend five hours in meetings today – on the press digest and future diary and with Sue Cameron, journalist; Tom Arnold, publisher and former Tory Party vice-chairman; the GIS executive and the IBA.

On Thursday, I drive with Nancy to Yorkshire with a bad conscience, knowing that interest rates are to be raised. They rise in the afternoon, but it seems to go quietly, even with Labour in conference in Brighton. I try to keep in touch with the office during the four and a half-hour drive. I drop Nancy off at the Hebden Lodge Hotel in Hebden Bridge before driving to Asda's Morley store and then to dinner in Asda's new HQ south of the river Aire in Leeds. It is heart-warming to see so much development going on in central Leeds while fishermen still cast their lines into the river. At the dinner, I am provoked into an assault on the media by Gerry Holbrook, managing director of the *Yorkshire Post*, which enlivens the conversation. Back in Hebden Bridge by 11.15 p.m.

I drop Nancy off in her native Halifax on Friday before returning to Leeds for a good two hours with the COI's regional staff. I am met by Frank Metcalfe, ex-*Yorkshire Evening Post* who is working for the COI on a freelance basis. The regional director's deputy is Peter Craven, also ex-*YEP*. I find the office in good heart. There is remarkably little recrimination in the press over the rise in bank rate.

While I am in Leeds, the No. 10 press office is gathering in Hebden Bridge for my tenth anniversary weekend there. After visiting Nancy's sister and my brother, I lead the convoy to Far Flat Head Farm for dinner.

On Saturday, the press office – Mike Bates, the duty press officer, fielding calls on his mobile phone – friends and a few journalist friends walk to Stoodley Pike in a drizzle. The higher we approach this imposing memorial to the Treaty of Paris of 1812, the more we enter the clouds. Suddenly the Pike, with its viewing gallery thirty feet above ground, emerges out of the mist. We return to Hebden Bridge via Weasel Hall, which sounds like something out of *The Wind in the Willows*, to get a magnificent, elevated view of the town. During the afternoon, some go off to Walkley Clogs, a sort of commercial working museum, to see all sorts of clogs being made from timber lying in the yard and leather.

Dinner at the Hebden Lodge is an unqualified success with splendid food. The cheesecake is the largest I have ever been served. My brother and his wife, John and Christine and Christine's parents all join the jolly party. Among the many gifts is a World War II tin hat, which I am advised to wear regularly, such is the nature of our trade.

A wonderful weekend comes to a close with a morning's walk up the Heptonstall hillside on which Cavaliers and Roundheads fought, to a hamlet with a sign on the terrace of houses proclaiming its name – Slack Bottom. This is a temptation too large to resist; I photograph the party bending over, backsides to the fore, under the sign. We return for lunch at the Hebden Lodge via Heptonstall village and inspect the ruins of its ancient church and Sylvia Plath's grave before capturing another good view of Hebden Bridge and Upper Calder Valley from Brockholes, my playground as a boy, with its gnarled oak woods, steep grassland and quarries. All very nostalgic. In the afternoon, we go our separate ways – Nancy and I to Moffat in southern Scotland for a week's break while the Tories are in conference.

WEEK 41: 9–15 OCTOBER

In Scotland for four days. I don't go into the office until Friday, to prepare myself for next week's Commonwealth Heads of Government Meeting in Malaysia.

Monday takes us from Moffat to Glencoe via Glasgow, Erskine Bridge over the Clyde, to Helensburgh and Rhu, where we got engaged. Then Arrochar, Crianlarich and Tyndrum and down Glencoe to our hotel, the Creag Dhu (renamed the Lodge on the Loch – Loch Linnhe, that is). We have time for a look around Fort William.

With the cloud down over the mountains on Tuesday, we visit Glencoe village and the National Trust Visitor Centre. We have coffee at the King's House Hotel on Rannoch Moor and walk up to the White Corries ski lift before lunch in Glencoe. In the afternoon, we go beachcombing in front of the hotel for pebble eggs in a wide range of colours on a shoreline that is of great geological interest. Loch Linnhe is bathed in moonlight.

Wednesday's breakfast is disturbed because Ross Benson (*Daily Express*) says I am at odds with Bill Heseltine, the Queen's private secretary, because I don't think she should have an Australian private secretary. This is news to me. I tell the press office to tell all and sundry – including the Palace – that this is pure invention. I neither hold nor have expressed such a view. That done, we are off to the mill shops in Spean Bridge and Fort William to buy presents and visit Fort William's West Highland Museum. There, we learn that Flora MacDonald, of Bonnie Prince Charlie fame, emigrated to the USA and came home to die. After walks on the lower slopes of Ben Nevis, I retire to the hotel to read my brief for Friday's press conference on CHoGM.

Thursday sees a long drive home to Surrey, taking eleven hours, including a visit to my elderly aunts in Fleetwood. After the shores of Loch Lomond, we are in Glasgow for 10.40 and Kendal around 1 p.m., where I ring my aunts to tell them we are on our way. We leave Fleetwood at 3 p.m. and are home for 7.15 with 550 miles on the clock. I have never driven so far in one day. Press office tells me all is quiet.

Friday is an easy day back in the office and by 7 p.m. I have cleared the decks. By the time I get home, there is news of a late plummet on the Wall Street stock exchange. I give a briefing on CHoGM which provides some good lines for Saturday's papers. I have a meeting with Romola Christopherson, a former deputy and now head of information at the Department of Health, on GIS matters, and get my jabs for Malaysia, while the PM is making a stunning speech at the Tory Party conference which earns her a ten-minute standing ovation. I wish she would do more of this.

Geoffrey Tucker (former Central Office agent and now a PR consultant) comes in to tell me I need to sort out what I propose to do in retirement. He kindly offers to help.

On Saturday, I spend a lot of time briefing myself in case of a London stock exchange crash. I also check with Paul Gray on the state of the public expenditure round. It seems likely that the Star Chamber to sort out departmental spending stalemates will meet next week. It comprises Geoffrey Howe, Norman Lamont, Nicholas Ridley, Kenneth Clarke, John MacGregor and Norman Fowler. All this promises a lively time on the flight to Malaysia.

Sunday is a beautiful autumn day and a press full of foreboding about a stock exchange crash and the end of 'pure Thatcherism'. Bruce Anderson even foreshadows the age of 'Fabian Thatcherism', whatever that means. This is a load of old rope and I shall so demonstrate when I get back into my briefing stride. I feel better prepared for this CHoGM than the previous five and doubt whether it is going to tax me unless there are unfortunate events at home.

WEEK 42: 16–22 OCTOBER

We leave for Kuala Lumpur in the RAF's trusty VC10 with the world trembling on the brink of a stock exchange crash, if you believe the broadsheets. Some of the tabloids ignore it on their front pages. The issue dominates the morning and the stock exchange does fall by about 10 per cent, but the pound remains fairly firm. At the end of the day, it is clear that the press is more panicky and alarmist than shareholders and dealers. I suggest to the PM that she might say during the refuelling stop in Bahrain that she is pleased to see the media doom-mongers have been largely confounded. I spend much of the sixteen-hour journey reading the FCO's profiles of Commonwealth countries. This is the first flight with the PM for Foreign Secretary Major. I sort out my appalling diary with my secretary en route. In Bahrain, I find that Bronte (heather honey) liqueur, to which we are partial, is sold out.

We arrive on Tuesday in Kuala Lumpur at 1.25 p.m. local time. I am duly installed in the Shangri-La Hotel, with its beautiful view of the racecourse. We have a quiet lunch in the PM's suite before we all take a break. At 5.30, the PM goes off to an inconsequential meeting with CHoGM's host Prime Minister, Dr Mahathir – inconsequential, that is, if you ignore their argument over the procedure for electing a new Commonwealth Secretary General. They also sign a drug trafficking agreement – the tenth the UK has so far achieved. At the end of it, the PM looks drawn. She and her husband have a bad nose and chest cold, causing much snuffling on the flight. We shall be lucky to escape the germs.

The media reception is more a meeting of heads of delegation. The PM learns that Rajiv Gandhi, Prime Minister of India, is in difficulty over an election he has declared, and will be prevented from attending. My final briefing of the press at 9 p.m. is a quiet, civilised affair.

Wednesday is a quiet day because the media are preoccupied with a major earthquake in San Francisco. The FCO inform us about it just as the PM's party is entering the conference hall for the colourful opening ceremony. A loss of life is feared because bridges have collapsed. From that moment, it is clear that CHoGM is going to be of marginal interest in Britain tomorrow.

This in no way eases the pain of having to listen to first Mahathir and then a most nauseating Brian Mulroney harping on about

South African sanctions and their alleged success. I write a note to Andrew Turnbull saying, 'This is a pretty comprehensive MOAN.' I later ask Foreign Secretary Major whether it was as bad as he thought it would be. Worse, he said. The British delegation does not applaud the knocking speeches. I describe it at my 3 p.m. briefing of the press as 'par for the course' at Commonwealth conferences.

Benazir Bhutto (PM of Pakistan) is an impressive figure in bright green and a head shawl, which she has continually to adjust during her speech. We have lunch with the PM in her suite and I give a press briefing at 3 p.m. and a fuller one at 6 p.m. on the PM's panoramic speech on global trends. By then, the Nigerian Emeka Anyaoku has been elected Secretary General. He introduces himself to me in the lobby of the Pan Pacific. I congratulate him and wish him every success. The press office team have dinner at a restaurant on the recommendation of Mike Bates, our FCO expert, where the gargantuan choice leaves me feeling very fat by 12.30 a.m.

Thursday is South Africa day. It is the occasion for the ritual bashing of Britain in which all – black, white and brown – indulge themselves to the full. Bob Hawke, the Australian PM, plays a pretty disgraceful hand. He sees the PM over breakfast in her suite and makes no mention of a five-point plan to intensify financial sanctions. The PM only hears about it when she is given a paper just before rising to make her speech. Her response is tough – and necessarily so. The Foreign Secretary is shocked at the way the debate went and wonders whether Britain would withdraw all Commonwealth aid.

In her speech, the PM contrasts UK efforts to reduce poverty and hunger while the rest are prepared to increase it. She refuses to have anything to do with further sanctions, calling for carrots not sticks – incentives for South Africa to reform further.

I thoroughly enjoy giving out the line to the media that, whatever people say publicly to the PM, privately they are prepared to acknowledge that only Britain has influence with South Africa and is exercising it successfully. It leaves the journalists a bit stunned. After this, CHoGM turns to the environment. The PM sees the

Sultan of Bahrain – a defence procurement protocol has been signed – before going off to speak at a dinner.

According to custom, the heads of government 'retreat' on Friday to a resort – Langkawi – for a break. It has been an easy CHoGM so far, bearing in mind that I have always told those who wonder what it is like to be the odd man out among fifty that it is wonderful when you are right – and smilingly provoke them, saying we usually are. But we are now fighting on a number of fronts – at the moment over the environment as well as on sanctions against South Africa.

On the environment, the PM is very much against setting up a Commonwealth fund. Any additional money that is required should be dispensed through existing UN institutions. It is not easy to get this across when we are in the conference doghouse. The PM sends a message in the evening – the press team remains in Kuala Lumpur – to say that in spite of my efforts, TV has still got it wrong. Earlier, she had a rickshaw ride and took part in traditional Malaysian dancing with Benazir Bhutto at the retreat's concert.

On the South Africa front, John Major battles for fifteen hours to get a reasonable communiqué and manages to protect the UK position all along the line. He is proving a delightful Foreign Secretary to work with.

With the conference still at its retreat, the press office has a jaunt to the Genting Highlands, which my secretary Anne describes as Blackpool in the clouds. This is the second weekend running I have been out with my staff, and again getting limited views – this time from the top of a 6,000 ft mountain instead of Stoodley Pike at Hebden Bridge. We descend to visit a batik factory, a scorpion farm where they gas them and mount them in plastic, and a pewter factory, where I buy a dish for Nancy.

We get back to Kuala Lumpur for 2.30 p.m. for a satay lunch and then a press briefing on events at Langkawi – among other things, the PM playing with Benazir Bhutto's baby. I have dinner with Sue Tinson, who is with an ITN team making a film.

When the cat's away, the mice do play. And on Sunday, the press office team, including Martin Smith, the COI's radio expert, has a trip to the coast – to Melaka – through palm oil and rubber plantations with a professional guide. He takes us to a Malayan house with a well in the kitchen and no doors; to Buddhist, Taoist and Confucian temples; and to listen to a professional folk singer in the ruins of the fort. Fascinating.

Back to Kuala Lumpur and trouble. The retreat has gone reasonably well and the PM feels able to sign up to the conference statement on South Africa, subject to reservations which are recorded on four points without much explanation. The PM and Foreign Secretary decide to put out their own statement spelling out the reservations and I am left to present it to the media at 6 p.m. The immediate reaction is predictable: indignation – even outrage – among the Commonwealth buffs, notably John Dickie of the *Daily Mail*. But it only hots up after dinner when the Foreign Secretary is given a going-over by the diplomatic correspondents – habitués of the FCO. He gives better than he gets, but the issue has taken off in a big way. Britain is not apparently to be allowed free speech in the Commonwealth.

WEEK 43: 23–29 OCTOBER

Another row over South Africa. Mahathir, after reporting on the Langkawi retreat, comments on the British statement elaborating on the official communiqué and invites other comments. They do not flow easily, but eventually Hawke, backed up by Mulroney, lodges a protest and asks for an explanation. The PM says she is astounded and appalled that the Commonwealth is complaining about free speech. I let Reuters know of this before briefing the rest to make sure an objective account is immediately on record.

I get to work on the media about noon, when I also report on the drugs trafficking debate. The row rumbles on all day, with the PM giving terse sound bites and John Major lots of interviews. The PM is brassed off with Hawke and to a greater degree Mulroney but plugs away at meeting people and finds no one complaining about her statement to her face. We all go to a farewell dinner and concert in the Shangri-La. The atmosphere reminds me of the false camaraderie at TUC conferences.

At last, CHoGM is over. On Tuesday, the communiqué is approved within ten minutes – much to the PM's satisfaction – and the heads of government felicitations are soon over. An ebullient, tough and some say cocky PM gives the usual six radio and TV interviews before 10 a.m. This is followed by a press conference, which ends CHoGM on a high media note with lots of copy. And so we depart for Doha, Qatar, for refuelling – an eight-hour flight, during which the PM rehearses material for PMQs and her statement to the House on CHoGM. I am feeling excessively plump and cannot face the Emir of Qatar's dinner in his £250 million sumptuous white marble palace. I wonder how such an obvious tough egg can manage to have such a beautiful palace. He certainly does not have much social grace.

By Wednesday, we are utterly confused by all the time differences and the UK putting the clock back this weekend into the bargain. No wonder: we are back in No. 10 for 4.30 a.m. I have a shower and change and set to work on the usual backlog of paper, running to two briefcases before the newspapers arrive. It is clear from them that Alan Walters remains a problem, with the mischievous publication by the *FT* of an article he wrote eighteen months ago (with publication twice delayed) arguing that the ERM is a first step towards a common currency. I cobble together a briefing line as follows:

1. The article is ancient history and obviously much delayed;
2. It was intended for publication long before Walters returned part-time to No. 10 as the PM's economic adviser;
3. Whatever officials, part- or full-time, may say – and they should give advice confidentially – ministers decide;
4. The government has decided to enter the ERM when certain conditions, as stated at the EU summit in Madrid, are fulfilled.

This is helpfully portrayed as reflecting the Chancellor's view that Walters should shut up. (I have been telling Walters that for years.)

I have a very enjoyable lunch with Eric Varley, former Labour Energy Secretary, whom I served. He says he is wanted for a job at the NCB by the chairman, Bob Haslam. I hope that comes to pass.

Home for 7.45 p.m. with masses of presents.

On Thursday, high drama. Chancellor Lawson resigns on the day the PM faces PMQs for the first time since the recess and has to give her statement on CHoGM. I find it curious that just before the PM's 9 a.m. briefing for PMQs she is closeted with the Chancellor alone, allegedly to discuss what to say about Alan Walters. I learn later that he has hinted at resignation. Cabinet takes place without a hint of trouble and both Foreign Secretary Major and Kenneth Baker come in to see me, the latter to moan about Kuala Lumpur. At lunchtime it is all quiet, but when I get over to the House at 2.40 p.m. for the PM's final PMQs briefing, Charles Powell tips me off with a note saying he thinks the Chancellor has resigned.

It turns out he asked to see her at 2.25 p.m. to tender his resignation and, thoughtless or vindictive beast that he is, to announce it at 3.10, just before the PM rises for PMQs (and before the markets have closed). He is asked to desist until 4.30. Against this background, the PM's performance over seventy-five minutes – PMQs and CHoGM statement – is magnificent: commanding, authoritative and, in the case of Kinnock, crushing. The PM briefs me alone about the resignation before I go back to No. 10 to prepare with the staff what turns out to be an invaluable Q&A brief for the formal announcement and my briefing at 7.45. During that briefing, Alan Walters brings this dramatic day to a close by resigning too. God save me from political and official sensitive flowers.

Friday's press is, as expected, bad, apart from the *Star*, *Sun*, *Express* and *Mail*, though even they are critical in some respects. The rest see the PM on the rack in a first-class political crisis. I must say she does not look to be in a crisis when she sees Jean Rook from the *Express* at 10 a.m. It is a very good woman-to-woman interview, but I shall no doubt get it in the neck from the other media for giving her an exclusive on this of all days. This is one of the problems of arranging interviews well in advance to prevent media critics from saying we just play the media for advantage. I might have arranged for Chris Moncrieff, political editor of the PA, to sit in on the interview – as he does for radio and TV interviews at summits – to ensure that any news content is sent to all outlets, but it would not have been the same interview.

I give one of my best talks for a long time at a lunch given by the marketing department of ICI. They seem to appreciate it. Then, after briefing the Sunday lobby, I am late for briefing the PM for her Walden interview tomorrow because I have to pick up my car from servicing. Terry Perks and Sarah Charman have done most of the work before I get there. Before I get away at 8.15 p.m., Murdo Maclean pops in to ask me to try to get closer to his boss, the new Chief Whip, Tim Renton.

No rest for the wicked. I go in to the office on Saturday at 6.30 a.m. to prepare the final briefing for the PM's Walden interview at 10 a.m., taking in the day's papers. While I am digging away, Kenneth Baker calls and I give him a piece of my mind about ministers – notably Lord Hailsham, who criticises Charles Powell, myself and the press office in forthright terms entirely on the basis of gossip. And this from a legal eagle who is supposed to have a reverence for fact.

The Walden interview is a poor affair in terms of substance but presentationally it is marvellous. The PM looks good, shows she is still the Iron Lady after the week she has endured, and remains undented at the end. She stonewalls on the Chancellor's reasons for resigning and why she didn't sack Walters and repeats the Madrid requirements for any entry into the ERM. The real value of the interview is the demonstration of her mood and strength after a traumatic week.

After a nine-hour sleep, I find the Sunday press much as expected. The Chancellor gets a bit of a drubbing, but there are two worrying aspects to the coverage:

1. The interpretation put on Lord President Howe's speech on the ERM last night; and

2. Kenneth Baker's revelation that he advised the PM to make Douglas Hurd the Foreign Secretary in preference to Tom King.

Have these damn politicians no thought for the credibility of their government?

I have two chats with the PM on the phone morning and evening. During the latter, I am able to tell her that I have had a remarkable number of calls praising her Walden interview. I get to work on the garden before lunch and awake from a post-prandial nap to learn that Michael Heseltine says he is not going to stand for the party leadership against the PM, and Howe says his hat is not in the ring. So far so good, but the government is in a febrile state. To repeat: God save me from politicians, full stop.

A crowded Monday (30 October) ends with three parties: Mike Bates's farewell on his return to the FCO; a PM reception attended by a number of my friends; and the Node dinner – an annual reunion of supposedly rising civil servants and private sector executives who were together for ten days on a course in 1978.

Before that, I get through this tally of meetings after writing the press digest: press office admin; PM's week-ahead meeting in the Cabinet Room; long-term diary meeting; the lobby; speak to BBC trainees (11.15 to 12.50); lunch with journalist Christopher Fildes; brief the FPA and then lobby; and finally with Mark Lennox-Boyd, the PM's PPS, on internal No. 10 problems and presentation, including Charles Powell, who seems to want to do everybody's job.

The PM has lunch with the 1922 Committee's executive and by all accounts they are positive and supportive. As if I did not have enough ministerial problems – Howe being a recurring one – Norman Tebbit, of all people, is critical of the PM's leadership and style of management. There is no doubt about it: ex-ministers as well as ministers can be absolute bastards to the person who gave them office. Lord Whitelaw rings me to say he proposes to stay quiet but will speak up when the PM thinks it would be helpful. If only they were all like Willie.

On Tuesday, I scurry around, with Terry Perks away ill with flu, before the lobby gives a dinner in my honour. First, I have a good chat with Tim Renton, who does not seem to have heard my point of view on my alleged rubbishing of Howe as Deputy PM or the allegation that I am the scourge of ministers – as if they were not good at scourging their colleagues. The PM scores easy runs in PMQs. John Major gives a competent performance in an economics debate as the new Chancellor, and the old one – Lawson – is indiscreet.

Among the guests at the lobby's dinner for me are John Wakeham and Norman Tebbit. The oration is given by Lord Moncrieff of Bratsk (Siberia), as Michael Jones introduces the PA's political editor. He is hilarious, shouting at a phenomenal rate of knots, and has everyone in tears of enjoyment. A sort of Quaker meeting follows, in which lobby members speak as the spirit moves them. Julia Langdon and Geoffrey Parkhouse sing a ditty about me to the tune of 'Hello, Dolly', which, summarised, has the lobby telling their editors to hold the front page until I lose my temper, when a story is guaranteed. I have enjoyed my ten years with them.

The ditty, composed by Bill Russell (*The Scotsman*), goes like this:

> Hello, Bernard
> Well, hello, Bernard,
> It's so nice to see you there at four o'clock
> You're looking hell, Bernard,
> We can tell, Bernard,
> That the Lady's thrown a fit
> You're in a state of shock.
>
> We feel the room swayin'
> And we're all prayin'
> That you lose your temper like you always do.
> So

Hold the page, fellas,
Bernard's in a rage, fellas,
That means we've got a front-page lead for you.

Hello, Bernard,
Well, hello, Bernard,
It's too bad you're not here to hear this song
We are lobby hacks, Bernard,
And the fact is, Bernard,
We're a hundred years of age
And still we get you wrong.

We feel the room shakin'
And our hearts achin'
'Cos they say your job is going to Robin Day.
So let us state, Bernard,
Dammit, we hope you'll never go
Dammit, we hope you'll never go
Dammit, we hope you'll never go away.

CHAPTER 11

NOVEMBER 1989: A REAL CHALLENGER

Government in a nervous, frenetic state – and the PM doing far too much – as the month ends with Labour eleven points ahead and speculation about a real challenger instead of the declared stalking donkey, Sir Anthony Meyer. The PM adds fuel to the fire of speculation by saying she won't fight a fifth election, having yet to win a fourth.

It seems that Cecil Parkinson is responsible for a story that the PM can rely on only four Cabinet ministers – himself, John Major, David Waddington and Norman Lamont. Kenneth Baker blurts out that the government has been divided for eighteen months on EC policy. Only eighteen months?

In a month in which the Berlin Wall falls, the PM flies to the USA twice: to address the UN General Assembly and then for a Camp David meeting with President Bush. Privately, she lets rip about the EC. Publicly, thank God, she is more measured. In a meeting with President Mitterrand in Paris, she finds an ally – initially, at least – against a reunified Germany. Her approach to the fall of the East German government is not to rush any fences.

WEEK 44: 1–5 NOVEMBER

Everyone seems delighted with last night's lobby dinner. I am soon back to earth on Wednesday with a row with Kenneth Baker, who did not like my line on the Chancellor's speech. He said it was incompatible with the panic-stricken backbench feelings on

Europe, the EMS and the ERM. The PM had already used my line in an interview with Don Macintyre (*Sunday Correspondent*) before I deployed it. I am getting fed up with Baker's frenetic activity. He is so unbalanced. I recognise he is a member of the Cabinet as well as being chairman of the Tory Party and therefore entitled to ring me to criticise. But I have never had this before from a Tory chairman.

I give the American correspondents what I think is a sparkling briefing. They turn up in force, like vultures over a battlefield, because the government is in turmoil. I have a 'make-it-up' lunch with Ian Aitken of *The Guardian*, who disagrees with his editor's line on 'withdrawing' from the lobby – i.e. not attending my briefings. I have sometimes, unhelpfully from Aitken's point of view, said that *The Guardian* is split on the issue. He canvasses Michael White, *The Guardian*'s amusing political writer, as the next editor.

My wife and I end the day as guests of Mr and Mrs Howell Thomas – he a PR man – at Andrew Lloyd Webber's *Phantom of the Opera*. It is a wonderful evening's entertainment.

By Thursday, the steam is going out of Nigel Lawson's resignation. I record in the press digest that the *Daily Star*, *Sun* and *Today* have a go at him. But just when things appear to be looking up, Terry Perks interrupts the PM's PMQs briefing with a cutting from *The Scotsman* about an insider trading scandal likely to break on Channel 4. This is news to all of us. Then media gossip mentions Cecil Parkinson, Transport Secretary, by name. The PM drags him out of a meeting. He immediately calls his solicitor – Carter-Ruck, the libel specialists – and issues a statement that was judged necessary because of the possible effect of the rumour on the markets. Unhappily, I do not have a text of the statement when I see the lobby at 11 a.m. As a result, it is a bruising affair, but the story soon fades away.

On Friday, our thirty-third wedding anniversary, my wife and I take seven hours from noon driving to Harrogate – the worst long-distance journey I have had because of congestion and diversions. This leads to a very quick change for a dinner at Rudding Park given by the PR firm my friend David Illingworth works for.

In the process of my quick change, the PM rings the Moat House Hotel to say that she has sent a letter of thanks to Lord Stevens for the Express Group's support. I take the opportunity to press the case for separate *Express* and *Telegraph* groups, since Conrad Black, the *Telegraph*'s owner, continues to stalk the *Express*. She seems cheerful in spite of all the trouble and wishes us a happy wedding anniversary.

On Saturday, we drive from Harrogate to Lymm to visit John and Christine. After a huge lunch, John and I (when not dozing) watch New Zealand slaughter Wales in an Rugby Union international. Dinner is at a hotel near Manchester Airport.

Just to show how unpredictable the roads can be, we have the fastest ever run home (three and a quarter hours) to Surrey on Sunday. Nigel Lawson is given an easy ride by Brian Walden on *Weekend World*. This results in a flurry of phone calls, but I don't react much. There is greater interest in the PM's statement to the *Sunday Correspondent* that she won't fight a fifth election – i.e. she might fight a fourth in 1991–92, which she has yet to win.

WEEK 45: 6–12 NOVEMBER

Some nasty aspects to Monday's press. *The Independent* and *Mirror* put the worst possible interpretation on Lawson's performance on *Weekend World* yesterday and the PM's ill-advised remark that she is unlikely to stand for a fifth time as Tory leader in an election. The two questions put to me by the lobby are:

1. Isn't she guilty of lying over Lawson's resignation, as charged by *The Independent*?
2. Isn't she now a lame duck PM?

Having rehearsed my line with the PM at 10 a.m., I explain to the lobby that there is nothing incompatible in the PM saying she didn't know why Lawson resigned and him saying he did it because he asked her to get rid of Alan Walters. The PM finds it incredible that a

Chancellor would resign over an adviser. As for lame duckery, I laugh it off, making the point that she said it was unlikely she would stand a fifth time but that would surely be subject to popular demand.

The PM is preoccupied with Lawson's treachery (my word) when I see her after an interview with Kelvin MacKenzie, editor of *The Sun*. She confirms that Howe and Lawson threatened to resign if she did not set a date for ERM entry at Madrid. She didn't and they stayed.

I have lunch with the BBC's Brian Barwick and John Motson at the Reform. This takes me back to my ten years covering Halifax Rugby League Club from 1952.

On Tuesday, I feel as if I could do without a trip to the UN in New York, though flying by Concorde takes some of the drudgery out of it. The trip generates a lot of interest in the content of the PM's speech to the General Assembly tomorrow. This puts me in difficulty, as I want to preserve some news for then. By and large, I suppose I succeed while at the same time stoking up interest.

We do not leave by helicopter for Heathrow until 6.20 p.m., so I have to cope with an extraordinary event after PMQs. Neil Kinnock follows the PM out of the Chamber and tells her that her answer to a question on Pol Pot by Alex Eadie, a former Energy minister, was 'a bloody disgrace'. In reply, I am told, the PM and Mark Lennox-Boyd tell him they have sent a letter to him, to which he replies, 'Yes, and it says damn all,' and then stalks off. This soon reaches the media, who are agog. I give a frank briefing to the regional lobby before we leave for Heathrow.

Concorde's food is good, but the front seats are not as comfortable as on the VC10. Our maximum flying height is 58,000 ft and the lowest outside temperature is -62°. We have dinner with the UN Secretary General, Javier Pérez de Cuéllar. And so to bed at 4.30 a.m. London time.

The PM wears a purple suit and looks good in delivering her address to the General Assembly after an hour's rehearsal. The audience is generous with its applause and she looks quite girlish receiving it in a rather impersonal auditorium with not the best acoustics. Simon Walters asks me early for a copy of the speech and seems enthusiastic about it when he gets it.

After her speech, she goes across the road for a meeting with Pérez de Cuéllar and the Nigerian president of the assembly. So many want to shake her hand at the reception that I fear she will be late for an interview with the *New York Times*. Her interview with them might be taking place in the New York Central Synagogue from reading the galaxy of Jewish talent on the newspaper. The PM does not believe in a united Germany but manages to cover that up better than her impatience with the EC. We are back in London for 10.20 p.m. London time after a 3-hour 22-minute flight.

On Thursday, we find just how much sting has been taken out of the Lawson resignation. Not even a frank interview by Kenneth Baker with *Le Soir*, Brussels, in which he tells the truth – there has been a basic disagreement in government for eighteen months over EC policy – causes ructions. Kinnock and his MPs are unable to capitalise on this because the PM just refuses to add to what she has already said.

All of this is overshadowed by two things:

1. The collapse of the East German government; it opens up its borders while I am having dinner with Paul Potts, deputy editor of the *Daily Express*, who is concerned about both the PM's position and the Express Group's situation, with Conrad Black having acquired 9 per cent of it.
2. Pulling nuclear power stations out of privatisation of the electricity industry; I think this is sensible and what the government should have done from the start, though I recognise the presentational problem of excluding nuclear power.

Lord Weidenfeld calls on me, proposing I should write four books when I retire. I refer him to my agent.

On Friday, Nora and Beryl Stocks, who were with me at Hebden

Bridge Grammar School, visit me at No. 10. While I am greeting them, I get a message from the PM that she will go out at 11.30 a.m. to say a few words about Eastern Europe. This means that the Stocks sisters get a close sight of the PM in her natural habitat, as it were. Then Murdo Maclean, private secretary to the Chief Whip, takes them over to the House for an environment debate before my guests are whisked in with me to see Mr Speaker, Bernard Weatherill, who entertains us over champagne. I then take them to the Reform for lunch. They return to No. 10 at 6 p.m. for a drink after visiting the Cabinet War Rooms. Altogether a wonderful day for them, thanks to Murdo.

The excitement over the fall of the Berlin Wall overshadows the decision to pull nuclear power out of electricity privatisation. I give a talk to a GIS induction course.

On Saturday, Nancy and I have lunch with Mr and Mrs Ian Gillis – he the head of information at the Department of Energy – at their home in Weybridge. We have a jolly chinwag about Halifax – all four of us come from there – illustrated by photos of the *Halifax Courier* and *Hebden Bridge Times* and a National Union of Journalists (NUJ) event at Crimsworth Dene above Hebden Bridge.

Last of the Summer Wine – filmed in Holmfirth, near Huddersfield – is getting better and better. This evening's TV account of a golden wedding is hilarious.

WEEK 46: 13–19 NOVEMBER

As No. 10 weeks go, this promises to be a quiet one, though with a sting in the tail – an Anglo-French summit in Paris on Saturday. Winter and fog are upon us and it takes me ten minutes longer to drive into No. 10 at 6.30. There is continuing massive coverage of the dramatic events in Eastern Europe, but our line – the need for a cool, calm and collected approach – seems to be succeeding.

The PM's week-ahead meeting is preoccupied with how Kinnock will attack her in PMQs. Ten wasted years, I suggest, and now out of date into the bargain because of the events in Eastern Europe.

I spend a lot of time pointing out to the media the passage in her Bruges speech last year looking to a wider, looser Europe stretching to Prague, Budapest and Warsaw.

Tuesday's press gives good coverage to the PM's speech at the Lord Mayor's banquet last night. Predictably, the *Mirror*, *Guardian* and *Independent* slate it, while the *Daily Express*, *Daily Telegraph* and *Times* praise it in various ways. I make good progress in preparing a note for the lobby on the forthcoming Queen's Speech, for clearance with departments, but I am concerned about the state of my diary and the extent to which I am overworking.

On Wednesday, I don't have much time to worry about it. I am overworked. This is what I got through after preparing the press digest and finishing my Queen's Speech brief: morning lobby, which arrives just as Cabinet is ending with its clearance of the public expenditure White Paper, on which Chancellor Major later briefs me; the usual meeting with American correspondents, who try to trap me into indiscretion over a unified or neutralised Germany; lunch with Charles Anson in his 22nd-floor eyrie at Kleinwort's, with its magnificent view up the Thames to Westminster; watching in the House an excellent presentation by the Chancellor of his first and very difficult public expenditure White Paper, during which he answered forty-one questions in an hour; a meeting with Lord President Howe, ostensibly on televising the House from next week but touching ever so lightly on the fallout from his speech after Lawson's resignation; a meeting with the information minister of Bahrain, who presents me with a bowl of phials of scent; and the PM's party for speechwriter Ronnie Millar's seventieth birthday. Phew!

The PM is in South Wales on Friday with Sarah Charman, so I make good progress with eliminating the backlog. The media's main interest is in Eastern Europe and the effect of developments on the EC. I tell the Sunday lobby that the UK's thinking and approach have been consistent: to encourage the spread of freedom and democracy without destabilising Mr Gorbachev; not to rush any fences; and to press ahead with the EC agenda set out in Madrid. We are not seeking to break our promises, but we recognise that there are some in the EC who want to rush matters. Home for 8.30 p.m.

After all that, I take stock on Friday. I am worried that not just I but we are doing too much, and that I, at least, am skimping too much. I am unhappy about it. The new Home Secretary, David Waddington, kindly invites me to lunch at Lancaster House with the Bahraini minister for information, with whom I get on well.

John Major gets a good press for his presentation of the public expenditure White Paper, though there are some who fear that a £5.5 billion increase in spending, plus another £4 billion from raiding the reserve, will fuel inflation. With the exception of the *Mirror*, the tabloids highlight greater public spending on the NHS, roads, railways, education and the homeless. The broadsheets highlight the gloomy forecasts, and *The Guardian* and *Independent* lay them on with a trowel.

On Saturday, I go to the office at 3 p.m. for a Paris summit with President Mitterrand, having, it seems, succeeded in playing down expectations as to both substance and disagreement at the summit. The PM walks from the British Embassy to the Elysée Palace next door at 8 p.m. While she is in talks, Ambassador Ewen Fergusson and his wife throw a party for guests and staff. The PM and new Foreign Secretary Douglas Hurd return at 11.15 p.m. to hold a twenty-minute press conference. It goes well because it soon becomes clear that the talks have only been a preliminary tour of the issues raised by Eastern Europe.* The media must have felt robbed. TV gets her to comment on two IRA outrages earlier in the day.

On Sunday, I get home at 1.15 a.m. to find some curious goings-on in the avenue, with partygoers apparently switching from a car to a van. I awake to find the press OK, except that Michael Jones has an unhappy quote from a No. 10 insider about Howe and Baker indulging in disgraceful sniping. I suppose I shall get the blame. The press are gloomy about the economy and taxes.

---

* President Mitterrand initially supported the Prime Minister's stance against a unified Germany.

At the end of the day, the garden looks much better for my attention given to it between a lot of media calls about last night's summit.

WEEK 47: 20–26 NOVEMBER

The broadsheets forecast trouble at the Strasbourg EC summit next month after the PM's account on Saturday night of the wholly undemocratic nature of the proposals by Commission President Jacques Delors for the EC's development.

It is also clear that someone has been lunching with Gordon Greig (*Daily Mail*) and Trevor Kavanagh (*Sun*), who come up with a tale that the PM can rely on only four members of the Cabinet – John Major, David Waddington, Norman Lamont and Cecil Parkinson. It turns out that Parkinson had lunch with them last Tuesday. Kenneth Baker was attacked in *The Sun* the following day.

Lord Whitelaw rings me to say he proposes to break his silence in a press gallery speech, with a message to the party and government to 'belt up and win'. I think it is OK, but I recognise that it will reflect badly on Howe as the new Deputy Prime Minister. At lunch with Guinness, I give them a frank account of the state of the government and its need to stop kicking itself in the teeth.

I spend much of the morning rehearsing and rewriting the PM's speech in the debate on the address tomorrow. At a lunch reception in lieu of the usual eve-of-session dinner, the PM gives Parkinson a very hard time indeed. Rostropovich performs at No. 10 in the evening.

On Tuesday, the Commons is televised for the first time, after the Queen's Speech setting out the legislative programme ahead. Will Parliament ever be the same again? I doubt it. To start with, the PM changes her style, giving way to thirteen interventions in her speech on the address. Mr Speaker became a bystander as she set out the order in which she proposed to take points of order. This made for a much less tidy speech than usual, but it was more theatrical. The broadcasters bent the rules a little by showing some reaction shots, one of them the PM laughing, which will do her no harm at all.

Ian Gow, the PM's former PPS, makes a wonderful speech

proposing the humble address in which he ribs a lot of people, including Sir Stalking Horse himself, Anthony Meyer, who is challenging the PM's leadership. Later, the talk in the lobbies is of a more substantial challenge to the PM's leadership. We shall see, but it will be an awful pity if there is a contest.

Wednesday is an incredible day which leaves me very crabby. We are all trying to do too much and ought to slow down. Yet what do we face next? A flight to Washington to see President Bush and an overnight return.

A majority of the press thinks that after a nervous start the PM won the debate on the address – not that you would have thought so had you heard the BBC's 6 a.m. news. After completing a weighty press digest, bearing in mind the introduction of TV to the Commons, I face a lobby looking for a stalking horse. I have a plain-speaking lunch with Ronald Butt (*The Times*) because of his recent coverage of the PM and her works. A most fractious GIS executive follows on GIS development.

I sit in on a much delayed *Times* interview on the PM's return from a visit to Canterbury; then I have a meeting with Lord Whitelaw and Lord Stevens on the future of the Express Group; and finally I give a briefing to the media on tomorrow's visit to Camp David.

I don't feel up to the trip to Washington – tired and somewhat depressed about the political situation. I leave with the party at 12.45 p.m., comforted by the knowledge that I am up to date with work and admin. We fly out over a sun-baked England and then over Labrador and New England under snow.

Over lunch en route, the PM gets her dander up about the challenge to her leadership. She is determined to fight and win. That's the spirit. But I tell her that once the leadership election and the Strasbourg summit are out of the way, we should sit down and plot the government's way forward.

I give the travelling press a briefing on board, but I have little new to say. I have already fed out the same line at least ten times.

You can imagine my chagrin when we learn that it is snowing in Washington and that somehow I have failed to bring a topcoat. It proves to be very chilly on landing. After a visit to the Ambassador's residence, I give yet another press briefing in the Sheraton.

Dinner with Ambassador Sir Antony Acland and his wife is followed by a hilarious attempt to get the PM to be more positive about the EC. As the wine – or, in her case, whisky and soda – flows, she sounds ever more bloodthirsty about the institution. Then at about 3.30 a.m. London time I make a dramatic exit for bed, saying, 'Prime Minister, if that is what you propose to tell the American TV breakfast programmes about the EC, there is only one thing I can do and that is to go out into the garden and shoot myself.'

(Several years later, Sir Antony said my departure was followed by a long silence as presumably the party awaited the fatal shot. It was broken by the PM, who said, 'Don't worry. He doesn't mean it, you know!')

After five hours' dozing, I get up at 6 a.m. local time for the PM's customary interviews with the four breakfast TV channels – ABC, CNN, NBC and CBS. She is on her best behaviour and the interviews are notable not for what she is asked but for what is ignored. That is what is supposed to be the Anglo-American issue of the moment: the PM's refusal to integrate with the EC. She tells America that she is no lame duck and doesn't intend to become one. This is meat and drink to Chris Moncrieff, who sits in on the interviews as usual for the benefit of all the British media.

We then fly by helicopter to Camp David on top of the Catoctin Mountains – I in company with my old friend Marlin Fitzwater, the President's press secretary. Mr and Mrs Bush shake my hand as the party files out of the helicopter. The Americans kindly lend me a huge parka to ward off the cold.

We are quartered in Holly Lodge – Camp David is a series of chalets named after trees – next door to Laurel, where the talks are taking place. Just after noon, the principals emerge and drive to Aspen, where the Bush family have a residence. After a quick debrief from Charles Powell, I ring Chris Moncrieff – the press have remained in Washington – to give him a substantial report for him to share with the rest of the media. The press conference is a non-event and the subsequent radio and TV interviews are memorable only for their search for a stalking horse.

After a quick meal and an equally speedy briefing for the British Sunday press, we fly back home. We arrive at 6.25 a.m. on Saturday and I feel awful with a bug of some sort. My system seems to be poisoned, so I go on short rations and soup and to bed at 7.15 p.m. The press coverage of Camp David is reasonably good, based entirely on my many briefings.

After twelve hours' sleep, I feel better physically on Sunday. An *Observer* poll gives Labour an eleven-point lead and 66 per cent think the PM should resign, up from 58 per cent a month ago. The visit to Washington is written down, if covered at all, except for the news that the UK and US do not see eye to eye on the repatriation of Vietnamese boat people. Sir Anthony Meyer adamant he will challenge his leader.

WEEK 48: 27 NOVEMBER–1 DECEMBER

A new week starts with the pressure of events and travel showing. The PM faces an interview with the BBC's *Panorama* programme, fixed up weeks ago. She is never enamoured of these occasions, but today she mildly rebukes me for giving her more work. She has had enough of life's hurdles at the moment and wishes she was not confronted by *Panorama*. She is clearly nervous of putting a foot wrong.

Yet today's press devotes few column inches to the presumed leadership challenge. The week-ahead meeting is taken over for a time by Kenneth Baker's determination to rehearse her, however irrelevantly, for the interview. We waste a good twenty minutes on war widows' pensions, even though I have no indication the issue will arise. I move in and out of the PM's briefing before I go off to lunch with John Deans (*Daily Mail*) and Rob Gibson (*Daily Express*).

Chancellor John Major, looking rather unhappy, comes in during the afternoon as sterling weakens against the D-Mark. Then the PM gets flustered briefing herself for *Panorama* and almost unprecedentedly takes forty-five minutes over changing and makeup. In the end, the interview goes far better than I expected, though she heckles the interviewer too much and tends to ramble. But she looks good – tough, animated and confident. What more could I ask?

I feel able to tell the PM on Tuesday that she is in a stronger position today than she was twenty-four hours ago because of the interview. It gets a lot of coverage in today's press, though focused almost entirely on the party leadership. This is borne out by the warmth of her reception at PMQs.

The other issue today is the release by national newspaper editors (except the *FT*) of a code of practice with a heavy aroma of hypocrisy. For example, the *Daily Mail* says it has operated by it for years. I advise the PM to welcome any manifestation and acceptance of responsibility by the press and to look forward to its being exercised, starting this day.

By the end of Wednesday, I feel I have achieved a lot even though I am still not on top form after catching the US bug. I am encouraged to find that the PM and the government have had their best press perhaps for this year and certainly for months. Coming on top of yesterday's *Panorama*, her performance at PMQs has rallied opinion. But lots of problems remain – notable Vietnamese boat people and war widows' pensions.

I write my speech for today's lunch with the Institution of Practitioners in Advertising before briefing the lobby and American correspondents. I get the impression that my talk and Q&A session goes down well with the advertisers.

While the PM is seeing visitor after visitor – the last is Herr Genscher, the German Foreign Minister – I make valuable progress in clarifying GIS recruitment options. I get away at 7.10. I must do this more often.

The big story on Friday (which dawns with a heavy hoar frost) is the leak of a paper for a select committee on the Rover privatisation. It seems that the government went behind the back of the EC to give British Aerospace a £30 million 'sweetener' to buy it. Much to my surprise and relief, Nicholas Ridley volunteers a statement to the House. This goes rather well, but it does not stop Kinnock asking the PM before the statement if she knew about the 'sweetener'. As occurs only too often, she refuses to answer directly. Afterwards I tell her that we shall now be pursued on the issue and that I would like her to say, 'Yes, in general terms.' This leads to an argument in which I express myself rather toughly but eventually persuade her to answer the question.

That apart, it is a quiet day. Lady Porter, Tory leader of Westminster City Council, comes in to pick my brains about presentation, and Sir Denis Barnes, my Permanent Secretary at the Department of Employment, rings to ask whether he should give Robert Harris an interview for his book about me. I say, 'Yes, please.'

The PM and EU Commission President, Jacques Delors, agree to avoid the most controversial issues, so the Sunday lobby does not get much out of weary me. I have not had a drink for a week, but I do not feel well and take paracetamol in the afternoon.

My spirits rise because of one of the best meetings I have ever had with GIS heads of information. The discussion is excellent. There is a great pulling together and sensible talk about career paths and high-flyers. Mike Devereau, Director-General of the COI and a rebel, says at the end that it was an eye-opener and that such a meeting could not have been held twelve months ago. I regard this as progress in my first year as head of the GIS, though there is a serious problem over pay, especially at the higher levels, even though wastage rates are not high at less than 10 per cent.

The *Express* claims an exclusive about government movement on war widows' pensions, which the rest follow up.

On Saturday, Lech Wałęsa, leader of the Solidarity movement in Poland, is late because of fog for a meeting with the PM at

At a press conference in our Embassy in Belgrade in the early 1980s.

At the United Nations with David Hannay, now Lord Hannay, Ambassador to the UN.

With Marlin Fitzwater, who succeeded Speakes as press secretary to Reagan and was later press secretary to George H. W. Bush.

To Bernard Ingam:
... A legend and good friend Marlin Fitzwater
4·18·91

Pictured with Marlin Fitzwater, with his message below.

Press conference in Hong Kong, 1984, en route from Beijing, where agreement was reached on the handover of Hong Kong in 1997.

Mrs Thatcher inspects the teddy bear presented to me by the lobby on my birthday in Toronto in June 1988.

Cutting my birthday cake on the plane returning from Canada in 1988.

Mrs Thatcher with her press office and COI colleagues, 1990.

Mrs Thatcher with her private secretaries and advisers, 1990.

Mrs Thatcher with NATO/BAOR forces on Lüneberg Heath, Germany.

At work in the Paris Embassy on the day the PM learned she had not got the super-majority required in the leadership election.

Meeting Prince Michael of Kent before my installation as president of the Television and Radio Industries Club, with Ned Sherrin, who preceded me as president.

Pictured with Charles Anson, former press secretary to the Queen and a member of the No. 10 press office when I went there in 1979. We are on the marina in my native Hebden Bridge in 1990, on a weekend trip with the press office and friends.

Lady Thatcher confers an honorary doctorate on me at Buckingham University, where she was Chancellor. In my retirement, I was also awarded honorary doctorates at Bradford and Middlesex Universities.

Chequers. The PM calls for Britons to invest in Poland. President Bush's 'seawater summit' in Malta is nearly wrecked by a Mediterranean gale.

On Sunday afternoon, I am told to get into the office as rapidly as possible because the PM is leaving early for a NATO summit in Brussels because of continuing fog. A car is waiting for me to take me to Northolt and we are in Brussels by 7.45 p.m. After a briefing on the summit, the PM goes to bed suffering from a bad cold.

The party has dinner with Foreign Secretary Hurd. It is a sombre affair. All kinds of gloomy predictions are being made about the future of Europe. West Germany, a united Germany, European defence and a pull-out of American and Canadian forces. For the second time in less than a week, I tell a minister – this time the Foreign Secretary – that there is nothing I can do in the state of despair the conversation has left me in but to go outside and shoot myself. The dinner party counsels caution, which is kind of them. The fact remains that Europe is in a bad way.

CHAPTER 12

DECEMBER 1989: PRECIOUS LITTLE CHRISTMAS CHEER

The PM easily sees off Sir Anthony Meyer in the leadership election, by 314 votes to 33. But no one cares to rule out another challenge before the next election. After all, Meyer polled thirty-three votes, with twenty-four spoiled papers and three abstentions.

Much of the month is spent wrestling with German reunification, European integration and the repatriation of some Vietnamese boat people and right of abode for some Hong Kong folk. The government – and the Tories – are far from united.

The month begins with a gloomy UK government full of foreboding about the future of NATO at a NATO summit in Brussels. And President Bush stirs it up by setting conditions for German reunification and apparently advocating greater EU integration. Meanwhile, Chancellor Kohl looks set to bully through German reunification.

There is precious little Christmas cheer around, with a blood bath in Romania with the fall of the Ceauşescus and the Americans ridding Panama of the awful President Noriega, who surrenders to, of all people, the Papal Nuncio. On a happier note, Chancellor John Major thinks we have managed over the month to sound more positive about the EU.

WEEK 49: 4–10 DECEMBER

Monday finds Brussels cold, frosty, slightly foggy and with traces of snow on the ground. I feel better after six hours' sleep, but the PM seems to be in as bad a way as Europe when I see her at 8 a.m. after breakfast. She is coughing, spluttering and sneezing and should not be here.

We go to the NATO HQ at 9 a.m. for a familiar briefing from our Ambassador, Michael Alexander, a former private secretary to the PM – familiar in style in that he goes on and on in a didactic kind of way, with occasional friendly flare-ups with the PM. She goes down for the meeting at 9.30 to a warm reception from the staff but has to hang around until 10.20 when President Mitterrand makes his semi-regal appearance – the last to arrive, as is his entitlement as a head of state rather than a mere PM.

The morning is relatively uneventful, with President Bush giving the sort of run-down we got from Ambassador Alexander. Most contributors emphasise the continuing importance of NATO. I brief the media at 12.15 p.m. with Andrew Turnbull. After a quick lunch, President Bush drops his bombshell, spelling out the terms for German reunification and contemplating Delors's proposed reforms and urging further and faster European integration.

Chancellor Kohl wants this to be the last word, but three PMs – Giulio Andreotti (Italy), Ruud Lubbers (Netherlands) and Mrs Thatcher – voice their concerns about borders. The PM's concluding press conference is tricky because the Americans have not briefed on Bush's statement. We are back in London for 5 p.m., with the press clamouring because of a false rumour that the PM had breakfast with Bush and the claim that she is isolated over German reunification and European integration.

Tuesday brings the Tory leadership election. The PM triumphs with 84 per cent of the vote to Sir Anthony Meyer's nearly 9 per cent. The voting is 314–33, with twenty-four spoiled papers and three abstentions. This is by any standards a major victory, though Meyer attracted a surprising number of votes. There is nothing in the press about Meyer's alleged private life, reported to me by Brian Hitchen, editor of the *Daily Star*, before we left for NATO. When I tried to pass on this report in the plane, the PM told me she didn't want to hear it. This lady is no gossip.

The press have the PM rebuffed, shocked, surprised and isolated by Bush's remarks on EC integration. I write a strong line for the II a.m. lobby, which I deploy with vigour and a somewhat weary passion. The PM wishes, I say, that some other member states were as keen on integration – i.e. achieving a real single market – as we are. And she cannot believe that the USA wants a socialist, centrist and bureaucratic EC.

The PM easily copes with Kinnock at PMQs, flooring him and others – or perhaps bushwhacking might be a better term – with the news that President Bush telephoned her at I p.m. to say that he was astonished that the British press had so misinterpreted him.

On Wednesday, the PM gets a good press apart from, predictably, the *Mirror*, *Guardian* and *Independent* and some indifferent comment in the *Daily Telegraph*. But even her enthusiastic supporters have their doubts about whether she has seen off any further challenge before the next election. Much will depend on the progress of the economy.

I work out a briefing line at 9 a.m. and have a word with the PM in her flat at 10.15. Her cold is mending and she is obviously relieved about the election outcome. At noon, I give a candid briefing to American correspondents on the EC and then try to prepare for the forthcoming summit in Strasbourg. I have never had such a volume of paper for a summit.

I lunch with Robin Esser (ex-editor of the *Sunday Express*), who is hopeful he will emerge again in the Express Group on the back of a Conrad Black takeover. At dinner, Brian Hitchen doubts whether Black will get the Express Group.

On Thursday, I note we are entering a testing three days. The Tory Party is not as one over the EC. There is probably still a majority who know where their bread is buttered with Mrs Thatcher as leader, but there will likely be more who wish she would be more positive and less abrasive about the EC.

The PM resumes PMQs with supportive comments from both sides of the House, notably from Labour's old anti-EC warhorse, Peter Shore. Earlier, the Cabinet, via Kenneth Baker, let it be known of a plan to help war widows. The Chancellor, briefing me on Cabinet, says he thinks the party has now accepted that Howe is yesterday's man. The PM does not seem depressed and shares my excitement about the approach of Christmas and a break.

At 6 p.m., we go from Wellington Barracks in Birdcage Walk in a helicopter to Northolt for Strasbourg. London by night looks vast and prosperous. We arrive in a cold, frosty Strasbourg in time for one of my typical late-night summit media briefings – a bear-baiting session with me in the role of growling bear – prodded by John Palmer (*The Guardian*) and David Usborne (*The Independent*). I make it clear I am not in the business of games.

On a cold and frosty Friday morning, I give a 10 a.m. briefing which I think is informative – the PM's ideas for improving relations with the EC. There is also a strong rumour that the PM is keen to have the European Development Agency on that site of excellence, Cambridge.

By late afternoon, the PM is in a minority of one over a proposed intergovernmental conference on the EC's future. France and Germany are also reported to be at odds over Germany unity, which the PM thinks is a long way off. Lying behind all this negativism is the PM's positive outlook on Eastern Europe and a real single internal market. She has a fifteen-minute discussion with Mitterrand, waiting for the conference to begin, entirely on German reunification and Kohl's heavy-handed determination to unite the two Germanys. Mitterrand is alarmed about the likely consequences. I get to bed at 2 a.m.

On the final day of the summit – Saturday – the press don't know whether to write that the PM has capitulated, been crushed or is just biding her time. Or is she trimming? I have created the mystery by refusing to brief on the German question because I don't know which way the cat will jump. Will she suddenly break the surface with an ultimatum on the whole concept of reunification?

After a reasonably successful morning working on the communiqué, and an early finish, the PM remains true to her convictions while sounding more pro-Europe. But it is going to be a long, hard grind turning our reputation for negativism into a positive approach, though events in Eastern Europe may help. Judging by Kohl's overbearing and bullying approach, the Franco-German relationship cannot really survive intact over the coming year.

A reasonably satisfactory press conference is followed by seven radio and TV interviews in which the PM expresses herself with considerable force, tempered by some positivism. Back in No. 10 for 4.15 p.m. and home for 7 p.m.

I sleep until 8 a.m. on Sunday and then I am promptly furious. It is clear from the *Sunday Telegraph* that Charles Powell has leaked the idea of a four-power meeting in Berlin. I tell Andrew Turnbull that this old pro is thinking of hanging up his boots if this goes on. Charles rings me and denies responsibility for the leak but says he had a word with Julia Langdon and Geoffrey Parkhouse about a passage in the PM's summit contribution about a four-power consultation.

I am very brassed off about this freelance activity on my patch. Under my regime, No. 10 has never gone in for selective leaking but an iron determination to give all an equal service in the dissemination of news. How on earth can I convincingly represent the PM's views day in and day out when another source exists?

Otherwise, the Sunday press is a mixed bag and my conversation with George Jones (*Daily Telegraph*) and Robin Oakley (*Times*) confirms that they still do not know what to make of the summit. I try to set the PM's reputation in the context of her ten years' effort to sort out the EC and put it on the road to a common market. This seems to go down well. I don't put my nose outside today and crash on with writing Christmas cards.

WEEK 50: 11–17 DECEMBER

I score a high strike rate for yesterday's briefing in today's press in trying to turn our EC stance from negative to positive. The two journalists I briefed yesterday – George Jones and Robin Oakley – reflect my argument, and Chris Moncrieff puts out an ebullient piece on the PA. We must be carrying conviction.

I hope that over time and with a good performance by the PM in PMQs tomorrow she will be regarded more positively. I think Charles Powell feels guilty about his performance in Strasbourg.

The PM's interview with the *FT* is easier than expected in spite of the somewhat reptilian presence of one, Sam Brittan, who tries to take over. I ignore him.

Lunch with Conoco, the US oil firm active in the North Sea, finds me letting my hair down about the Americans and notably James Baker, Secretary of State, who eats humble pie with the PM for President Bush's words on EC integration.

Dinner with Jeffrey Archer, where Jim Naughtie and his wife argue with me about the BBC. Lady Young, the only woman to have served in a Thatcher Cabinet, has a real go at the BBC and all its works.

Tuesday is a mixed day. The press digest is very thin in spite of the first repatriation of fifty-one Vietnamese boat people – that is, those who are judged not to be political refugees. It goes more smoothly than I thought it might. Nonetheless, it generates condemnation both at home and abroad, where few countries have undertaken to help with their resettlement.

I bash on with Christmas cards before a boat people lobby and later see Geoffrey Tucker to talk over the political situation. Only three turn up for my European briefing. I really ought to kill it if they are not interested. The PM faces a bad-tempered Kinnock at PMQs over the boat people but then dominates the House with her statement on the Strasbourg summit. She accuses the opposition of not understanding the situation. The regional lobby gives me the chance to give them a very full briefing on the topic of the hour: the PM's softer line on the EC.

Wednesday's press brings a terrible fuss over the Vietnamese boat people, but the *FT*, *Guardian*, *Daily Telegraph* and *Times* adopt a more rational approach. Surprisingly, the *Express* turns sour. *The Independent* remains incorrigibly opposed to the PM and all she does. So what?

The day begins with Brian Hitchen interviewing the PM, having powerfully anointed himself with aftershave and bearing red roses for a blue lady. He has a splendid way with him and gets all he wants, plus photos. He does rather well in getting her to talk about a Britain fit to live in. I hope he does not go off at half cock on the threat from ambulancemen, who meet tomorrow on what seems likely to be abortive talks in their dispute.

I do not detect at the 11 a.m. lobby any great interest in the boat people. My American correspondents briefing has more life in it, and I tell them that America has disqualified itself on the boat people issue by refusing – or not offering – to take more of the refugees.

Lunch with Martin Adeney, ex-BBC, who has taken over the ICI media operation. I also see a Professor Nash from Leeds, where I am to give a lecture next November. In the evening, I see the Mexican Ambassador about his President's visit.

Thursday brings signs of a Tory revolt over the right of abode for Hong Kong lay personnel. I see the Chancellor after Cabinet and we agree things might be looking up for the government even if there is bad news today on earnings, unit costs and the trade deficit. He agrees with how we have turned the presentation of our approach to the EC over the past fortnight, and this leads on to consideration of entry into the ERM. He does not believe that the ERM matters one way or the other economically, but the politics of it are important and conceivably crucial. What, he asks, if we do not enter before the next election? It is not a great leap of imagination to suggest Kinnock will say, 'Get the election over and Labour will take us in and all will be well.' That might be nonsense, but possibly appealing nonsense. This raises the question that if the trade deficit and inflation are moving the right way (down), might it not make sense to announce entry in six months' time in a surprise coup, possibly in a broader tolerance of 2.5 per cent either way? That, he says, would take a lot of tricks and would convince everybody that we are going to be at the heart of Europe. It would also help to convince people to invest here.

Another GIS drinks party at 6 p.m., which goes well even though half the press office staff are hard at work processing paper. I leave for home at 7.15 p.m.

I am greeted on Friday in the hall of No. 10 by the custodian, who accuses me of being improperly dressed. News travels fast. In fact, I arrived to park my car on Horse Guards only to find I had left my passes at home. Fortunately, the policeman on guard recognised me and let me off.

The press is notable for a revolt by Norman Tebbit against right of abode for any Hong Kong folk. I hold fast to the established policy of safeguarding the prosperity of Hong Kong by giving those who make it tick a right of abode here should they feel they need it. This line is followed somewhat sketchily by the PM on a visit to Bristol.

The Sunday lobby is pretty boring before Michael Jones rings me to say I am being maligned by Lord Young in a book for foisting a senior information officer on to him. God, these people are petty. Michael Jones agrees. I try and fail to leave early and then take an hour to get home because of heavy traffic.

On Saturday, I desperately do some Christmas shopping before showing Ken Dodd, a former Halifax and *Guardian* colleague, and his wife around No. 10 and then entertaining them to lunch at home. It is a wild Sunday, with the rain lashing the windows. It settles down after lunch, but I am confined to the house.

WEEK 51: 18–24 DECEMBER

Government has that end-of-term feeling, with masses of announcements, statements and answers to PQs piling up for this final week of this session of Parliament. This just shows you how badly government is conducted. It really is not good enough that the machine still crowds all these developments etc. into the last week. Good publicity is lost in the welter of information that pours forth.

The press has little of note beyond a Chief Whip-induced obsession with Hong Kong folk seeking right of abode. Then, during the course of the day, the Archbishop of Canterbury calls on the government to halt sending people back home until an international agreement is reached on finding homes abroad for them. This will surely only add to Hong Kong's problems as the main goal of Vietnamese boat people.

I write a *Sunday Express* article for the PM before embarking on three media briefings, a lunch, MIO and a talk with Mr Oh and Mr Soo of South Korea. John reports that it is snowing on the summit of the M62 between Halifax/Huddersfield and Rochdale. Nancy has gone to bed with flu.

On Tuesday, Cabinet decides its policy on the right of abode for Hong Kong citizens after an hour's debate, with some reservations from Home Secretary Waddington and Industry Secretary Nick Ridley. The PM is almost alone in speaking of our duty. The feeling is that the policy will not get through, though the PM at least will try to sell it. Interestingly, Labour is resisting right of abode, along with right-wingers.

I am visited at noon by an aged Scottish artist to deliver an awful portrait of the PM. My deputy says it is really of Faith Brown, who impersonates Mrs T.

It is difficult to hear the PM at PMQs because of the noise. While Eduard Shevardnadze, the Soviet Foreign Minister, is meeting the PM, I have dinner with David Illingworth to discuss the proposal that I should join a PR firm in Yorkshire in some capacity when I retire.

On Wednesday, Charles Powell tells me as soon as I get into the office that President Bush telephoned the PM at 7 a.m. to inform her of action in Panama to get rid of President Manuel Noriega.

We get out a statement in time for the 8 a.m. news. The PM then becomes unusually hyperactive about the media. Should she go outside to say a few words? I think she should for four reasons:

1. To get on American breakfast TV;
2. To show that someone at least supports the USA;
3. To remind the wayward Americans who they can count on as they curry favour with Germany in Europe;
4. Because of the PM's need to justify her support for Bush.

The BBC ask the PM all the awkward questions. They will say that this shows how good they are at the journalistic game. I sometimes wonder who needs enemies when they have got the BBC.

In talking to Paul Potts, I draw his attention to an extraordinary BBC doctrine that BBC Scotland must reflect Scotland's lack of political balance by allowing anyone to attack the government, providing they say nothing new, without right of reply. I hope the *Express* goes to town on this.

For the rest, the government news factory churns it out, losing lots of good publicity in the process. By majority vote, the press office goes Indian for its Christmas dinner. I am becoming a real old conservative in my preference for English food.

As news continues to pour out of the government, events in Panama and Romania are heavily reported as the old orders collapse.* I write a presentation stock-taking note for the PM until four lobby officers – Geoffrey Parkhouse, George Jones, Chris Moncrieff and David Hughes – come in for a Christmas drink. Robin Butler drops in while the party is in full swing to wish us a merry Christmas, which we are obviously having. I walk for twenty-five minutes along the bracing Embankment to Blackfriars Bridge, because the ambulancemen's

---

* US forces invaded Panama on 20 December, leading to the surrender of President Noriega on 3 January 1990. The Romanian Revolution began on 16 December, resulting in the overthrow and, ultimately, the execution of President Nicolae Ceaușescu and his wife Elena on Christmas Day, ending forty-two years of Communist rule.

dispute has disrupted traffic, to see Nick Lloyd, editor of the *Express*, with another civil servant about starting a Buy British campaign.

Nancy lets me know that while shopping at Sainsbury's she told striking ambulancemen who were collecting funds to go back to work because they were depriving charities of money. In spite of the invigorating walk to the *Express*, I do not feel on top form. I may be going down with flu and so leave the PM's party early.

On Friday, President Ceauşescu falls in Romania, while I do some last-minute shopping for presents. By late morning, Sir Percy Cradock, chairman of the Joint Intelligence Committee, is reasonably satisfied Ceauşescu has been deposed. The PM agrees to go outside to say a few words to the media. To my mortification, the BBC are there but somehow not ITN, which causes extreme anger at ITN, who claim they have been commercially disadvantaged. I blow up at ITN because I am fed up with trying to help the media only to be battered when something goes wrong. The press office seems to get no credit for its assistance. I regret firing into David Mannion, but the press office make it clear they enjoyed my blast and only regret that from time to time they could not blast away a bit themselves.

I give my secretary Christmas lunch at the Howard Hotel. And who occupies the next table? Why, Nick Lloyd and Paul Potts, similarly thanking their secretaries for their work during the year.

On Saturday, it is clear there is Christmas carnage in Romania. It is dreadful what is going on. That is really all there is in the newspapers. The US intervention in Panama is very much down-page. Otherwise, it is a domestic day, with last-minute Christmas and birthday shopping, during which I get soaked by the bad weather.

It is Nancy's birthday on Christmas Eve, with calls from the family and friends to wish her well. I send a resumé of the Romania-dominated papers to the PM at Chequers. Then I learn that Charles Powell, who is treating me warily, has informed the duty press officer about the plight of our Embassy staff in Bucharest. We get them out eventually. For the rest, it is gardening, listening to music and generally enjoying my wife's birthday.

WEEK 52: 25–31 DECEMBER

By the time I go to bed on Christmas Day, it seems that Ceaușescu and his wife are dead, but the FCO has no official confirmation. If it is true, I rather agree with the White House's premature comment that it is a pity they were not put on trial.

Meanwhile, Noriega seeks refuge at the Vatican's Embassy in Panama, which is a bit rich for a man described by the BBC as a dictator, murderer, tyrant, drug runner, womaniser and pornographer. All this on Christmas Day. Some Christmas.

I seek solace in my presents and music – Beethoven's choral symphony and the *Phantom of the Opera* tape Nancy has bought for me. I am so tired that the music all too easily moves me to tears.

Newspapers are not delivered on Boxing Day so I have to go out to buy them from Mr Patel. I get the tabloids and *The Times*, all of which are full of the fall of the Ceaușescus. It is a truly mild day and the sun warms my back as I garden until noon. The balmy weather is good for racing at Kempton Park, where Desert Orchid triumphs even though his trainer and others say he was not on top form. Nancy's brother, Raymond, and his wife, Simone, come for tea.

My garden fills me with a sense of achievement. With a bit of luck it will be as good as I can make it before I return part-time to work. I begin writing my speech for Calder High School's forty-year anniversary dinner. At noon, I go into work hiding the unsightly gardening blisters on my hands. The press officers look rested. I send off the article I have written for the PM to the *Sunday Express*. The editor, Robin Morgan, seems to like it.

In the course of the day, I find that David Beveridge, Scottish Information Office, has got the OBE in the New Year honours list. It is good that the GIS is being recognised. Beveridge did a sterling job in Lockerbie [after a US airliner was blown up by terrorists over the town in 1988]. I persuade the staff to leave at 6 p.m. by driving them to the station.

I get to the office on Friday by 10 a.m. and shift what little is left to do before our usual media briefing on the honours list. It is far more entertaining and newsy than most. In addition to David Beveridge, Chris Moncrieff and George Bull are also in the media honours. I finish my Calder High School speech and my secretary gives me a Lochnagar haggis for the New Year. Home for 6.30 p.m.

On Saturday, we have a fast drive to Lymm in Cheshire to spend the New Year with John and Christine. After visits to relatives in Halifax and Triangle, we take Nancy's sister, Miriam, and her husband, Ted, to lunch at Far Flat Head Farm. Both are looking disturbingly frail. Back in Lymm, we go for dinner on New Year's Eve to the Moorside Hotel, where John and Christine held their wedding reception.

CHAPTER 13

JANUARY 1990:
GORBACHEV IN TROUBLE

The Soviet empire is breaking up – and so, it seems, is the government, with Norman Fowler leaving with a knighthood 'to spend more time with the family'. How many more will opt for the bosom of their families? Polls put Labour anything from twelve to thirteen points ahead.

Mr Gorbachev is in real trouble. After giving way in Lithuania, he faces threats of civil war in Armenia, Nagorno-Karabakh and Azerbaijan. The month ends with scare stories he is to quit. Apparently, he only threatens to do so.

For the rest, the ambulancemen make sullen strikers, and the teachers and local government workers, through the NUT and NALGO, make belligerent noises. And, to cap it all, Ford workers settle for 10.2 per cent, in a blow to inflation and jobs.

Lord Chief Justice Taylor shows no appetite for the government's proposed national membership scheme in his report on the Hillsborough football disaster. This effectively kills it for the time being. As was to be expected, the football authorities bleat about the need for more government money. They have learned nothing from ninety-six deaths.

The month ends with a storm that kills forty-seven people.

WEEK 1: 1–7 JANUARY

We see in the New Year at the Moorside Hotel, Bramhall. John, who has to work today, finds he cannot get breakfast until 9.30 a.m. after the late night. He leaves in a fairly ratty state to try to find the first-born of the new millennium and to cover a murder in Leigh, Lancs. We have a huge lunch with Christine and her parents in Bramhall before a five-hour drive home in mostly heavy rain. Not much in the news. Thank goodness for a quiet holiday.

The Chancellor helps to fill Tuesday's papers with economic forecasts. I have to write letters to nine people I know in the honours list. I also give Lord (Douglas) Houghton, ex-MP for my native constituency, Sowerby, a ring to see if he has a message for me to take to Calder High School. He obliges. At ninety-one, he sounds to be in fine fettle. Sheelagh Jefferies (COI) rings to tell me Henry James's wife, Sylvia, has died. Henry James preceded me as press secretary to Mrs Thatcher, having been brought out of retirement because she came to office without a press secretary.

I remain at home on Wednesday, but my secretary sends me down a briefcase of papers to digest and I reciprocate with another case of documents I have read. Norman Fowler, Employment Secretary, is to announce his retirement 'to spend more time with the family' and goes with a knighthood. I prepare for tomorrow's GIS visit to the Northern Ireland Information Service in Belfast.

Anne Nash and I fly to Aldergrove for our day with GIS colleagues there. We are met by Andy Wood, the director, who was a No. 10 press officer I inherited from the Callaghan regime. He introduces me to the protection officers assigned to me for the visit. We go straight to Stormont House for an initial meeting with senior staff. After that, we go for drinks at Andy Wood's home and then for a sumptuous dinner in Carryduff with Dr Brian Mawhinney, junior minister. He gives us a briefing on his talks with all shades of opinion. While the real problems seem to be with James Molyneux (Ulster Unionist) and John Hume (SDLP), we gather the most powerful man is probably still Ian Paisley, who might be 'delivered' by Peter Robinson (Democratic Unionist Party). It is a valuable account of what is going on in Northern Ireland politics.

We breakfast in Stormont and I am reassured by the press office about being away from base. There is little to cause concern except that Mr Gorbachev's position looks increasingly difficult because of events in Armenia and the Baltic States. He cancels a projected visit by Neil Kinnock. Poor chap. Mr Kinnock has bad luck with his trips abroad.

At 9 a.m. I go up to Stormont Castle to talk to the information division for seventy-five minutes on what we are trying to do with the GIS. They seem to appreciate it. We are then taken for a tour of Belfast, including a National Trust pub, the Crown, which has been preserved, including its lovely coloured windows. Lunch is with the head of prisons and a political adviser, who confirm Dr Mawhinney's view last night that the situation should be much better in twelve months' time and much changed by 1995.

We call on the RUC and the Army information teams in Lisburn and then I say my goodbyes to my protection officers, who have given me confidence and made me feel comfortable. We fly back to London by British Airways instead of the much better British Midland.

On Saturday, Roy Hattersley, deputy Labour leader, brings forward proposals for constitutional reform of the House of Lords, freedom of information and privacy. Donald Macintyre (*Sunday Correspondent*) tells me Sir Percy Cradock has been to China, where he was once our Ambassador.

By evening, it is clear the broadsheets are up to no good in the ambulance dispute. Geoffrey Goodman (*Mirror*) rings to say Robert Harris has seen him to try to dig up political dirt on me for his book.

Sunday's main problem is the press's interpretation of a briefing by the Health Secretary on the ambulance dispute. Kenneth Clarke spends his lunchtime on the radio knocking down the nonsense. Reports of Sir Percy Cradock's visit to China also need straightening out. I send a press digest to the PM at Chequers before we go for a walk on the Downs. Dennis Skinner MP, the so-called Beast of Bolsover, is on BBC's *Desert Island Discs*. His obsession with the working class is a bit much.

I do hope we can keep 1990 reasonably quiet. Famous last words.

WEEK 2: 8–14 JANUARY

A new year's work begins in earnest and we are thin on the ground, with my deputy seeing a specialist, Sarah Charman on holiday and Philip Aylett with the PM at Warwick University. That leaves only Peter Bean, Audrey Nelson, who is on a six-week secondment to No. 10, and me. Fortunately, Terry returns for 10.30 to take the first of two ambulance lobbies, both of which are dedicated to causing trouble for the government and the political death of Kenneth Clarke. Terry puts up a stout defence after a word with Romola Christopherson, head of information at the Department of Health and another former deputy of mine in No. 10. She is quite unfazed by the weekend reporting.

I have to delegate the first lobby because George Russell (IBA) and Alastair Burnet (ITN) come in to update me on their attitude to the Broadcasting Bill. On the whole, things seem to be OK. I then see the Japanese Ambassador preparatory to Prime Minister Toshiki Kaifu's visit on Friday, followed by lunch with the American Ambassador, Henry Catto, at La Gavroche, where the prices are hideous but the salad splendid.

After my briefing at the FPA, Geoffrey Smith (*The Times*) comes in to grill me on the PM's relations with Reagan and Gorbachev for his book. Home for 8.30 p.m.

On Tuesday, things get tougher, even though the newspapers are quite light. Sir Robert Reid gets a mauling from the press for leaving it until just before he gives up his post as chairman of British Rail to criticise the government for failing to give the railways enough money and moral support. At the same time, the press think the government should act on his criticisms.

The ambulance dispute gets tougher, too. I hold the fort at the 11 a.m. lobby before the PM rehearses her line at PMQs with a bouncy Kenneth Clarke. I break off my engagement with the 4 p.m. lobby when they try to negotiate through me. I say that there is no more money coming and it is time for the ambulancemen to settle. All this is fully reported on the 9 p.m. news. Now people know where they stand.

Earlier, the PM voiced concern about demands for more money for the disabled, with millions of pounds already being distributed. The DSS information division lobby me on this and I give them short shrift. They are clearly worried because they have told the disabled lobby more money is on its way.

I see the European lobby and then the regional lobby. I fear I am not in the best of tempers and reveal my distaste for the charades some journalists play. I do not like at all Tony Bevins's delight at Labour MP Dale Campbell-Savours putting the boot into Michael Forsyth, a junior Scottish Office minister, when the Speaker loses control of the House.

On Wednesday, George Jones interviews the PM and gets two things out of her: a somewhat optimistic view of 1990 economically; and a wish to visit South Africa after an appropriate interval following the release of Nelson Mandela, now elevated from hope to expectation.

Over lunch, the PM entertains the new, young and bright team from *The Economist*, with whom she relaxes and speaks her mind, especially on the German question and the Germans' propensity to dominate.

The main news story of the day is the renewed effort to get the Northern Irish political parties together. The PM is very cautious about it after the *Daily Telegraph* has gone overboard about a meeting. Another attempt will be made to get talks going, because the Unionists recognise that the Anglo-Irish agreement is not as fearsome as they thought.

I do both lobbies today. They would have passed quietly but for a 10.2 per cent pay offer to Ford workers. This presents a serious threat to inflation and jobs. Talking about inflation, over dinner, a Yorkshire PR firm that wants to employ me when I retire offers me £25,000 for two days' work.

My appointment as a fellow at Newcastle University is announced on Thursday. It is so mild that I walk to the House, Treasury and for dinner without a topcoat. Our main concern is excessive pay settlements after the Ford offer. The ambulancemen remain sullen and disruptive, and the NUT and NALGO (teachers and local government officers) make belligerent noises. The Cabinet discusses the issue and the PM follows this up at PMQs. In my briefings, I put the stress on the job-losing nature of union pay demands.

Earlier, I saw Robin Renwick, our Ambassador in South Africa, who filled me in on the proposed moves following Nelson Mandela's release and a degree of associated relaxation in South Africa – President de Klerk to see the PM at Chequers; the Foreign Secretary to go to Namibia and South Africa; and the PM to go to South Africa when it is judged she can have most beneficial effect.

After the 11 a.m. lobby, I write a brief for the PM's appearance on *The Wogan Show* and finalise the details of my Newcastle appointment. I persuade the Vice-Chancellor at Newcastle to downgrade me from professor to fellow until my retirement. Just imagine what the press would make of Professor Ingham as chief press secretary.

In the afternoon, I report to departmental establishment officers – man managers – on my first year's stewardship as head of the GIS. They seem very impressed with what we have done. At a British Management Data Foundation (BMDF) dinner at the Army and Navy Club, I open the batting on pay settlements. They are all concerned about our inflationary culture but are curiously disinclined to accept any responsibility for it.

On Friday, I describe the PM's contribution to *The Wogan Show* last night as 'a great triumph'. Dominic Morris, private secretary for parliamentary affairs, confides in the corridor that several in No. 10 thought I had gone mad letting her go on *Wogan* but admits that she did brilliantly. Her performance certainly repaid all the work we did in rehearsing her.

Peter Bean, our new press officer from the FCO, also did well last night: he frustrated the media and Michael Cole, Harrods' PR man, in their attempts to get a picture of the PM with Mohamed al-Fayed, the controversial owner of the store.

Pay takes second place in the media to Mr Gorbachev giving

way in Lithuania, and thereby probably starting the undoing of the Soviet empire. There is a great deal of editorialising on pay, which employers at last night's BMDF dinner interestingly did not put down to the unions any more. Some of the press think the government should hold firm against the ambulancemen and the public sector.

When Mr Kaifu visits the PM at 11 a.m., I go off to speak at the COI to a very entertaining induction course.

We drive to Hebden Bridge on Saturday for my Calder High School speech. After visiting all our relatives, I arrive at the school at 7.30 to see old colleagues in the form of Donald Crossley, the artist whose work I promote in Westminster; Beryl Chatburn (née Pickles); Professor Norman Riley; Ian Hellowell; Joyce Hartley; and Ina Lord (née Marsland). It is all very nostalgic. The evening goes on and on because of the long gaps between courses. I propose the toast to the school for twenty minutes until 11.25 p.m. I get an excellent reception and lots of laughs and, it seems, a good time was had by all. Bed at 1 a.m.

We have an uneventful drive home in time for the 1 p.m. news. I get up to date quickly and find Robert Harris (*Sunday Times*) and Adam Raphael (*Observer*) writing, respectively, unhelpfully and helpfully about the lobby system. My brother Derek rings to say that our cousin, Malcolm Horsfall, thought the school dinner last night was a good do.

WEEK 3: 15–21 JANUARY

A MORI poll gives Labour an eight-point lead. There is threat of civil war in Armenia, Nagorno-Karabakh and Azerbaijan. Gorbachev sends in troops and the KGB during the course of the day.

Week-ahead meetings are becoming interminable under Kenneth Baker's influence. He wants Hong Kong legislation out of the way by the summer recess so that it does not interfere with the Tory Party conference – an idea apparently the product of his meeting with the brash Tim Bell, PR consultant. In the evening,

I get a presentation of new 'values' polling which shows that the government has a hard fight on its hands to win back C2s.

I have lunch at the Savoy with Peter Norman (*FT*), then briefings of the FPA and lobby before chairing MIO. I am beginning to feel the pace, and my row with Charles Powell has knocked a lot of enthusiasm out of me.

On Tuesday, the media complains about a dearth of news. 'What on earth can we write about?' they say. 'Give us a story.' There is little to give them apart from events in Eastern Europe and the USSR.

We struggle to work out what Kinnock will raise at PMQs. To our astonishment, he raises pay policy, apparently completely misunderstanding the nature of an incomes policy embracing norms and the public and private sectors. He fair caps me at times. I do not exactly appreciate the PM flying a kite about higher compensation for homeowners for road and rail projects, because we are unbriefed on it.

In the evening, the press office goes over to Buckingham Palace for our annual visitation for drinks. I am delighted to learn that Charles Anson, the FCO press officer I inherited from the Callaghan regime, is being lined up as the next press secretary to the Queen. Before we go to the Palace, I finalise my report to Robin Butler on GIS development.

I am preoccupied on Wednesday morning with the PM's visit to the National Children's Home in the evening. I began interesting the press in this yesterday and it is now clear that someone in DSS has briefed *The Times* on the need for many more runaway fathers to pay maintenance for their children. This is useful because it titillates the appetites of the evening newspapers. Once her speech at the event is finalised, I go out and sell it in a big way. It proves to be a successful operation.

I lunch with Biddy Baxter and David Hatch at the BBC to discuss plans for a GIS/BBC radio seminar. I think we shall have a good joint meeting. The BBC's wine is somewhat potent, so I rather somnolently preside over a meeting of the GIS executive on recruitment.

On Thursday, the government wins the 10 p.m. vote on the implementation of the community charge by forty-six votes. The PM had said that if the government got a twenty majority, she would have two drinks with the whips. Earlier, there were all kinds of palpitations behind a calm exterior about the outcome. I did not understand the lack of scare stories about the charge – indeed, no high noon build-up to the votes. Perhaps the size of the majority explains this.

In the briefing for PMQs, we are far from clear what Kinnock will lead on. It turns out to be the poll tax, as the PM calls it in an unguarded moment. The result of his line of questioning is to give the PM the opportunity to hammer home the point that a high community charge will be the fault of local authority spending.

Friday takes me to Edinburgh to brief the Scottish Information Office on GIS developments. It entails getting up at 5.15 a.m. to be in a blustery, wet Edinburgh for just after 9 a.m. Under the chairmanship of Fred Corbett, director, I give a 75-minute briefing, with questions, in two halves – one morning and the other afternoon. Altogether the outcome is pretty satisfactory, although I am always worried when I go outside London because of the GIS's lack of mobility. They do not have the chance to get the same experience of different government departments as in London. High winds make for a rough flight back to the office for 7.20 p.m.

On Saturday, Terry Perks accompanies the PM on her visit to Paris to see President Mitterrand so that I can have a break. Sarah Charman goes into No. 10 to cover the filming of the redecoration of the reception rooms. On a wet and miserable Sunday which rules out a walk, I send a note to the PM at Chequers on one of the emptier sets of Sunday newspapers I have seen for a long time. There is next to no coverage of the Paris summit. Altogether a restful weekend, if you ignore all the reading the job entails.

WEEK 4: 22–28 JANUARY

Speculation about the mildest winter since the mid-1970s seems a bit premature, bearing in mind the forecast for the weekend.

Week-ahead meetings have become undisciplined under Kenneth Baker. I perform a useful task in getting all concerned to think about the presentation of the PM's tricky meeting with MEPs on Wednesday. It is tentatively decided that the Foreign Secretary should handle it. Baker reiterates his desire to get the Hong Kong legislation out of the way by the summer recess so that it does not interfere with the party conference.

I take Lord Whitelaw's counsel on my problems with Charles Powell. What can I do if I think the PM's interests are being damaged by a chap who has gone over the top? And can you help a PM so lacking in tact? He thinks I should soldier on to the next election, about which he is by no means sanguine. I still think she will win with a majority of thirty, but nobody knows at this stage.

On Tuesday, the PM has a meeting with the Home and Environment Secretaries on Lord Justice Taylor's report on the Hillsborough football disaster. As expected, he has shown no enthusiasm whatever for the proposed national membership card scheme. Ministers agree that they cannot now go ahead with this particular scheme but decide to keep the enabling legislation on the statute book and to conduct tests on other membership schemes and keep the idea in reserve.

After the PM wipes the floor with Kinnock at PMQs, I go to Cardiff by train to talk to Polish journalists under the auspices of Geoff Rich, editor of the *Western Mail*. My encounters with British journalists evoke some tough words from me about the British media. The Polish journalists are desperate to get Britain involved in Poland. Please invest in Poland, they say.

It does not take long on Wednesday for the Taylor Report to leak, and the media are agog over it. I manage to come out of my 11 a.m. lobby in reasonable order, but I fear the PM is in for a towelling at PMQs tomorrow, given that Taylor has rejected the idea of a membership scheme, which was very much her own.

The PM is interviewed by three journalists from the *Wall Street Journal* and gives an excellent account of her views on German reunification.

After the lobby and the American correspondents, I hare off to Bloomsbury Baptist Church to speak to the Cosmopolitan Women's Club about my job and the past two momentous years. I am the only man among 200 women – frightening. They send me packing with a bottle of malt whisky in a gorgeous tin.

Rupert Murdoch visits the PM after lunch on his return from Poland, Hungary, Romania and Czechoslovakia. He fires her with enthusiasm to go east.

Thursday brings the great storm. I am not aware of its intensity until around lunchtime, when it roars down my office chimney. It calms down by 6.15 p.m., when the Home Secretary calls an emergency meeting of ministers, which I attend. By then, twenty-seven people had been killed (thirty-four by the 10 p.m. news) and traffic is at a standstill around Whitehall and Westminster for hours.

After the ministerial meeting, I issue a statement promising financial help. I then try my luck with the car, taking Ian Beaumont, press officer manager, home. I am home for 9.20 p.m.

The day started with my anger over a BBC *Newsnight* piece the night before which quoted No. 10 confirming the demise of the football membership card scheme. I write to John Cole (political editor) protesting about this erroneous statement. His colleague John Harrison says he will try to sort it out and seems to have a jolly good try doing so.

The opposition have a steady go at the PM over the Hillsborough Report in a bad PMQs. David Nicholas, editor of ITN, comes in on his sixtieth birthday to air a problem over ITN/commercial TV companies' relationship.

I am flat out from 7 a.m. on Friday because my deputy and Philip

Aylett are with the PM in Lancashire and Sarah Charman is on a recce in Dublin, where the next EU summit is to be held. This is my agenda: compile press digest; attend week-ahead meeting; meeting with Lord Privy Seal, Lord Belstead; lobby at 11 a.m.; meeting with No. 10 private secretaries at 11.30, at which Paul Gray fills me in on pay review bodies; follow-up to last night's emergency meeting on the storm; lunch with Liz Drummond, press secretary to Westminster City Council and former No. 10 officer, to see if she might be interested as a Scot in taking over the Scottish Information Office. She seems to enjoy working for that handful Lady Porter, leader of the council.

It seems that, while forty-seven people were killed in the storm, the government handled it well, but Labour thinks the government did not give adequate warning in spite of a broadcast referring to the possibility of structural damage. The Met Office feels more needs to be done by way of liaison with the police, utilities, farmers etc.

It is raining in Purley on Saturday but snowing, according to relatives, in Lymm and Halifax. Indeed, my brother reports eight inches on his farm after tea. I read, watch racing at Cheltenham and Doncaster and Rugby League.

MORI and Harris polls give Labour surprise leads of twelve and thirteen points respectively. I would not have thought events could lead to such an adverse movement. There are a lot of stories around about a defence review which I am sure will come about, but I cannot hint at it.

I clean up the debris after the storm – no structural damage, thank goodness – and then write a speech for a press gallery lunch next month.

WEEK 5: 29 JANUARY–4 FEBRUARY

The Hillsborough Report is published on Monday. In response, we fix responsibility for the wellbeing of soccer on the football authorities and clubs. I am sorry to say that, like the opposition parties, their customary reflex action is: who is going to pay? We're going to be bankrupted; we shall go out of business; the government must show its responsibility, too (by finding the money). All this after ninety-six deaths! Home Secretary Waddington is ably firm in the Commons, and the PM acknowledges this in conversation while waiting for the arrival of President Salinas of Mexico, at 7.40 p.m., just as I was leaving for home.

It takes longer to read the Monday newspapers than any other day because of the hotchpotch of stories that the press have had time to dream up over the weekend. The most devastating news from the weekend was Halifax crashing in the Rugby League Cup at Hull. Awful. Lunch with Fernand Auberjonois (the *Toledo Blade*, Ohio), who shows interest as a Swiss in going to my native Hebden Bridge in the summer to write about the place.

In the usual PMQs briefing on Tuesday, we have great fun with the text of my forthcoming speech to the parliamentary press gallery. To my surprise, they all think it is very mild! The press give the football authorities and clubs a real going-over after the Taylor Report. It is pretty savage stuff, with leaders to match. The PM is thoroughly brassed off by *The Times*'s sports reporter, who accuses the government of neglecting the hooligan problem, and we try to get Sports minister Colin Moynihan to write to the editor.

The main worry today is a series of parliamentary answers on Colin Wallace, an information officer working in Northern Ireland and allegedly engaged in disinformation in the 1970s. I do not like this at all.

Just before I leave for home, we have a scare that Mr Gorbachev is to quit. It soon turns into 'threatens to quit'.

I have a great deal of work to get through on Wednesday. The Colin Wallace case continues to cause trouble, more evidence of his work having been found in the government's possession. President Bush is about to make more cuts, which gets me into a false position with the American correspondents because I do not tell them Lawrence Eagleburger, Deputy Secretary of State, came to No. 10 about this on Monday. All the pay review bodies and the teachers' committee reports have to be mastered before their publication to-morrow. And then, late in the day, C4 reports that the Post Office is to be privatised – it isn't, but its postal monopoly is to be restricted, thereby increasing competition; and I am trying to sew up a three-way switch of heads of information which, if we pull it off, Robin Butler thinks will be a coup – i.e. Brian Mower from Home to FCO; Adrian Moorey from DTI to Environment, and Jean Caines from Environment to DTI.

In addition, I introduce Robin Morgan, the new editor of the *Sunday Express*, to the PM and give an interview about my job to *The Independent*'s Mark Lawson, an untidy fellow who comes to No. 10 as if dressed for an expedition to the Pamirs.

The overriding issue on a very wet day is the Colin Wallace affair. It is an almost classic case of the first law of modern journalism: where there is no sin, create it. We have an avalanche of absurdity as every conceivable angle is raked over, new (or old) questions asked and new mysteries created.

We advise a very jumpy PM ahead of PMQs to keep it simple: it has nothing to do with the present government, and all the spying allegations have already been investigated. We urge her to say she has come to the House to correct errors of fact and clarify situations, none of which bear on Wallace's (wrongful) conviction for manslaughter, for which he served six years in prison.

Towards the end of the day, while I am holding a farewell drinks party to say thank you to retiring information officers – the first – we hear of a speech by President de Klerk and the release of Nelson Mandela.

Overnight brings news that de Klerk is going for broke – doing almost everything the Commonwealth's Eminent Persons Group asked for. The press office seems to be in a panic over the media pressure and I have to tell them that we are not going to be ruled by them.

Eventually, we put out a statement on Friday, followed up quickly by Terry briefing the lobby. Then, at the end of the morning session of a GIS training seminar, I get the PM outside to say a few words to the media, who, on the whole, behave well, given that Gallup gives Labour a 15.5-point lead.

On Saturday, the heaviest rain of the winter turns to sleet, thunder and lightning, and I get sopping wet out shopping. I am a bit dizzy, coughing a lot and generally below par. Perhaps it is the depths-of-winter syndrome. Consequently, I try to rest watching England Rugby Union beat France by the largest margin since 1914. I hope they win the Grand Slam.

The Sunday papers are rich in social/class comment following the libel settlement between two editors, Andrew Neil (*Sunday Times*) and Peregrine Worsthorne (*Sunday Telegraph*). Michael Jones portrays his editor, Neil, as the anti-establishment outsider. I know how he feels.

Charles Powell has clearly been talking to the *Sunday Correspondent* and *Observer* to no effect and much disadvantage. It is becoming blatant and cannot go on. By 11.30 a.m. I have sent a summary of the papers to the PM at Chequers.

Between watching Spurs beat Norwich, I shift a lot of admin and reading and subedit a government report on inner cities that I find rather stilted. I then knock off to watch Michael Palin and *Poirot*.

CHAPTER 14

FEBRUARY 1990: THE RELEASE OF NELSON MANDELA

Four topics dominate the month: the release of Nelson Mandela, which the PM watches on TV; Gorbachev winning a vote in reform and plurality in the USSR; the PM's concern about Chancellor Kohl's dictatorial approach to German reunification and the need for the two Germanys to take account of others and existing treaties; and a shock 15.4 per cent mortgage rate announced suddenly by Abbey National to go with arguments over whether the ambulancemen have settled for 17 per cent or for 13.1 per cent over two years, as claimed by the Department of Health. It is not the best background to the Mid Staffs by-election.

Otherwise, Chancellor Major opts for a cautious Budget strategy while bearing down on inflation and is optimistic about 1991.

WEEK 6: 5–11 FEBRUARY

On Monday, the press concentrates on the USSR after a big demo in favour of reform, and the impending release of Nelson Mandela. I begin the day with a talk with Andrew Turnbull about Charles Powell's activities. We decide to keep a dossier prior to a showdown.

At the week-ahead meeting, the PM wants the ambulance dispute out of the way without surrendering, wrapping the dispute up with a two-year deal. At the 11 a.m. lobby, I face an *Independent* story that the PM favours an officer class for the police. The story is not all it is cracked up to be, but it has elements of truth.

I lunch with Keith Renshaw (*Sunday Express*) at his usual place in L'Epicure. It is rather boozy, so I am well-oiled by the time I get to the Arvon Foundation's literary dinner at the Savoy. There is an astonishing collection of people supporting Arvon, which has a base at Lumb Bank in my native Hebden Bridge, but only myself and Donald Thompson MP and his wife are the real local thing.

Poetry readings keep the evening going until 11.30, when I slip out to find the PM returning to No. 10, where I am staying overnight. We drink together until 1 a.m.

On Tuesday, I am inevitably rather fragile. This is the problem with chatting into the early hours with a PM who never seems to want to go to bed. And those damn chimes by the Horse Guards clock wake me up at 4.45 a.m. At the PMQs briefing, it seems likely that Kinnock will lead off on an HM Inspectorate's report on the state of our schools. Sure enough, he does so, but with only one sheet of paper to support him, according to Dominic Morris, private secretary for parliamentary affairs.

The PM stings him by implying that he has not read the report. And before we know where we are, the Wombat, as he is called, loses his rag – or wool, as the PM puts it – and is foaming at the mouth. The PM remains calm amid the storm and so wins hands down.

I then pop over to the Department of Transport to see Cecil Parkinson, who wants to tell George Russell what was wrong about a C4 programme that libelled him with allegations of corruption. Home for 8.45 p.m.

On Wednesday, press gallery chairman Michael Jones feels like I did yesterday, having been out on the town last night with Murdo Maclean and ended up in Hastings through falling asleep on the train. This entails a £40 taxi to his home in Orpington. Nonetheless, he discharges himself well in introducing me as speaker. The gallery take my talk in good part and there are lots of laughs from an audience including the Chief Whip and several MPs, notably Austin Mitchell, who lives near my brother's farm outside Halifax.

Nick Jones (BBC) asks me for an interview after the lunch and deals with me very fairly on Radio 4's *PM* programme. But I have no illusions about my popularity in media circles, and the BBC's *World Tonight* gives an early taste of their vitriol. Anthony Howard puts my remarks down to my alleged disappointment at not succeeding Peter Jenkins as labour editor of *The Guardian*. Absolute nonsense.

At the press gallery lunch, I get a message from Peter Bean to say that Mr Gorbachev has won the vote on political reform and plurality in the Soviet Union. Michael Jones promptly conveys this to the lunch. This makes 7 February 1990 an important day, and it will be the main story tomorrow. One of the top four in the Soviet hierarchy comes in to see the PM.

My speech gets a lot of coverage in Thursday's papers. The *Daily Telegraph* and the *FT* are sober, apart from Simon Heffer's sketch in the *Daily Telegraph*; *The Guardian* pretty fair, though flowery; *The Independent* sour and paranoiac – which is what they say I am – and *The Times* wonderful, with a cartoon. I also get coverage on the BBC's *PM*, *World Tonight* and *Today* programmes, where Chris Moncrieff from the PA stands up for me like a true friend. Sir Marcus Fox, a Yorkshire MP, says, 'Good old Bernard.' I write to him saying, 'Good old Marcus.'

Andrew Turnbull calls in to laugh with me at *The Independent*, and the PM reads *The Times*'s account and calls for a copy of the speech. The fun is perpetuated when I welcome the 11 a.m. lobby to Rottweiler Hall, since *The Independent* says the gates at the end of Downing Street are to protect the public from Rottweiler Ingham.

The PM is in Rottweiler form at Cabinet over German reunification and gives strong backing to Mr Gorbachev. PMQs are a non-event, with Roy Hattersley deputising for Kinnock.

Friday brings the reckoning. *Today* and the *Daily Telegraph* have particularly nasty leaders about my speech. I think some criticism was inevitable and I am not too concerned. After a visit to the dentist because of an ulcer on the gum, I then compile the diary for the two weeks ahead and read a report from Anne Nash on progress in pursuing our GIS agenda. We need to start planning for the GIS weekend conference in Bath.

After lunch with George Bull, I have a monumentally long Sunday lobby on child benefit, tax reliefs for working mothers, German reunification and arms control, and Mr Gorbachev. Altogether a tough week, but I think I have achieved something for the GIS and struck a blow for accuracy, fairness and balance in journalism.

On Saturday, Charles Powell rings me to say President de Klerk is trying to get hold of the PM, who is in Torquay for the Young Conservatives conference. Eventually, Pik Botha rings Charles to let him know Nelson Mandela is to be released tomorrow. I get a statement together for Peter Bean, the duty press officer.

Coverage of my press gallery speech continues in *The Independent*, a letter in *The Guardian* and a splendid though not particularly accurate article in the *FT* by Hazel Duffy, who recently interviewed me. The strapline on the last claims I am carving out a place in history!

Sunday brings the long-awaited release of Nelson Mandela. It takes me into the office in a gale and rainstorm for 4.30 p.m. to talk with the PM, who has earlier seen the media on her visit to Ellesborough Church near Chequers. She has nothing new to say, so I call off any media event outside – a decision that is received with ill grace. But they have already got their sound bite.

I watch Mandela speak with the PM in her flat. He goes on a bit and is somewhat disappointing in maintaining the armed struggle and calling for continued sanctions. But we agree this was perhaps inevitable. On the other hand, he is very positive about de Klerk and his hopes for negotiations and the maintenance of peace during the process. I feed reaction out to Chris Moncrieff for the simultaneous benefit of all news outlets.

And still they argue over my press gallery speech. The *Sunday Times* does it proud, and there are echoes in the *Sunday Express, Mail on Sunday* and *Observer. The Times*'s Atticus column as near as dammit seeks a benefactor to help me sue the *Daily Telegraph*. Let's keep the law out of it.

WEEK 7: 12–18 FEBRUARY

Another week starts with a fearfully busy day, what with the release of Mandela, German reunification and the visit of the Polish PM, Tadeusz Mazowiecki.

Our failure to produce the PM for interviews last night is interpreted as a disappointment with Mandela's speech. In fact, the PM thinks it is just about what was to be expected from a member of the ANC, while noting his positive views of de Klerk and the need for peaceful negotiation.

Charles Powell and I work out a forthright briefing line which contrasts the support given to Mr Gorbachev for leading the USSR out of repression to, we hope, democracy with the refusal to support de Klerk.

On Germany, I seek to win credit for the UK for the idea emerging from Kohl–Genscher talks in Moscow of a four-power conference with the two Germanys to try to ensure that all interests are taken into account. It emerges after my FPA briefing that the Polish PM is especially exercised over German reunification and is anxious to see Polish–German borders enshrined in law.

The PM is extremely concerned about the arrogant attitude of the Germans at this stage and has been in no way soothed by Charles Powell's meeting with Kohl's adviser in Bonn on Friday.

On Tuesday, the PM is in hot water at PMQs, with uproar in the House when she says Labour Party policy is possibly driven by the ANC. It produces the noisiest scenes of the newly televised House. The BBC is responsible for some tendentious reporting at 6 p.m., about which I lodge a severe protest.

PMQs actually begin quietly, with Mandela's release and a

possible four-power meeting on Germany, which the *Daily Mail* says was the UK's idea. I am very anxious that the PM should repudiate the idea that the new family doctors settlement justifies in any way the exclusion of expensive patients from their lists. Alas, there was no opportunity. Only noise. In the evening, the PM goes briefly to a lobby party, where she praises my press gallery speech to Michael Jones. She then slips out with her detectives when I am not looking. I catch them up in time for a drink with her in my room before she receives the Polish PM.

I must confess that by Wednesday I am almost on autopilot briefing on East–West relations; Germany reunification and the need to take into account existing treaties and agreements, such as the CSCE, NATO, Warsaw Pact and the EC; and the need for carrots not sticks for de Klerk. All this comes at the 11 a.m. lobby, then the American correspondents and subsequently and separately with the *Wall Street Journal*.

Then the Abbey National drops a bombshell – a 15.4 per cent mortgage rate, which is no help to anyone and almost certainly means the Tories will lose the impending Mid-Staffordshire by-election. Life is not going to be easy for the PM at tomorrow's PMQs. On the other hand, Westminster City Council has come in with a moderate community charge, which gets less play than I expected. In short, a busy St Valentine's Day.

On Thursday, Labour fluffs what is predicted as a difficult PMQs with:

1. Mortgage rates at a record level (Abbey National);
2. A government shocked by a rate it says was not called for and about which it was notified only twenty minutes before the event;
3. Contradictory economic indicators.

Kinnock can manage no more inventive question than 'When is the PM going to cap mortgage rates?' This is easily dealt with and all the media hype about the PM facing tough questions looks lame.

Perhaps I should not be surprised about this damp squib since the 11 a.m. lobby shows a lack of steam in the mortgage rate story. It also fails to pursue what I think is the real political story of the day: hard evidence that someone, presumably in the FCO, is trying to stir up trouble between the PM and Foreign Secretary Hurd. They meet before Cabinet and kill the issue. I have an excellent meeting with Chancellor Major after Cabinet. He is confident that the economy has turned, notwithstanding money supply figures. For the rest, I sort out the picture story of the No. 10 refurbishments; have another GIS party for information officers; and have dinner with Frank Melville (American correspondent).

John, our son, is thirty-two on Friday. He and Christine arrive at 10.15 p.m. – he having been held up writing a feature for the *Express*.

Before their arrival, I have the usual busy Friday – mapping out the weeks ahead; handling the PM's speech on the second annual report on inner cities; meeting with Anne Nash on GIS issues; and writing a speech for a Shepherd's (Yorkshire building firm) lunch in the cellar of the Stafford Hotel. It is the least satisfactory of my Shepherd's lunches, partly because I have a bad cough, which I am treating with whisky.

The Sunday lobby is neither here nor there but goes on a long time. I get away at 7.15 p.m. feeling tired, but John and Christine cheer me up and we eventually get to bed around midnight.

After a walk on Chipstead Downs, where recent gales have blown over some trees, including yews, John and Christine go off to visit the Royal Pavilion in Brighton. They return saying it is fabulous. We are booked for a birthday dinner at the Green Rooms in Croydon. After a thirty-minute wait for a table and some rude treatment, we walk 100 yards down the road for a slap-up birthday feast. The evening is recovered from disaster.

On Sunday, the PM takes a tough and uncompromising stance on German reunification at the Board of Deputies of British Jews luncheon and the need for the Germans to take account of the interests of others. The *Sunday Times* goes rather hard on this and rather frightens the PM. Charles Powell rings to say she would like me to adopt a more conciliatory tone.

John and Christine leave after an early lunch and are back home in Lymm for 4.20 p.m. It was good to have them for the weekend.

WEEK 8: 19–25 FEBRUARY

A boring week in prospect after recent excitements. Internationally, it is busy, but there is not much at home to divert minds from the economy. Yet the economy figures much less than I expected in today's press. The PM's speech to the Board of Deputies of British Jews on German reunification gets a good show.

The week-ahead meeting is dominated by concern over the disaffection of Andrew Neil (editor, *Sunday Times*), whom Kenneth Baker went to see on Thursday, apparently to no effect. The point of the PM's concern is the attack on her in yesterday's leader as negative and out of touch.

I attend a meeting of the honours committee, lunch with a Swiss journalist, brief the FPA (curiously, no German journalists there) and the 4 p.m. lobby and preside over MIO before drawing breath.

I am concerned about the government's inability to back up my contention that the Germans and Japanese are increasing their investment in South Africa. We must find it soon.

At Tuesday's PMQs briefing, I tell the PM we need to get over positive messages at PMQs – notably, fixing responsibility for high local spending (and poll tax) on local authorities. Environment Secretary Chris Patten comes up with an excellent brief relating existing rates to the community charge. This enables the PM to tell the House that comparing this year's rates with a predicted average community charge shows a 35 per cent rise – getting on for five times the rate of inflation. The figure can be worked out for every local authority.

This keeps me busy throughout the afternoon after I see Health Secretary Kenneth Clarke in his room about the ambulance dispute, which after twenty-two weeks has gone to ACAS [conciliation service]. The National Union of Public Employees will no doubt try to portray the proposed settlement as a 17 per cent rise, whereas the increase in the pay bill, according to the Department of Health, is only 13.1 per cent. I get this into the public domain, only to be told by Paul Gray, the PM's economic private secretary, that he doubts whether the Department of Health figure is high enough. Oh dear. I fear we shall end up with the ambulance workers being seen as winners, with all the implications for other pay negotiations.

I have an extremely lively briefing for American correspondents on Wednesday morning on Germany and South African sanctions. Why, they ask, when you need friends in Europe, don't you shut up about South African sanctions? I derive enormous satisfaction from telling them that their attitude is typical of the hypocrisy to be expected from liberal wets – never stand for anything, least of all equal opportunities for black people, if other things get in the way.

I am a guest of Conoco at the Institute of Petroleum dinner, one of the great dinners of the year. Energy Secretary John Wakeham gives an excellent speech, and John Greenborough (Shell) winds up with a wit that has them rocking in the aisles.

I sit between Dan McGeachie, Conoco's UK PR officer, and Harry Sager, over from Houston, and regale them with the government's views on the German question and our misgivings about the way they, and particularly Chancellor Kohl, are going about the business of reunification. I walk back to No. 10, where I am staying, from Park Lane at 11.30 after a chat with Malcolm Thornton, MP for Crosby. The chill and my brisk pace do me good and I am in bed for 12.30, having whipped through Thursday's newspapers.

Thursday brings the pre-Budget Cabinet, after which the Chancellor gives me a thorough run-down on the strategy, for which he wins the support of his colleagues. They reaffirm a strategy bearing down on inflation and a cautious, prudent approach to Budget details. All ministers counsel caution. Many want something to help mothers who go to work – e.g. tax allowances on crèche charges. A number argue that the government cannot afford and has no need to raise interest rates further, and Foreign Secretary Hurd urges the Chancellor to do nothing to hurt C2 Tory supporters and, if possible, to do something to help them.

In presenting his strategy, the Chancellor predicted a gloomy 1990 but the possibility of a fast recovery in 1991. As a result, I would not be surprised if there is an election next year, however bleak it looks now. I think the PM believes she is in a fundamentally strong position after all that has been achieved during the past ten years.

On Friday, the Cabinet makes for gloomy reading in all bar the *Daily Telegraph*. The press continues to get it right about the ambulance dispute – they lost – but whether that will help to win the men's acceptance in a ballot is another matter.

I have to put my skates on this morning because of an Anglo-Italian summit. At the summit press conference in the steam bath of No. 12 Downing Street (the Chief Whip's office), Prime Minister Andreotti gives his support to the PM on both German reunification and South African sanctions.

I lunch with John Knight (*Sunday Mirror*) at the Savoy Grill. He is excellent company and too generous with the drink. This makes for an articulate and forthright Sunday lobby. Heaven only knows what they will make of it. Later in the afternoon, I write a brief for the PM for her interview with four *Daily Mail* writers on Monday and play with her speech associated with the inner cities report next Wednesday.

On Saturday, I am relieved to see that Mark Lawson's *Independent Magazine* article on me, with my face plastered all over the cover, is not too bad. I have a simultaneous telephone chat with Gus O'Donnell, the Chancellor's press secretary, and Paul Gray about an article by Philip Stephens in the *FT* claiming that the PM is leaving it to the Chancellor to decide when to enter the ERM. While a thunderstorm rages outside, I try to relax by snoozing and desultorily watching a Rugby League Cup tie. My peace is disturbed by Charles Powell ringing to say the PM has just had an excellent 45-minute telephone chat with President Bush prior to his receiving Chancellor Kohl at Camp David.

The Sunday papers take a lot of reading. They have clearly got my point about German unification bringing new uncertainty to early British entry into the ERM. I have also trailed the likely lifting of sanctions when South Africa ends the emergency.

Two bits of news today are: Kohl apparently disagreeing with Bush on some aspects of reunification, notably reassurance for the Poles. I watch England hammer the West Indies' bowling and Nottingham Forest get to Wembley on aggregate over Coventry.

The doctor tells me on Monday that I have Dupuytren's contracture – otherwise known as the Vikings' Disease – the hardening of tendons in the hand, creating something of a claw with the fingers. She arranges for me to see a specialist. I arrive at No. 10 in time to take the 11 a.m. lobby, which concentrates on the poll tax. This is followed by the PM's interview with *Daily Mail* journalists. Two of the four – Ann Leslie and Margaret Stone – are not exactly friendly. I do not think it is a success, partly because the PM is repetitive.

I lunch with Hugo Young of *The Guardian* in the back room at the Garrick, where the boys are. He seems to be recovering from his wife's death but he is much thinner. The afternoon consists of an uneventful FPA briefing; another lively council tax lobby; and hanging around for the PM to sort out her Wednesday speech on inner cities.

On Tuesday, I get the PM to inspire a question at PMQs on the *Mirror*'s campaign to denigrate NHS reforms by suggesting expensive patients, such as the elderly, will be thrown off doctors' lists. This is causing stress among the elderly. I give George Jones a rather impassioned briefing on this.

I am then involved in speechwriting for the PM's visit to Bradford tomorrow; two lobbies on the sole topic of the moment – the poll tax – and trying to get the alarmingly increasing pile of reading under some sort of control.

Norman Tebbit brings the month to an end by suggesting that the PM was shaken last night when he disclosed at a supposedly private meeting with her that eighty-plus MPs would vote against the Hong Kong Bill on right of abode. Her principled response – we don't rat – could not have come as a surprise to Tebbit.

Mr Gorbachev steams ahead by securing executive presidential powers. I do not, I fear, steam ahead much myself. I shift a lot of paper even though shorthanded – my deputy and Sarah Charman are with the PM in Bradford and have to return by train because snow closes the Leeds Bradford Airport at Yeadon. But I have the unhappy task of telling two very senior heads of information that they have not got the director's job at Environment in the face of the minister's preference for another. My meeting with heads of information on recruitment after the Civil Service Commission becomes an agency in 1991 is not very satisfactory either, because of concerns about financial management.

CHAPTER 15

MARCH 1990: HAS THE GOVERNMENT HIT ROCK BOTTOM?

Has the government hit rock bottom? It is a good question, with polls giving Labour a lead of up to twenty-eight points; a heavy defeat in the Mid-Staffordshire by-election; the announcement that Peter Walker, Welsh Secretary, intends to resign; and even tales of a meeting of Tory MPs to get rid of the PM.

The by-election defeat, in which Labour turns a 14,000 Tory majority into a 9,000-vote victory, proves conclusively that the public do not like the community charge with a 15 per cent interest rate. The PM remains resolute and I seem to spend the month defending the tax.

Yet even though all this may be ominous for the government's future, confidence in Neil Kinnock inheriting the earth is very low. The political atmosphere is unreal.

By way of some consolation, Chancellor John Major's cautious Budget is generally well received by both Tory MPs and the press. And Chancellor Kohl gives way on the German–Polish border issue, perhaps demonstrating the power of the PM's arguments.

WEEK 9: 1–4 MARCH

Is this the low point? I ask this at 6.45 p.m. when my secretary hands me a note saying Labour's lead is 18.5 per cent – the biggest yet. West Oxfordshire Council has lost its Conservative majority because most Conservative councillors have resigned over, among other things, the poll tax. The Cabinet resolves to soldier on because they don't have any alternative and, in any case, are convinced of the superiority, if not perfection, of the community charge to rates.

The PM, God bless her, is not to be moved. She also sees off Neil MacFarlane, a former Sports minister with whom I got my wires crossed, when he has a go at me at the outset of a meeting with Tory MPs. It might be marvellous if they removed me now, but the PM won't. At the 11 a.m. lobby, I put on a display of confidence in the community charge which I half feel. But it will only work if the Tory Parliamentary Party discovers a new appetite for office.

I have dinner with Brian Mower, Home Office director of information and a former deputy to me in No. 10, to brief him as I see it – very frankly – about his new job as Douglas Hurd's press secretary at the FCO.

On Friday, I have the strong suspicion that the PM has decided that, having done eleven years, she is going to enjoy herself and to hell with all you lily-livered wets. That's my girl. I check this impression with John Whittingdale, the PM's political private secretary, so that I strike exactly the right note with the media.

After that, I drive out to Whitgift School, near where I live, to tell their Hansard Society about my job. It is the first time I have been to this rather old-fashioned institution. The society gives me a good hearing after sherry in the headmaster's study and a public school lunch – spaghetti and apple pie and custard. Back then to No. 10 to brief the Sunday lobby. It is a lively rush through outstanding problems in the hope that we might put some of them to bed.

On Saturday, Wandsworth Council helpfully comes in with a moderate community charge that gives the government some respite, but everybody is waiting for the PM to pronounce at the Tories' local government conference. She stands firm while saying she will review the operation of the community charge next year. I do some gardening on either side of watching Scotland beat Wales with some difficulty, leaving England *v* Scotland in a fortnight to decide the Rugby Union championship.

In the evening, I have a rush of calls about Welsh Secretary Peter Walker's apparent intention to resign. I speak to the PM on the phone, but I am going to have to temporise until she gets her thoughts together.

I have inevitably a very disturbed Sunday morning, so that I do not finish reading the papers until just before lunch. Yet what is amazing about the government being in the slough of despond is that no certainty comes out of it that Labour (or more precisely Kinnock) will win the next election. This is in spite of an expected 9 per cent inflation, opinion polls and fears that Britain might have to raise interest charges if Germany raises its rates.

Peter Walker, or someone on his behalf, has done his best to help the opposition by leaking his intention to resign. In a flurry of internal calls, I cobble together a statement before the impending resignation is announced at 11 a.m.

WEEK 10: 5–11 MARCH

I have two meetings with the PM on Monday: the first at 10.45 a.m. to clear my lines for the 11 a.m. lobby – resolution is the order of the day – and the second at 5.45 p.m. In the evening, I can tell her that I have not had much trouble with the media on the community charge. The problem lies not so much with inflation and high interest rates but with the Tory Party. She has not been well served by her colleagues. I report that I have sought to get over the fairness of the community charge in that the top 10 per cent of wage earners are paying fifteen times more to local government than the poorest – a pretty progressive tax by any standards.

You would not have thought the government is in a crisis. The lobby briefings are mediocre and Arthur Scargill's alleged shenanigans with money dominate the press. The best thing to happen to me is lunch with Jonathan Holborow of the *Mail*, a competent man with a mind of his own. He suggests that the Walker resignation leak might have been via an agricultural correspondent. (Walker is a former minister of agriculture.)

On Tuesday, I take the line in briefing the regional lobby that there is a great deal to be said for persevering with the community charge. It has everything a political animal could wish for, and sooner or later it will be accepted. I must surely be getting through the government's resolution by now, but what we need is the opportunity to present the basics in a broadcast.

It is interesting that Kinnock does not lead on the community charge at PMQs or go anywhere near Scargill in his troubles. The media seem determined to make charges of corruption stick against both Scargill and the NUM General Secretary, Peter Heathfield.

The PM thinks the press is full of good news today, notably with Kohl climbing down over the integrity of Polish borders, which he was linking with the Poles abandoning claims for reparations. I use this to demonstrate the power of the PM's arguments. Far from being on the periphery of Europe, she is at the heart of forward movement.

We are living in an unreal atmosphere in which, for all the government's problems, no one seems to believe that it is on its last legs or Kinnock is to inherit the earth.

The PM's main event on Wednesday is lunch with the Newspaper Society, representing the provincial press, in Drury Lane. I go over to the House to link up with her, only to be directed to the wrong place – Old Palace Yard instead of Speaker's Court – with the result that the bird has flown, so to speak. I immediately commandeer a No. 10 car and make a late entrance, with the whisky already flowing. I have a jolly time sitting between Michael Unger (*Manchester Evening News*) and James Evans (Thomson). The PM is in good form, makes all the right noises and gets on well with the company. She is far from beleaguered. Subjects covered are the EC, the Broadcasting Bill, journalists' standards and the government's sparse use (4 per cent) of the provincial press for advertising.

Among all this, I do two lobby briefings in the morning and one in the afternoon and take a GIS executive to organise the Bath weekend conference.

Thursday is pretty successful in every way, after a frightful rush to produce the press digest for the 9 a.m. meeting as there is so much to divert attention: Kohl gives in to the PM's wishes; Scargill is in desperate trouble amid news of a great deal of inward investment, notably in Scotland and on Merseyside; Militant is causing mayhem over the community charge; and Kinnock fluffs it yet again at PMQs. On my way back to No. 10, I see Dr Brian Mawhinney, Northern Ireland minister, who is highly delighted with the PM's performance at PMQs.

I manage to get most of our positive messages out through the lobby, but I have yet to hammer home that the 'rich' pay fifteen times more to local government than the 'poor'. I am supposed to stand in for my deputy at Lord President Howe's lobby briefing because he is off to Scotland for two days with the PM, but manage to make my escape and leave it to Sarah Charman. Later, we have a little party for the staff. David Illingworth (PR officer) and Mike Lomax (Pilkington) give me dinner.

Friday brings *The Economist/Independent* conspiracy. It surfaces in an article by – guess who? – Tony Bevins, *The Independent*'s resident conspiracy theorist, modelled on an article by his former protégé, Andrew Marr, about an MPs' meeting to get rid of the PM. I find it interesting how a Bevins byline on anything conspiratorial devalues it. He is clearly obsessed with ousting the PM.

The questioning on this was more persistent at the 11 a.m. lobby than at the Sunday lobby, but by then I had rubbished the idea. With Terry away, I have to do everything either side of a lunch with Paul Potts of the *Daily Express*.

There is little cause for concern in Saturday's papers before I go to Sandown Park races. I learn of three newspaper surveys of Tory MPs following up *The Economist/Indy*, showing that only 25 per cent support the idea that the PM should go. To which the PM says, 'Poppycock.' Michael Jones fills me in on the detail, which I relay to Terry in Scotland with the PM. When Peter Bean rings me in the evening about the alleged move against the PM, I tell him to inform the media that this is a media game and we are not playing.

The Sunday press is much as expected, claiming that 25 per cent of Tory MPs want the PM to resign before the next election. I tell her what I propose to say: all this was started by *The Economist/Independent* and predictably followed up. But it is media-driven and we do not intend to join in. Instead, the PM intends to go on governing as she has for eleven pretty successful years. She approves and is helped by Cecil Parkinson, who makes a TV appearance telling Tory backbenchers to stop bickering.

I shift paper and watch Liverpool draw with QPR in an FA Cup quarter-final. I end the day very tired. I am doing too much and must slow down.

WEEK 11: 12–18 MARCH

Is this the calm after the political storm of the weekend? The USSR dominates the scene, with Lithuania going for independence – the first Soviet republic to secure it – and the Congress of Deputies delaying Gorbachev's appointment as chief executive by a token day.

I have lunch with Angela Rumbold, Tory MP for Merton, who hails from Pudsey, at the Trade House, a renovated warehouse in Southwark. It is remarkable what can be done with old buildings.

In the evening I go over to the House for Michael Jones's inauguration of Mr Speaker as president of the press gallery. It is a jolly affair with lots of old faces and Chris Moncrieff's typical oration.

Tuesday is a marvellous day – some winter! – even though I manage to smash my specs when they fall out of my pocket on to a tiled floor. I also have a worried night because I agree on the spur of the moment to go on the record about the way *The Independent* has produced a damaging, in financial terms, story about a Tory plot against the PM. I find it fascinating that *The Independent* wishes to quote me at all times (even second-hand) yet fails to identify any source for the alleged plot.

My remarks are taken up in a big way by the *Express*, and Chris

Moncrieff runs them on the PA. I take considerable satisfaction in getting this out into the open. The *Express* also leads with a claim that the Tories are targeting Kinnock because he is seen as a liability. He certainly misses his chance to put the PM on the rack after a weekend of political intrigue and polls.

On Wednesday, having worked myself up to having an operation on my right hand, a local specialist, Dr Hashemi, tells me that my growths are benign. One is Dupuytren's contracture and the other a long-standing tumour in my left thumb. He shows no inclination to operate and leaves it to me to decide if and when they cause discomfort or impediment. This is a load off my mind.

While I am waiting outside the PM's study just before 9 a.m. on Thursday, Andrew Turnbull comes up with a message from the Home Office apologising for not telling us sooner that Farzad Bazoft, a 31-year-old Iranian-born journalist working in Britain for *The Observer*, has been executed in Iraq for spying just over two hours earlier. He was investigating reports of a big and unexplained explosion south of Baghdad before joining a press facility visit at the invitation of the Iraqi government.

I am soon preoccupied with the fallout. Leaving aside the effect on Anglo-Iraqi relations after the PM joined international pleas for clemency, it turns out that Bazoft had been convicted of demanding money by menaces in the 1980s and served twelve months in prison. It is inevitable that this will come out sooner or later. At 4.45 p.m., we get a call from Brian Mower to say that the *Express* is on to it. Peter Bean, duty press officer, confirms the facts, as supplied in a note from the Home Office, at 10.30 p.m. Earlier, the Foreign Secretary reported to the House that Bazoft had offered himself to British intelligence but had been turned down.

I am extremely busy trying to get control over the reading and admin and eventually succeed. Sheenagh Wallace, a former No. 10 press officer, rings to say she has had an awful day because her cataract operation has been cancelled. After my experience on Tuesday, I think I know how she feels.

To my astonishment, on Friday, *The Sun* claims an exclusive about Bazoft's criminal past, even though the news is plastered all over the front pages of the *Express* and *Daily Mail*. I am not, however, clear to what extent they have followed up *The Sun*'s story. This is going to cause a bit of a stink, because the media are sensitive to anything averse being said about one of their kind. The Sunday lobby is, however, not very moved by it, except Nigel Nelson of *The People*.

This is the Sunday lobby just before the Budget. These are always the most difficult, but – again surprisingly – I am not unduly troubled.

The PM gives an interview at my suggestion to Tony Smith (*Sunday Express*), who wants to be helpful. She gave him value for money and I rather enjoy the occasion. I have lunch with the Dutch Ambassador to introduce me to his new information officer from Washington.

On Saturday, I buy a new car, and England, on a warm, sunny day, fail to win the Grand Slam. The early spring has my horse chestnut in bud. I wish I knew how the press came to know of Bazoft's conviction. It is known that Anthony Beaumont-Dark, Tory MP for Birmingham Selly Oak, knew about it. Was he told by a journalist? The PA also reveals it knew about the conviction on Thursday but could not confirm it with No. 10 until 10.44 p.m. It is all very strange.

Sunday's press writes off the Tories in the Mid-Staffs by-election and are assiduously promoting Michael Heseltine. There is also lots of Budget speculation. The *Sunday Correspondent* says the *Express* got a call about Bazoft's criminal record from a government department. I ring Paul Potts to see if I can elicit anything. He says he was given a hard time by the *Mail on Sunday* yesterday and has his own suspicions about who talked to the *MoS* and the *Sunday Correspondent* before the *MoS* approached him. Sooner or later I shall be blamed for it all.

Nancy and I go to the BAFTA Awards at the Grosvenor House in the evening. John Thaw gets the Best Actor award and Pauline Collins Best Actress. It is a good night.

WEEK 12: 19–25 MARCH

An eventful Monday. Three issues lead the press: Budget speculation, Lithuania, and the remarkable triumph of conservatives in East Germany. Kohl clearly has done well in his campaign, with 48 per cent of the vote. This will almost certainly speed up reunification. As so many newspapers say, the East Germans have abandoned socialism and any halfway house for capitalism.

Sarah Charman accompanies the PM to the Ideal Home Exhibition while I, after lobbies, draft a speech for the PM's visit to the Association of Combined Youth Clubs on Wednesday. I have lunch with Ray Tindle, owner of the Tindle Group of local newspapers. He says his company is doing well and again offers me a managerial post when I retire. I delegate the FPA and 4 p.m. lobby to finish the speech.

Nancy joins me in the evening at the PM's reception, at which I score a triumph: on my suggestion, she has invited both Sir Leonard Hutton and a very modest and retiring Cyril Washbrook, who together opened the batting for England. I have a good chat with both of them and also with the cast of *Coronation Street* (of which Sir Leonard says he is a fan); Keith Waterhouse; Thora Hird; and Simon Jenkins, who has just become editor of *The Times*. We have dinner with Harold Bolter (BNFL) and his wife, Sheila.

Tuesday is Budget Day. I read the text for the first time after the 11 a.m. lobby. The contents have held beautifully against leaks, though one or two concepts have been written about without much conviction. I find the Budget well judged. The tight summary of the main measures at the beginning and the peroration are extremely well done and the measures are easier to understand than in some Budgets I could mention.

The only question, which has been worrying Paul Gray for a week or so, is whether it will prove tough enough for the markets. As it turns out, they think it errs on the soft side of tough. But it is warmly welcomed by backbenchers, and Kinnock clearly has difficulty attacking it. He is thrown back on his old laments – interest rates and the community charge. So far, so good. We shall see how the press handle it. In the evening, the press office goes to the Chancellor's party in No 11. I congratulate him on his work.

The Budget gets a better reception from the press than I expected. Virtually all, apart from *The Independent* and *Mirror*, have a good word to say for it, even if they are not entirely complimentary. The main reservation about it remains: is it tough enough? The City does not think so by its actions in the exchange market.

I deal with this laconically at the 11 a.m. lobby and with somewhat more spirit at 4 p.m. My main point is that the scribblers do not seem to understand that interest rates are high at 15 per cent; that we are one of the few countries with a budget surplus; that the Budget is taking £1 billion out of the economy over a full year; and that the community charge is removing more purchasing power.

We are late going to the Association of Combined Youth Clubs lunch because Scottish Secretary Malcolm Rifkind wants to get his hands on more money from a backdating measure introduced in relation to the community charge in the Budget. I do my best to tighten the purse strings with the PM on the way to and from lunch, and at the end of the day Paul Gray and I think we have won by dint of some very tough briefing by me at the 4 p.m. lobby.

On Thursday, at about 8.50 a.m., just as I am completing the press digest, Paul Gray calls on me to say Rifkind is incandescent about my 4 p.m. briefing yesterday and wants to see the PM. I am a little concerned because, while counselling toughness on spending, Paul Gray and I actually tried to help Rifkind. He obviously does not accept that.

I give the PM a great deal of briefing on our role, including the press office's note of my 4 p.m. lobby. I make it clear I think I am being used by Rifkind as an excuse to push for more money.

While the PM stands up for me, I find the Scottish press astonishingly anodyne, apart from *The Scotsman*, which has chosen, with *The Independent* and *Guardian*, to boycott my lobbies. I also learn later from John Whittingdale that Tory Central Office in

Edinburgh got a call from the *Glasgow Herald* saying that they had heard that Rifkind had been to see the PM on the issue and there was a prospect of a Scottish Office briefing at 6 p.m. All this points to a great deal of Scottish Office briefing yesterday and even tentative preparation for a statement heralding Rifkind's success. It carries on today, but we keep mum.

I tell Fred Corbett, director of Scottish Information Office, after their announcement of their climb-down, that I shall not forget this event and will not lift a finger to help Rifkind in the future. I have dinner with Geoffrey Goodman from the *Mirror* and Peter Thornton, editor of IRN (Independent Radio News).

I suppose they will call 23 March Black Friday. Like the PM, I awake at 6 a.m. to find Labour has turned a Tory majority of 14,000 in Mid-Staffs into a 9,000-vote victory. This comes as something of a relief to the PM, who had heard that the Tory candidate had pledges of only 13,000 votes, whereas in fact 18,000 voted Tory.

The message is clear: voters don't like high mortgage rates and high taxes, as evidenced by the reaction to the community charge – a point I make at a snide, off-hand, sneering Sunday lobby. In preparation, I go up to see the PM at 8.55 a.m., just before the Foreign Secretary reports on his visit to South Africa. We sort out a line for me to take.

At 10 a.m., the PM has an interview with *Der Spiegel* which for me is distinguished by her refusal to have any truck with ganging up on Germany in the EC. The day has been very hard going, and I fall asleep after another GIS lunchtime drinks party for information officers. But there is a lot of goodwill towards me in No. 10.

The news coming in on Saturday gets worse and worse politically, with reports of opinion polls giving Labour leads in the higher twenties. I am also in trouble with our Ambassador in Bonn, Sir Christopher Mallaby, over the interview with *Der Spiegel*, especially a passage saying the PM had heard Kohl saying in Strasbourg he would not confirm the Oder–Neisse line as the German–Polish border. Oh dear. Kohl, however, has been very provocative in Brussels in trying to steamroller us all into a federal Europe.

Like the political climate, the temperature falls, with our horse chestnut coming into bud. There is a heavy hail shower before lunch. The Sunday press present a right mess, opinion polls giving Labour leads of anything from nineteen to twenty-eight points. *The Observer's*, at twenty-eight, is a record. Paul Gray also tells me that after her meeting last night with the Tory trio Messrs Baker, Bell and Reece,* the PM is calling for a thorough review of the community charge to help her natural supporters, and rigorous capping of local authority spending. She seems to have written off the accountability value of a more or less universal community charge.

In view of the weather, I get stuck into the backlog of reading matter, shifting enough to fill 1.5 briefcases, and draft a paper on presentation for the PM. It is a silly way to spend a weekend.

WEEK 13: 26–31 MARCH

The calm after the Sunday newspaper storm. They filled the news vacuum with polls, as the *Today* newspaper puts it more elegantly. Certainly, there is precious little left in the political situation after Lord President Howe calls on Michael Heseltine to stand up for the PM. Perhaps a change of fortune will come with the spring, which is bursting out all over very early.

We have an amicable week-ahead meeting until Kenneth Baker tries to persuade the PM to go on a walkabout with Chancellor Kohl at their summit on Friday. I stop the whole idea, saying it is too gimmicky. I lunch with Colin Webb, editor of the PA, on his birthday.

My Tuesday press digest is not a pretty sight and we gossip over it for nearly an hour. The opportunity for Kinnock at PMQs to damage the PM seems too good to be true. We believe the PM

---

* Kenneth Baker, Tory Party chairman; Tim Bell, PR consultant; and Gordon Reece, political strategist who advised on Margaret Thatcher's image.

will have a difficult time, yet she bowls along in a big way and wins hands down. Who would have thought it at 9 a.m.?

Her trouble is that it is her own side that is continually putting the boot in. Only last night ex-Chancellor Lawson bemoaned the failure to signal early entry into the ERM. We could have done without that plus a defeat in the Commons on community charge regulations and two defeats in the Lords on student loans.

My working day is taken up with meetings on community charge capping and future presentation. The Chancellor drops in to discuss my paper on post-by-election presentation and generally approves of it. He wants to enter the ERM sooner rather than later. I am not sure my paper will deliver that.

On Wednesday, Kenneth Baker takes me to lunch at the rather swish Lindsay House in Romilly Street. He is in good form and we seem to be thinking on similar lines about future presentation. The big question is how to break out of the cycle of trouble that has afflicted the government for about twelve months. We agree that we shall not do so before the local elections.

On my return to No. 10, I learn that the PM has spoken on the phone for fifty-three minutes with Mr Gorbachev. This leaves me with a tricky presentational problem at the 4 p.m. lobby, because the Russian leader was sombre and troubled about Lithuania. I get a reasonably easy run, however.

I brief the FPA on the forthcoming German summit before seeing departmental heads of information on how we might better cater for the regional lobby. Dinner with Nick Lloyd and Paul Potts.

On Thursday, Nancy and I are off to Bath for the GIS weekend conference. My niece, Sarah, has come to stay overnight with us on Wednesday, but I never see her because she has gone to bed before I get home and I leave early.

Before we set off, I find my briefing on Gorbachev has come out quite well. I finalise my paper for the PM on future presentational strategy which the Chancellor and Paul Gray have been mulling over and made detailed comments on. The paper sets out a strategy for the spring and summer and argues for two things:

1. An economic presentation group comprising the Chancellor, John Wakeham, Andrew Turnbull, Paul Gray, Gus O'Donnell and myself; and
2. A decision on entry into the ERM by midsummer.

The second point is the key. I feel a great deal of hope is being reposed on my ability to shift the PM on this.

We drive to Bath after a brisk PMQs. I must confess I am a little concerned about going to Bath instead of Bonn.

I need not have worried. The press is full of reasonable reports on the summit. Kohl once again reveals his petulant side by suggesting the Poles should apologise for their treatment of Germans. Once again the poison came out before the event.

After walking into the centre of Bath with Nancy, who is going sightseeing and shopping, I have two sessions with GIS members from the regions, morning and afternoon. On the whole, I find members less difficult than a year ago and more passive. This may be because they are more satisfied with their situation or because they know I am on my way out – as indeed I am, to retirement.

It is all conference on Saturday. We have a good constructive meeting from 9.30 a.m. to 1 p.m. in gorgeous weather. It is not a yes-man's session but there is a positive approach to the future of the GIS.

In the afternoon, we have a conducted tour of the Roman Baths, sampling its 10,000-year-old waters with their forty-two minerals. In the evening, Robin Butler addresses the conference dinner and declares his support for what we are trying to do.

CHAPTER 16

APRIL 1990: RAW
VIOLENCE

Will she last? That is the question of the month. Polls suggest the PM is the least popular for fifty years. American correspondents are fixated on her 'longevity'. The Chief Whip thinks the doldrums will last until the summer recess, and Tristan Garel-Jones tells the PM bluntly there will be another challenge to her leadership if things do not improve by November. We are in a right old mess.

To make matters worse, the month opens with raw violence – a poll tax riot in Trafalgar Square and a prolonged riot at Strangeways Prison in Manchester. All this with poll tax Bills, inflation figures and local council elections to come.

The PM is helped in her resolve by Neil Kinnock's Black Power salute at a Wembley pop concert attended by Nelson Mandela, which earns him a hammering in the press; the French swapping three Mirage fighters with Libya for the release of three hostages; an often comical visit to Bermuda for a relaxed summit with President Bush; a visit to the Dardanelles to mark the seventy-fifth ANZAC anniversary; and a remarkably quiet EC summit in Dublin.

We awake on Sunday morning to the full horror of the community charge riot in Trafalgar Square and Whitehall. In the early hours before going to bed, I ask Sarah Charman by phone to look after the PM at church in view of the likely turnout of the media. She does brilliantly and is rewarded with lunch at Chequers.

In spite of all this, we have an entertaining final session of the GIS conference with David McDonald and John Shaw, both administrators working in the GIS. Their message is clear: better organisation, better written work and better internal PR. We shall have to follow up these ideas. I am a little disappointed that the discussion was taken over by under-grading. This is not something that I can resolve in the time left to me.

After a quick lunch, Nancy and I drive my secretary to her home in Ruislip on a lovely spring day. We are home for 5 p.m. John rings to say he is covering the jail riot.

WEEK 14: 2–8 APRIL

On Monday, the press is full of violence – the Trafalgar Square and Strangeways Prison riots. On the latter, John gets a front-page byline in the *Express*. The Home Secretary makes statements to the House on both, and the main issue of the day is whether Kinnock has condemned the thirty-one Labour MPs who advocated disobeying community charge law. In fact, he doesn't, and this helps the PM.

She is in robust mood at the week-ahead meeting, with a whole lot of editorials calling on Kinnock to disown the thirty-one. She does, however, show some signs of being rattled by unusually saying she would like to cultivate more radio and TV editors. Hardly anybody turns up for the 4 p.m. lobby. They are too busy listening to Home Secretary Waddington on the violence.

MIO at 5 p.m. is largely a case of sorting out the main business to the Easter recess. I get away about 7.30 after meetings with George Russell, Sir Tom Arnold and Ian Gillis.

On Tuesday, the Strangeways siege continues and the government announces the capping of community charges. The Department of the Environment tries to put out a statement on the capping, which the COI refuses to circulate because it is 'polemical' – referring to the different political complexions of various local authorities. I support the COI.

At PMQs, the PM wants to reflect in her remarks the violent, intimidating tradition of the Labour Party. I tell that if she does that, she will have a parliamentary riot, too. Left-wing or perhaps union tradition, but not, please, the Labour Party. She takes my point.

Environment Secretary Chris Patten does not get much support for his capping statement from a sullen Tory back bench who are the government's worst enemy. Stanley Sparks, *Birmingham Evening Mail*, remarks on this at the regional lobby. The government is in a poor way and the Chief Whip, whom I see at 10.25 a.m., thinks it will continue until the summer recess. This is going to be a hard year indeed.

I see Robin Haydon, Heath's press secretary, and Sue Cameron, journalist, before having an early night.

On Wednesday, the death toll in the Strangeways riot remains unclear. Community charge capping is reasonably well received by the press. The American correspondents are fixated on the PM's longevity. They are very sceptical about the PM's continued political potency. The going gets harder.

I lunch with Martin Sorrell, CEO of the media organisation WPP, and Giles Shaw, Tory MP for Pudsey. We have a jolly time over two bottles of Gewürztraminer and I get the feel that Sorrell is giving me the once-over for the future. Whether he will want me after I drop my age – fifty-seven – is unclear. I announce new life peers, including Eric Varley on Kinnock's nomination. He deserves it.

In the evening, I attend the hail and farewell party at the Foreign Press Association for Brian Mower and Andrew Burns, who is moving on as the FCO press secretary. I thoroughly enjoy myself with the Americans and I agree with my staff later that it is time for me to take the pledge – again.

On Thursday, the GIS has a jolly good set-to with BBC Radio over nearly four hours at the BBC. On my return to No. 10, John Whittingdale tells me that a very bad Gallup poll tomorrow will show that the PM is the least popular for fifty years.

We have, I fear, made a mess of it – really blown it. Still, we shall just have to soldier on. But will the PM be there by the July recess? That is the question I put to Mark Lennox-Boyd, the PM's PPS, who calls in to see me as we arranged yesterday. He agrees to try to arrange for the PM to see Tristan Garel-Jones MP, a senior whip extraordinaire, to hear the hard word from him.

What is clear is that with community charge Bills, inflation, the Hong Kong Bill and local council elections to come, we are in a fine old mess and I do not believe it has yet touched bottom.

The Cabinet is a brisk affair, followed by an election presentation by Kenneth Baker and then a political discussion. There is then a more restricted meeting on the community charge. It now looks as if we are moving to targets and penalties for local government, much to the concern of the Chancellor, whom I see in his office at the Treasury at 2.15 p.m. He seems pleased when I tell him that I think my minute on presentation has moved the PM on public expenditure, defence and the ERM.

I attend the COI's launch as an executive agency and see lots of old colleagues.

There is no end to bad news. On top of Thursday night's opinion poll, Friday brings early forecasts of inflation rising to more than 8 per cent and poor producer price figures. Next week will bring no relief even if the House will be in recess.

The PM is bearing up well, determined to fight the good fight, judging from her early meeting with Andrew Turnbull, Robin Butler and Kenneth Baker, who comes to see me to coordinate a line.

By lunchtime, there is more trouble – the Irish courts turn down yet another extradition application. Ye Gods! Is there no end to Irish support for terrorism? Curiously, the Sunday lobby does not ask me about this.

I lunch with my former deputy Neville Gaffin, who is bronzed, relaxed and clearly earning good money in PR. He said, startlingly, that I should be able to earn much more than my present salary outside government. We shall see. I ring Sheenagh Wallace, who is washed out but recovering from her cataract operation.

Nancy and I go to Hebden Bridge for the Easter recess in my new car, which I bought last night. She spends Saturday afternoon after a fish-and-chip lunch with her sister Miriam, while I visit my brother and help around the farm. We have dinner with Derek and Mary at the Hebden Lodge Hotel, where the cheesecake is as brilliant as ever and the food wholesome.

The next day, the *Sunday Telegraph* and *Sunday Times* are pretty awful on the PM's chances of lasting. We get away from it all by walking up to Gibson Mill in the Hardcastle Crags valley. We are appalled by the litter and the mess to which hippies have reduced the 'no poll tax' colony in Windsor Terrace on my old newspaper round. This has become the rough end of Hebden Bridge.

After lunch with Ted and Miriam at Far Flat Head Farm, we go to Derek's, where I learn to my astonishment that Crystal Palace have reached the FA Cup final by beating Liverpool. John is beside himself. There will never be another day like it, he says. It is Palace's first FA Cup final and earlier in the season they lost 9–0 at Anfield.

WEEK 15 9–15 APRIL

Bright and sunny early, turning to drizzle at 6 p.m. We spend the morning walking along the canal bank to Stubbing Holme and then up the Colden Valley, via Mytholm, to the Arvon Foundation's Lumb Bank and then on to Heptonstall. I reach the conclusion that 'no poll tax' posters are to be found in the messier parts of town, including Queen's Terrace, where my maternal grandparents used to live. We also visit the old *Hebden Bridge Times* office, which is now an antique centre, and the old reporters' room. Nostalgia. After a fish-and-chip lunch at Miriam's, we visit Ogden reservoir, between Halifax and Keighley, and then Derek and Mary.

On Tuesday, we drive home in five hours. Nothing much doing at No. 10. The FCO has handled the release of French hostages in the Lebanon. It is sickening that the French have again done a dirty deal – very dirty this time because it involves the supply of Mirage jets to Libya.

I go back to work on Wednesday to find the PM chirpier. She has a meeting with Chris Patten to tackle the community charge problem.

There is curiously little to follow up in the press. Gorbachev is adopting a heavier hand with Lithuania, the Strangeways siege seems to be becoming less of a problem and the French get an editorial pummelling for swapping three Mirage jets for three hostages.

I give a hesitant media briefing at noon on tomorrow's trip to Bermuda, which is going to be the focus for so many 'Is Maggie finished?' stories. At lunch with two veteran American correspondents – Don Cook and Bill Tuohy – I blast off about the perfidious nature of the US State Department and many of our European allies. I don't think they are fit to lick the PM's boots in terms of principle and consistency of purpose. I sound very brassed off.

In the evening, I go with the PM and Denis Thatcher to Nick Lloyd's ninth anniversary party as editor of the *Express*.

Off to Bermuda on Thursday. Seldom have I felt so nervous about a summit – George Bush is to join the PM there. The PM feels the same. This is what the pressure does for those summiteers with political difficulties at home. We fly at 8.15 a.m. and have lunch on board with Denis; the US Ambassador, Henry Catto; and the Bermudan Minister for Health, returning home from a conference on drugs in London.

Both the PM and I work as never before on paper during the morning before I brief the travelling press on the trip over champagne. There is no doubt we are going into the lion's den. The media, including the Americans, see the PM on her way out.

During the afternoon, we have a series of meetings with the Premier and his Cabinet before going to the western extremity of the island to view a new dock, prison and an interesting museum in the fort. The official dinner is a noisy affair after a reception at Government House. The PM seems to have greatly pleased the Bermudans by visiting them. At 3 a.m. London time, the press try to give me a hard time at a briefing and this leads to some acrimonious exchanges.

President Bush arrives after we have breakfasted at the Governor's house and attended a church service – rather a good one conducted by two clergymen, one blessed with a splendid voice. While we wait, the Governor confuses us all with details of the ceremonial welcome. It is rather comic. Bush has his shirt-tail out and the gale blows off the hats of the Bermudan Regiment's guard of honour. The PM and President settle down to a good talk between 10.50 and 1 p.m., during which I have a chat with my opposite number in the White House, Marlin Fitzwater. Like me, he is thinking of retiring within a couple of years.

We both join the PM and President's party for lunch, where a very good discussion continues covering China, Hong Kong, Vietnamese boat people, the General Agreement on Tariffs and Trade (GATT), agriculture and the EU. At 3.30, Marlin Fitzwater and I brief the principals for the press conference – a tame affair, overshadowed by President Bush's news of a Soviet ultimatum to Lithuania. I preside and win three handshakes from the President for my performance.

This is followed by a reception on board HMS *Ivy*, a walkabout and dinner in Government House.

During a relaxed part of the afternoon, President Bush invites Denis to play golf tomorrow morning. DT, having seen the weather forecast, tries to excuse himself as not being up to their standard. It does not work. Bush says that he is just the sort of chap they want to play against.

Saturday dawns windy and wet, with DT awaiting the expected call to cancel the golf date. It never comes, so he goes off at 7.35 a.m. into the gale. The PM's party leave at 8.45 a.m. for HMS *Arrow*, of Falklands fame, to be briefed on its anti-drug operations in the Caribbean and for the PM to present a long-service medal.

We then go to Hamilton City Hall to meet the mayor and council and on to St George's, where an evil-looking town crier heralds the PM's arrival with bell ringing. The visit ends with a walkabout. I do a lot of briefing on board the plane home, including about the likelihood of a NATO summit. We fly up to St John's, Newfoundland, to catch the big winds and arrive back in London at 10 p.m. I pop into the office to pick up my car before leaving for home at 11.10 p.m.

On Sunday, the weather has followed us home across the Atlantic – chilly, hail and rain showers. I am able to send a note to the PM at Chequers saying the Sunday press is the best she has had for weeks. The trip to Bermuda has done her no harm – indeed, quite a bit of good. Not even the worst press can be nasty about it. I do a bit of gardening before sorting out the usual accumulation of paper. And then just before bedtime comes news that Nelson Mandela is to see the PM on his next visit to the UK in May; he is currently here for an emotional pop concert at Wembley. This gives the press office a lively night.

WEEK 16: 16–22 APRIL

Not much to trouble us in the press this Easter Monday, with the Soviets playing a waiting game over Lithuania and generally positive reporting of the Bermuda summit. Later in the day, the media go mad over Nelson Mandela at Wembley and Kinnock shaking his fist in the air like a black South African.

We buy garden plants and I put them all in before we have a thunderstorm accompanied by a tremendous hailstorm that leaves the lawns white.

Back to work at lunchtime on Tuesday. There is again precious little to worry about in the aftermath of Mandela's visit, but I think we need to give out a line, and Charles Powell and I draft one. Essentially, we affirm the PM's determination to go to South Africa at a time of her choosing; the objective would be to bring an end to apartheid and to urge Mandela to concentrate on stopping killing between blacks and to start negotiations with the South African government.

The press office goes to the Vitello D'Oro for a post-Easter lunch to catch up. I shift a lot of paper in the afternoon and take calls, one from Robert Maxwell inviting the PM to attend the launch of his new European newspaper. I shall recommend the PM to go nowhere near it.

On Wednesday, the PM and I lunch with the *Sunday Telegraph*. On the way there, she says she does not feel like visiting South Africa. I am not surprised. Mandela seems to be a busted flush, without, so far as one can tell, much influence to go with his patriarchal presence.

In the press, Kinnock gets criticism for what turns out to have been the Black Power salute at Wembley, and the NUT gets a real hammering in editorials for voting for a national strike in response to local redundancies. Against this background, we begin to contemplate tomorrow's PMQs with some relish, tempered by the knowledge that the Tory Parliamentary Party is not very good at politics.

Lunch with Peregrine Worsthorne, Bruce Anderson and Frank Johnson is entertaining, with much anti-German, anti-African and anti-big-spending talk. The lobbies hold no terrors because the media have not really found their Westminster legs after the holiday.

On Thursday, the government – as early indications suggest – wins the Hong Kong Bill vote by ninety-seven. I go over to the House for the division at 10.15 p.m. after a lively dinner with Lyndy Payne and her advertising friends. The PM is clearly pleased with the vote when she returns to No. 10, and congratulates the Chief Whip on his success.

Before the PM returns to No. 10, she has a private word with the Chancellor, which I suspect is about my ideas for future presentation. She tells me she has decided to ask Energy Secretary John Wakeham to be responsible for the coordination of presentation. I try to hide my delight – while making clear that I do not like the idea of avowing his role because it will cause difficulty in the House. She reasonably says she will have to tell Cabinet colleagues.

In the morning, Cabinet is given the hard word by the Chancellor about public spending, which is already oversubscribed. To my astonishment, this does not leak – at least not until Michael Jones gets to work on ministers.

My dinner with Lyndy Payne and friends largely consists of a wonderful exercise on what the PM should do if she wins a fourth term – the emphasis being on 'if'.

I call my son on his return from covering the NASUWT/NUT conference to find he has a tummy bug which has laid low 200 or so of the delegates. On the whole, the government has had a good week. Certainly, the opposition has had a bad one, what with Kinnock's Black Power salute, Gordon Brown going over the top on the Sheffield Forgemasters' Iraqi gun,* and Roy Hattersley seemingly an empty vessel in last night's Hong Kong debate.

I give a talk to forty GIS recruits – they get younger! – before lunch with the PM, when I manage to cause her to laugh. I give the Sunday lobby a substantial briefing on Europe in the context of today's visit by the Irish PM, Charles Haughey, before next weekend's summit in Dublin. The meeting turns out to be low-key and has to be dragged out to last ninety minutes. I find the *Sunday Times* is doing a leader on who is the real European: Margaret Thatcher.

By nightfall on Saturday, I am feeling luxuriously worn out because my next-door neighbour, Ken Bromley, orders 'two yards' of gravel to renew the drive to our garages. It arrives late and we work intensively from 11 a.m. to finish the job before lunch. After lunch and a nap, I mow the lawns and by teatime I am tired and stiff, which shows how unfit I am.

On Sunday, I go into No. 10 to see the PM on her return from

---

* On 11 April, customs officers in Middlesbrough had seized steel pipes intended to form the barrel of a massive gun on a ship bound for Iraq. With a barrel length of 130 ft, the assembled weapon would have had a range of 600 miles, making it by far the largest gun in the world. The export would have breached restrictions on the sale of arms to Iraq, and in the weeks following the discovery Labour demanded to know when the government had been made aware of the order. Gordon Brown, then Labour's shadow Trade and Industry Secretary, accused Nicholas Ridley's Department of Trade and Industry of 'slackness and complacency of almost criminal dimensions'.

Chequers at 6.45 p.m. Mark Lennox-Boyd has arranged for us to meet Tristan Garel-Jones MP, to tell her the horrible truth about the Tory Parliamentary Party, which is so well stocked with 'grandees', the disappointed who have not been preferred and the sacked. Garel-Jones says with admirable clarity that if things are not looking up by November there will be another leadership contest. In that event, the PM believes Sir Ian Gilmour will be her opponent. Garel-Jones says things have improved over the past two weeks but opinion is so volatile that it could be as bad as ever tomorrow.

The Sunday press is not all that bad but while Kinnock gets more hammering for his Black Power salute, the *Sunday Times* claims that Sir Geoffrey Howe did the same in Africa.

WEEK 17: 23–29 APRIL

I leave the office in a state of high dudgeon. Robin Oakley (*The Times*) rings to say that Tory MP Sir Hal Miller is alleging that I have been saying disagreeable things about him – notably that he had been duped over the Iraqi gun affair, had been present when Iraqis were involved and was taking money. I retorted that these were 'monstrous' allegations with no truth in them whatsoever. I ring Murdo Maclean, the Chief Whip's principal private secretary, to suggest that he tells Miller that if he has a complaint against me to write to the PM. I tell Andrew Turnbull what I have done. He would have played it more softly, but I am not going to allow MPs to get away with this sort of stuff and nonsense. To cope with all this, I had earlier left the PM's interview with the *Scottish Daily Express* after showing Nick Lloyd into the meeting.

Earlier, I lunched with Dugal Nisbet-Smith of the Newspaper Society and then tried to kill my Thursday press briefings for European correspondents since so few attend. This will put the cat among the pigeons. I also advised Gus O'Donnell, the Chancellor's press secretary, not to leak bad trade figures to try to condition the market. There is little to be gained and a lot of pain to be had from doing so.

Overnight, the Chief Whip acts swiftly and at 10 a.m. brings me and Hal Miller MP together in his office. Miller denies saying that I had alleged he was duped over the gun, was present when Iraqis were involved and was taking money. But he says he is fed up with being blagged off by junior civil servants and press officers and with disinformation from me. I make it clear I do not intend to put up with unfounded allegations against me.

He acknowledges he should have been more careful and accepts my assurance that I never said the things alleged. We agree to say publicly – as we do – that we both accept we are the victims of mischief. It all seems to go reasonably well, though Miller reveals he has borne a grudge against me for nine years or so because of what I am alleged to have said about him when he resigned as a PPS. I have no recollection of this at all.

After Tuesday's PMQs, we set off for Istanbul and Gallipoli to mark the seventy-fifth ANZAC anniversary. I have always wanted to go to Gallipoli to see the sites of great battles and, as on the Somme, to honour the dead.

At our huge and impressive consulate in Istanbul's red-light district, the PM plunges into the crowds on a walkabout. We hear that the Strangeways siege is to end tomorrow and of some horrific trade figures. I eventually put the media to bed with a briefing at 12.45 a.m.

On Wednesday, we breakfast at 5.30 a.m. in the consulate before a seemingly interminable helicopter flight down to the Dardanelles to the Turkish war memorial. I find the UK band quite the smartest at the ceremonial. Then on to the British ceremony at Cape Helles, looking out across the Aegean. Here, we meet six veterans, five from the UK and the sixth from Newfoundland. The youngest is ninety.

We lunch under canvas and congratulate the Archdeacon of the Aegean and Danube – what a job! – on his splendid service. I have a moving time with Australian PM Bob Hawke, identifying the young Australians who died this day seventy-five years ago. While Hawke is talking to the PM, I have a good chat with General Sir

Robert Ford, head of the Commonwealth War Graves Commission. And then I nearly come to grief. All the helicopters, including the PM's, leave for Istanbul as I am arriving at the assembly point. After haranguing Turkish officers, I suddenly hear a helicopter start up in the distance. I run towards it and find it is indeed waiting for me. Whisky is served informally on board by the pilot. I eventually catch up with the PM's party at Istanbul Airport, but it is a close-run thing.

Thursday brings very good media coverage of the Gallipoli ceremonies, which is some compensation for missed sleep these past two days. *The Guardian*, however, is disgraceful. It apparently tried to set up one of the veterans to ask the PM about the community charge, but, surprise, surprise, he didn't.

After Cabinet, I have a good talk with the Chancellor, who feels he is sitting on the edge of a volcano. I then digest the briefs for the EU summit in Dublin before going over to the House for dinner with John Wakeham. Our purpose is to find a way to involve him in what is hoped will be the government's recovery.

We decide to propose to the PM that he should be responsible for the coordination of presentation and the development of policy, including the canvassing of opinion of where the government should be in five years' time and how it should develop its appeal. The PM would announce she will take charge of the manifesto and then a month later, having divorced him from the preparation of the manifesto, authorise him to form groups to tackle individual aspects of policy.

On Friday, we are hit amidships by two leaks:

1. A conversation between Mark Lennox-Boyd and Tory MPs about the possibility of new legislation on the community charge; I don't regard this as sensational and get out a briefing line.
2. A claim in *The Economist* that the PM has told ministers that the community charge is unfair. Not true. She said people perceived it to be unfair and that perception has to be changed.

I write a minute for the PM on John Wakeham's proposed role and bring myself up to date with Anne Nash on GIS developments before entertaining a lively bunch of GIS information officers at lunchtime.

On Saturday, we are off to Dublin at 7 a.m. It is my first outing with Brian Mower, the Foreign Secretary's new press secretary. He speaks with authority and I think we shall prove to be a good team.

I think – though you never know – that I have got the PM in a positive position on EU political union, and at the end of the day, after five media briefings, she gives a very relaxed and good-humoured press conference. She brings out the insubstantial nature of what lies behind EU political union – i.e. establishing what it is by process of elimination. I manage to reinforce this point with a briefing on the PM's intervention in the summit on political union.

I am, however, very nervous about using the Queen to illustrate what political union is not about, yet it is an issue that needs to be faced and cleared out of the way. We ditch the usual post-press conference radio and TV interviews: They would have concentrated on the poll tax and Hong Kong. Home for 10 p.m.

On Sunday, I find coverage of Dublin better presentationally than I ever expected. It has not been portrayed as a defeat for the PM on political union.

The month ends with the hottest April day for years. Trees are fast coming into leaf, apart from the oak. Our ash tree is just making it. Is this heralding a summer soaking?

The PM continues to do well out of Dublin. There are some splendidly supportive leaders and articles, notably by Conor Cruise O'Brien in *The Times*.

My main task on Monday (30 April) is to resolve with Kenneth Baker fears in the GIS about the appointment of PR 'minders' for three ministers – David Waddington, Kenneth Clarke and John MacGregor. I tell him that the GIS is up in arms over this – the lack of consultation and the implication of GIS incompetence.

Baker is embarrassed by the publicity and claims that the three advertising men offered their services. They would be personal/party appointments and have no effect on the GIS. This, of course, raises the question as to how the government can ensure that all spokesmen speak with one voice. However, when I retail my conversation to departmental heads of information at MIO, they appreciate my raising the issue. We shall have to see how it works out.

After lunch with the Korean Ambassador, I see the PM late afternoon to tell her we must get a grip on things, and to this end I suggest we meet for ten minutes every morning.

CHAPTER 17

MAY 1990: A DAMP SQUIB FROM MICHAEL HESELTINE

The Chief Whip concedes that the atmosphere on the Tory back benches has improved during the month, but they are far from euphoric. I am excited by a better press for four weeks running.

This is partly due to a far better Tory performance in the local elections than expected; polls showing a substantial movement back to the government of the middle class and homeowners, though by the end of the month Labour is still thirteen points ahead; and something of a damp-squib campaigning intervention by Michael Heseltine, whose acolytes concede he wants to be Prime Minister. It becomes clear that the next election is wide open.

Our feet are kept on the ground by Mr Gorbachev's deepening troubles – we begin to wonder whether we shall go to the Soviet Union as arranged next month – and the appointment of Boris Yeltsin as President of the Russian Federation; and an IRA atrocity that kills two Australian lawyers in Holland by mistake.

WEEK 18: 1–6 MAY

A perfect May Day, apart from having Robert Maxwell's Mirror Group breathing down my neck. The *Sunday Mail* (Scotland) wrote a leader on the basis of banter at last Friday's Sunday lobby in which, in response to a question as to how I was going to stop the Scots grumbling, I am alleged to have said, 'Emasculate them.' Neither Terry Perks nor Peter Bean can recall precisely how it arose, but Jack Warden, an *Express* man and a Scot, confirms it was banter not to be taken seriously. I fear there will be questions in the House at PMQs this afternoon, especially as a Scottish MP has tabled an Early Day Motion.

How wrong can I get? The subject never arises at PMQs. Instead, the Tories fight back for once, with a rousing chorus attacking Labour over local government extravagance and incompetence. The PM goes on to give an absolute tour de force of a statement on the Dublin summit which was well received on all sides.

In the course of the day, I go over to the Department of Employment, as head of the GIS, to try to sort out Michael Howard's wanting his own PR chappie.

On Wednesday, it is exactly a year since Nancy's sister Kathleen died. I drive to work through May blossom – or so it seems.

For the second day running, I go to a government department – this time the Department of Energy – to tie up with John Wakeham his eventual appointment as coordinator of government presentation. I am able to tell him that Sir Geoffrey Howe has apparently been sorted out, but that the Chief Whip may be difficult over his appointment.

My briefing of the American correspondents ends on a telling note. They say no one has yet won an election with a tax-raising manifesto. If so, I say, the PM will be OK.

I have lunch with a wealthy Indian from Kerala who runs newspapers here for Indians. In the afternoon, I am landed with coordinating an answer to a PQ about PR consultants for each of three ministers and end up talking with Kenneth Clarke, Health Secretary, who, like John MacGregor at Education, does not want one. I find myself in the ridiculous position of trying to soften their approach.

Thursday is the day of reckoning: the local elections. I cling to my view that the outcome is too close to call because of community charge cross-currents. The prevailing consensus is that the PM is about to meet her Waterloo. This seems somewhat unlikely in those local authorities declaring low poll taxes. Waterloo seems even less likely when George Jones from the *Telegraph* rings me to say Gallup is reporting a 9.5-point movement back to the government over recent weeks. On top of this, I am told that next week the index of retail prices is likely to be lower than expected – i.e. below 10 per cent. This is because of the squeeze now being applied by high interest rates.

I go out to the Node reunion dinner in pretty good mood, though Rodney Brooke, secretary of the Association of Metropolitan Authorities, tries my patience with his entirely roseate view of local government. Earlier, my view was so rosy about it that I took a car to Purley to vote at 11.15 a.m.

The PM has another good PMQs before I have it out with Ian Hernon (*Sunday Mail*), who seems not to accept responsibility for feeding out the banter about my wanting to 'emasculate' the Scots.

On Friday, we go to Waddesdon Manor in Buckinghamshire, the French-style chateau, for an Anglo-French summit. Jacob Rothschild is the welcoming host. Before we fly by helicopter from Wellington Barracks, we learn that while the Tories lose Bradford, they are back in Wandsworth on a landslide and have captured Hillingdon. The PM issues a quick statement and I make sure she leaves No. 10 by the front door to smile at the media.

Tom King's helicopter lands next to the red carpet and covers it with dust and gravel. There is much vacuuming. There is not a lot in the summit apart from defence cooperation. The lunch is superb, with beautiful coffee cups.

I am back in time to bawl out the Sunday lobby on two counts: for suggesting I am incandescent with rage at Mark Lennox-Boyd after the leak of his conversation with Tory MPs; and for retailing Ian Hernon's banter. However, the atmosphere at the lobby is remarkable. Gone is the tendency to jeer at the PM. Even to Julia Langdon she is a new potent force.

It is clear from Saturday's press that the next election is wide open and that the likelihood of another challenge to the PM's leadership is receding. Charles Powell rings to say that the full text of President Bush's defence speech contains a warm tribute to the PM's championship of freedom over a decade. I get the press office to feed this to the *Sunday Times*, who are always in the vanguard of those wanting to write up the PM's comeback. By the end of the day we are in good stead. I watch racing and Rugby Union on the TV and then the Eurovision Song Contest.

The lovely sunny weather continues on Sunday when we go for a walk in Banstead Woods, where the rhododendrons have yet to reach perfection but the endless carpet of bluebells is a wonderful sight in the dappled sunshine.

The *Mail on Sunday* portrays me as the Rottweiler who has saved three Cabinet ministers from a fate worse than death – personal PR minders. It has got hold of my signal to the GIS fleet, publishing it virtually in full.

For the rest, this is the third week running that the PM has had a better press. Interestingly, *The Observer* puts next Friday's inflation rate at 9.5 per cent. I am not sure that this serves our purpose at this stage.

WEEK 19: 7–13 MAY

Little to concern us in Monday's press apart from football hooliganism on Saturday involving Leeds United (again) and Bournemouth; the failure of the Football League to act on warnings of potential trouble on a bank holiday weekend; and the near certainty that English clubs will not be allowed back into Europe next season. It is difficult to see how English clubs deserve a return and how Leeds deserves to be promoted.

We go for a bank holiday walk on Farthing Down, with its yellow carpet of buttercups – an hour and a half's ramble on an ice cream in brilliant weather.

I find it hard to get going in Tuesday's warm weather – so much so that Terry asks me if I am OK because I am so subdued. The truth is that I have acquired a taste for home, garden and walks.

There is little in the press digest to bother the PM. I suggest to her that, given the local elections have changed the political atmosphere, her own side should demonstrate renewed confidence at the first PMQs since the poll. They don't make a particularly good job of it, but they do greet Kinnock with shouts when he rises to bash away at the government over the economy. The Chief Whip acknowledges that there is a better atmosphere on his back benches, but they are far from euphoric.

Anne, my secretary, greets me with a doggy bag with bones, all tied up with blue ribbon and dedicated to 'The No. 10 Rottweiler'. Robert Maxwell rings seeking a message from the PM about the launch of his new European newspaper. I don't think I should try to deny him one, even though I do not think the PM should attend the actual launch.

It is all football hooliganism in Wednesday's papers. The football authorities come out of it rather badly and Home Secretary David Waddington, splendid man that he is, very well.

I get off a launch message from the PM to Maxwell and then have a general sort-out of admin and GIS issues before giving an exhilarating briefing to the American correspondents.

On my way to lunch at Bucks with a PR contact, I drop off Denis Thatcher at Overton's. He is full of personal gossip. I fill him in on my briefing of the Americans on our political situation.

I am somewhat lively in the afternoon – the lobby; a meeting with Robin Butler on John Wakeham's additional responsibilities, the announcement of which has been put back a week; and then to Brian Walden's party to launch his book of LWT interviews. I alert the Chancellor to the Wakeham appointment.

Michael Heseltine's article in *The Times*, widely trailed yesterday, is the most overt campaigning stunt yet by him. But where's the beef? We examine his article at the PM's 9 a.m. meeting on Thursday. The first point to be made is that Heseltine has accepted the principle of the community charge. Second, as a backbencher, he is entitled to put forward his ideas, but there is not much new in them. Indeed, he admits in the article that he has tried and failed to get them past the Cabinet from 1981. We make it clear we shall consider his views and generally smother him with faint praise and kindness.

After that, it is all plain sailing. PMQs go without much incident – Kinnock asks the PM whether she will put Heseltine in charge of reviewing the community charge. This is no doubt trading on the line fed me last night by Brian Walden that Heseltine could not refuse. I told him that the PM is not made that way – and neither am I.

Drinks and dinner with Murdo Maclean and the head of Interpol at the House. We have much fun with Heseltine's article. His acolyte, Keith Hampson MP, is operating on the terrace, admitting that Heseltine wants to be party leader.

Friday begins in the best possible way for the PM. The 6 a.m. BBC news summary says the media have universally condemned Heseltine for a lack of guts, his willingness to wound but not to strike and the lack of substance in his ideas. I speak to Simon Jenkins, editor of *The Times*, who is coming in to see the PM on Monday. He says Heseltine had two choices: either lie low or come up with an alternative to the community charge. Instead, he comes up with 'a dog's breakfast'.

The week is thus ending on another good note, with inflation coming in below expectations, including mine, at 9.4 per cent. Having got on top of things, working non-stop since 7 a.m., I set off with Nancy to Cumbria for one of BNFL's weekend seminars. The rail journey shows off the May blossom to advantage.

On Saturday, after a quick tour of BNFL's extremely smart new visitor centre with Harold Bolter, Nancy and I watch an immensely exciting FA Cup final in which Crystal Palace go to a replay next week with Manchester United. John is walking on air – soaring, in fact. In the morning, the seminar hears from Dr Roger Berry, BNFL's new environmental boffin; Margaret Evans, ex-Welsh

Office and now at the National Rivers Authority; and Stewart Lewis of MORI.

I write my speech for tonight's dinner after the Cup final excitement. There is not much new in it, but it seems to go down well. During the evening I was extensively lobbied about West Cumbria's failure to secure £6 million of EC money.

On Sunday morning – another gorgeous day – we have a sensible discussion about nuclear matters. I urge those taking part to tell a positive tale and get out of their defensive stance. I suggest a conference of environmental officers advertising their nuclear wares.

We return to Penrith to catch the train for Euston via Ennerdale and Cockermouth and are in Euston for 7.30 p.m. John is hoarse after his exertions supporting Crystal Palace.

WEEK 20: 14–20 MAY

Far too much fuss is made of Chief Secretary Norman Lamont's BBC *On the Record* broadcast, with claims that it contrasted with the PM's optimism on Saturday and her determination to cut taxes. Lamont wants to cut taxes, too, when it is prudent to do so – just like the PM. I don't think there is much sense left in journalism. But then I never was very good at making up stories.

The week starts in a relentlessly mundane way – the PM's week-ahead meeting at 10.30; lobby at 11 a.m.; drafting a letter to Harold Bolter in response to Saturday night's lobbying of me over EC money for West Cumbria; writing a feature for a Newbury paper on the community charge; an enjoyable lunch with Joe Rogaly of the *FT*; lobby at 4 p.m.; presiding over MIO at 5 p.m.

At MIO, we focus on the handling of the Strangeways riot. It is clear from all I hear, especially from Adrian Moorey, head of information at the Home Office, that the prison management and the Prison Officers' Association grievously failed the nation – and the GIS. I suggest writing a paper recording GIS concerns to try to prevent another PR disaster and to secure the position of the GIS in all disaster teams.

Simon Jenkins is in good form at his meeting with the PM – sympathetic on the EC but not on the community charge.

John is in Northern Ireland covering the Upper Bann by-election. In the course of the morning, I write the press digest, attend the PM's PMQs briefing, write the promised paper on Strangeways, and generally feel much better for not drinking. I resist the temptation at lunch with United Newspapers.

Tuesday's PMQs are not very successful – nor much of an event either, leave aside the hilarity caused by a Scottish MP who says 1990 began in January and today is May to catcalls. He never quite recovers.

After PMQs, the PM tells Kenneth Baker of her intention to appoint John Wakeham to coordinate government presentation. I don't think he likes the idea but goes along with it, as, I assume, Sir Geoffrey Howe does. It is going to be a minefield, but Wakeham knows it. Matthew Parris (*The Times*) writes an interesting piece on the Energy Secretary.

I am very tired on Wednesday, probably suffering withdrawal symptoms (from whisky). People also say I am grumpy. Grumpy or not, I have a busy day – attending the PM's radio interview with James Naughtie on Adam Smith. She brings real passion and conviction to the programme. Then I try to sort out *The Economist* (via Marc Schuster) on a story emanating from the disgruntled at the DSS over the appointment of an outsider to head the Social Security Benefits Agency.

After finishing the Newbury newspaper article, I am let off lightly at the lobby since the closure of part of the Ravenscraig steel plant in Scotland is announced. Not easy. I predict difficulty and that is certainly what I get in the afternoon thanks to Scottish Secretary Malcolm Rifkind, who uses the words 'deplore' and 'unreasonable' about the closure.

We sort out Kenneth Baker's objection to the presentation of John Wakeham's additional responsibilities at 6.40 p.m. after worrying with the PM over Ravenscraig – or, more accurately, Rifkind's response to it.

On Thursday, we are convinced that the PM will face an awkward PMQs over the extent to which she supports Rifkind's deploring the Ravenscraig closure. If Kinnock does not home in on 'deplore' and 'unreasonable', we think he will go for the PM over unemployment, which, after forty-four months on a downward path, has risen marginally – by about 1,000, seasonally adjusted.

Imagine my surprise when Kinnock does not ask a question but makes a statement of condolence to the family of the sergeant killed by a bomb at Wembley. This fair took the wind out of the PM's sails – and mine. The most intriguing question is what does Labour research show if Kinnock feels the need to take the line he did on such a day of opportunity for him?

The lobby has behaved pretty badly by clearly briefing Scottish MPs that I disowned Rifkind. This was raised four times on the floor during the usual Thursday statement on next week's Commons business.

Friday finds me worried about allegations that I have left Rifkind out on a limb over Ravenscraig. The press office tells me at 7.15 a.m. that a certain Ken Macintyre is quoting me as undermining Rifkind. I chase the BBC's top brass for forty-five minutes, via John Harrison, political correspondent, until the editor of the programme rings me at 8.30 a.m. By 8.50, I have a broadcast retraction. I have never even implied criticism of Rifkind.

I resolve that if I am to be treated in this way by inventive and mischievous members of the lobby, I shall refuse to say a word on the subject. I refuse point blank to discuss the issue at 11 a.m. without demur. The Sunday lobby, however, is shocked at my attitude and tries to persuade me to relent. I refuse. Not a very satisfactory briefing. The Sundays complain I am taking it out on them when they are innocent. I urge them to observe collective responsibility.

I leave at 7.35 well content with the day's work but troubled that the press office is still hard at it.

Saturday's press brings a *Telegraph* front-page lead on discord between Defence Secretary Tom King and his Minister of State,

Alan Clark, over defence cuts. I learn from the *Sunday Times* that Clark is embarrassed by the publicity. The tale about his ideas for extensive cuts is substantially true.

After a haircut and gardening until lunchtime, I ask Charles Powell to ring me from Chequers for a line on the PM's meeting there with President F. W. de Klerk. Armed with his account, I then brief the press individually by phone until 2.30 when I return to the garden. Don Macintyre of the *Sunday Correspondent* and Michael Jones of the *Sunday Times* have both got wind of John Wakeham's appointment to handle the coordination of government presentation.

The Sunday press is notable for its sober coverage of de Klerk's visit; reasonable reporting of the Wakeham appointment; and Kinnock's alleged failure to make any impact with his new mini-manifesto. Even the Labour leader's friends say he has a long way to go to convince the voters.

After sending a summary of the press to Chequers, I take about a dozen calls from the media in and among lunch, a deep sleep and gardening. John says he is shattered after a week covering the Northern Ireland by-election but appreciative of the experience. We are glad he is back.

WEEK 21: 21–27 MAY

I am quite excited after the fourth weekend running of a good press for the government – an excellent visit by President de Klerk and EC Foreign Ministers sorting themselves out (in our direction) on political union and sanctions against South Africa. At the week-ahead meeting, the PM is buoyed up by this and is brisk and businesslike on the presentation front. I wonder how long this will last. It is a pity that John Wakeham cannot attend because of an EC Energy Council.

We play to the lobby a recording of the PM's lunchtime remarks at the Chelsea Flower Show. She says she is not going to allow the red rose to be hijacked by anyone and certainly not by the Labour

Party, which has adopted it as its emblem. Sarah Charman deputises for Terry Perks at a PM interview with a women's magazine.

In the evening, Nancy and I go to the Chelsea Flower Show as guests of Ray Dafter, the energy editor at the *Financial Times*, but we have to leave early because she is not feeling well.

Tuesday's press is very bitty. Kinnock is seen as trying to distance himself from the Militant faction, which, he says, is behind the anti-poll tax group. He does fairly well out of PMQs by asserting that the government is the biggest taxer of all time. It's not true, but we have to work hard late in the afternoon to counter the claim.

I have a reasonable morning – the PM's PMQs briefing; a meeting with the Chief Whip, who seems relaxed; lobby at 11 a.m.; see Dan Pedersen (*Newsweek*) at 12.15; lobby at 4; regional lobby at 4.30 p.m.; and then a highly wasteful ninety-minute meeting with the heads of the civil service professional groups – economists, accountants, lawyers and statisticians – over the administration of funds for recruitment – whether by the departments or the individual management groups for the professions, such as the IOMU for the GIS. We and the statisticians hold out for the latter. Fancy all this high-powered representation over a mere £174,000.

A relatively uneventful Wednesday ends with a GIS meeting at the splendid new offices of the Department of Energy across the road from Buckingham Palace. John Wakeham gives a comforting little speech in which he acknowledges the need for a professional GIS, pledges his support, and acknowledges the need to keep the GIS out of party political controversy.

The PM leaves at 8.20 a.m. for Norwich and the Norfolk Broads, so we can get on with basic work. The lobbies are desultory and only two American journalists turn up for their pre-lunch briefing. I lunch at the Horseguards Hotel with Nick Guthrie and Nicholas Witchell of *BBC Breakfast*. They want the PM to appear on their programme, which is reported to pick up a peak audience of 1.4 million at 8 a.m. They tell me they find it difficult to get clearance for ministers to appear on the programme and ask me to report this to John Wakeham.

On Thursday, I am disoriented. I rush in to produce a press digest for the PM by 9 a.m., only to be told by my secretary that there are no PMQs today. All the energy seems to drain out of me. Our main worry is the grossly inflated accounts on the BBC and in the environmental columns of the press about the PM's speech tomorrow on global warming. I see her at 9.45 a.m. to sort this out and brief extensively on the subject at the lobbies.

By 5.45 p.m., I have cleared my in-tray in time to make hurried preparations for my eighteenth drinks party for GIS information officers.

A quiet Friday starts hectically to get out a press digest before the PM goes off to Bracknell to open the Hadley Centre for Climate Prediction. I have tried to damp down the highly inflated pre-reporting of her speech and continue to work hard on the evening press between 8.40 and 9.15 to get her views in better perspective. On the whole, her remarks are well received, but the government is never going to satisfy the Greens.

The digest shows how badly the Labour Party's latest policy document has been received. Only the *Mirror* praises it. Even *The Guardian* and *Independent* have reservations.

Sarah Charman accompanies the PM to Bracknell and then has lunch with her at Chequers before covering this afternoon's visit by the Prime Minister of Singapore, Lee Kuan Yew, with whom the PM always gets on well. I gather that the PM and her grandson, Michael, are a hit with the media.

Michael Jones reports that Labour's lead is down to thirteen points, in line with today's poll of polls. The middle class, home-owners, and the north, Midlands and Wales are reported to be moving back to the government.

Shopping and gardening take me to 4 p.m. on a glorious Saturday. There is good coverage of the PM's environment speech, and the PM and her grandson provide the press with a wonderful picture.

On Sunday, press scepticism over Labour's policies is matched by scepticism about the government's commitment to protecting the environment from global warming. That is, apart from Geoffrey Lean (*The Observer*), a regular environmental commentator, who thinks the government's embracing targets to 2005 is of great significance internationally. That is true because it leaves the USA isolated.

For the rest, I clean up the rockery, buy and plant flowers, have a nap, give Sarah Charman a driving lesson – or, more accurately, driving experience – to discharge my debt to her for all her looking after the PM, and then somewhat listlessly watch TV – *Blackadder*, a film about Dunkirk (fifty years ago today), *Mastermind* and Ken Russell's eccentric film about Mahler.

WEEK 22: 28–31 MAY

The press finds Mr Gorbachev in such trouble that I begin to wonder whether we shall go to Russia next week. They report empty shops, the Baltic states seeking independence, and six or seven people shot dead in Armenia. The Soviet Union (just) is in a terrible mess. And so are we, with the IRA shooting dead two Australian lawyers in South Holland, mistaking them for British soldiers. I also begin to wonder whether for our holiday we should drive in Europe.

I put these morbid thoughts behind me by taking a bank holiday walk with Nancy over a dry and dusty Reigate Hill. The view from the top of the downs of well-wooded England reminds me of medieval times and the music of Thomas Tallis.

John is in Sunderland covering a murder and, surprise, surprise, he is staying in Durham, where he went to university.

On Tuesday, my doubts about the PM's visit to Kiev next week are increased because of Gorbachev's crowding troubles: Boris Yeltsin secures the presidency of the Russian Federation.

We buy a new tapestry carpet during an almost entirely domestic day apart from clearing a lot of written work. I tell Donald Crossley, the Mytholmroyd artist with whom I went to school, that I have sold four of his paintings to journalists who love Yorkshire.

The press office breakfasts at the Ritz on Wednesday – my secretary's idea – at 8 a.m. It is the best breakfast value I have had in years. Thus fortified, we walk back to No. 10 across Green Park. By the end of the day I am up to date with work and am looking forward to a more restful week.

All the action is abroad: in Russia; at the Bush/Gorbachev summit; and in France, where they ban British beef because of BSE. Then at lunchtime comes news of a severe earthquake in Eastern Europe, though with mercifully few casualties because the shift was deep down in the Earth.

It takes me an hour to persuade the press office, which is notorious for staying on, to go home at 7 p.m.

On Thursday, we are told that this is the driest spring for nearly a century. The press is dominated by the US–Soviet summit that has yet to start in Washington.

Robin Butler rings me about a *Sun* story that No. 10 is at loggerheads with Buckingham Palace because the Queen won't hold investitures for British Empire Medals. This is not so and the press office does a good job in killing the notion.

I write minutes to the PM on her BBC World Service phone-in on Sunday and her chat tomorrow with John Wakeham. I then have a 45-minute meeting with John Birt, Director-General of the BBC. He tends to agree with my political judgements but frankly admits he faces a hell of a job imposing his views on the BBC. He is, however, determined to have the Labour Party as well as the government properly questioned. I urge him also to apply that doctrine to pressure groups. He says he is to issue a new guidance note on interviewing.

I have lunch with Marshall Stewart, ex-BBC, to prepare for the visit to Kiev. He is excited by the success of a recent business trip to Japan but frustrated by the difficulty of breaking into Europe to get Europeans on programmes.

CHAPTER 18

JUNE 1990: EUROPE
BANS BRITISH BEEF

If polls are anything to go by, this is a better month, with a sharp move-ment towards the government – from nineteen points down to a mere four. Can it last, we ask, as David Owen winds up the SDP and the community charge still troubles the government?

We make the visit to Russia, Kiev and Leninakan in Armenia, and the PM attracts thousands onto the streets. The FCO try – and fail – to get me to distance the PM from Mr Gorbachev in case he doesn't last. Mayor Popov of Moscow likens the Russians to a boy who has climbed a tree and doesn't know how to get down but knows he needs to – and soon.

Europe bans British beef because of BSE, but an EC summit in Dublin is concerned with other things and largely uneventful.

Two press stories occupy us on Friday: the French banning the import of British beef because of BSE, followed during the day by other EU countries; and a bogus tale that Britain is trying to put off prosecutions for dirty beaches because of water privatisation.

At 10 a.m. I join a meeting between the PM and John Wakeham. As so often after a quiet weekend or a break, she is mercurial and undisciplined. She is against going into the ERM and is discussing a new appeal for internationalism to avoid the creation of blocs dominated by Germany (she admits she hates the Germans) and Japan, about whom Lee Kuan Yew is concerned. She has had dinner with him twice over the past week.

In the evening, Nancy and I have a lovely dinner at the Reform with Dr Jim Wilde and his wife, Linda, who are over from Vancouver Island. I went to school with Jim in Hebden Bridge. Afterwards I drive them back to Horsham, where they are staying.

It is very quiet on Saturday, so I potter about in the garden and shift paper before watching a sorry display by England in a football World Cup warm-up with Tunisia.

The PM's BBC World Service phone-in on Sunday is an easy ride. Earlier, President Bush spent twenty minutes on the phone briefing her about his summit with Mr Gorbachev. I tell the PM there is astonishingly little in the press about the summit when I ring her at 10.50 a.m. It is sparsely covered by the tabloids, and Mr Gorbachev is written down and almost out by the broadsheets. The IRA get a terrible hammering in the editorials for their cowardly attacks on a boy soldier in Lichfield and a major in Dortmund. A number of writers do not see entry into the ERM as a panacea.

We learn that David Owen is to wind up the SDP – as he does later in the day – amid recriminations among his colleagues that the SDP has served his purpose. No doubt that is true.

I go into No. 10 for the PM's phone-in at Bush House. She comes looking for me because she has this horror of being late. The result is that, as usual, we are there too early. In the broadcast, she is kind to Mr Gorbachev and more than welcoming of overtures from Tehran. I get home for 7 p.m.

WEEK 23: 4–10 JUNE

Monday is a productive day. There is still little interest in the summit. The tabloids are far more excited by the demise of the SDP. I tell the PM at the week-ahead meeting that David Owen has a rather destructive history and I would not touch him with a bargepole. The PM has pulled a leg muscle overnight. I wonder how long we shall keep this quiet.

I do a lot of organising in the morning and have a rabies jab before the weekend trip to Russia that gives me a headache later in the day. If the press knew, they would claim the Rottweiler is rabid.

I give two lobby briefings and one for the FPA during the day. At the latter, I put French and German bans on British beef down to protectionism and warn them they will be in great difficulty if their cattle are found to have BSE.

Two new issues arise: Gorbachev's concern about our nuclear deterrent under the non-proliferation rules of the START treaty; and his threat to Jewish emigration. I don't take either too seriously.

Tuesday is a depressing day. I have to endure over an hour at lunch with a bitter, critical and Brit-hating Lord Cockfield, a former Thatcher minister who went native as an EC Commissioner. Then the ICI gives me a presentation on Britain's industrial failures without any refreshment to ease the pain. And the Lords throw out the War Crimes Bill, which leads to a large lobby attendance trying to work up a constitutional crisis. I tell them to calm down. The PM's torn muscle does not seem to be giving her any problems.

I get a long way behind with work because Geoffrey Tucker (PR consultant) comes in for a chat about the political scene followed by the EC/Cockfield lunch. On my return to No. 10, I have to write a minute for the PM on the Calcutt Report on privacy. It is tough but in my view fair, but it will bring forth howls of angst by the media. Fortunately, Simon Jenkins has signed it.

On Wednesday, *The Guardian* is trying to stir it up over Gorbachev's concerns about our circumventing the START treaty, which in the course of the day becomes an issue, with a report on Trident technology. The Labour Party make the running on CO_2 emissions, claiming to have a CBI leak which shows that the government has been inflating emission savings projections to get away with doing little. Bunkum, but it takes a long time for the government to come up with the facts. By then I have briefed two lobbies and the American correspondents on the trip to the USSR and ultimately a lobby on the CO_2 issue.

I go to the richly attended memorial service of Jock Bruce-Gardyne at St Margaret's. I was rather disappointed with Bill Deedes's tribute, which seemed to tail off after a good start. Lunch with Derek Lewis, ex-BBC, who is obviously enjoying his unexpected success in being elected an Ealing councillor and his role in Kew Gardens' PR.

On Thursday, I feel to have done a hard day's work on the press digest and clearing the decks before we depart at 10 a.m. by helicopter from Wellington Barracks to catch a flight from Heathrow to Prestwick – a flight that is remarkable only for my feverish attempt to read myself in on the trip East.

Before a speaking engagement in Turnberry, the PM has a meeting with US Secretary of State James Baker to hear about his meeting with Eduard Shevardnadze, Soviet Foreign Minister. He says the Kremlin is still working out its approach to the idea of a united Germany joining NATO.

I host a table at the Turnberry lunch and am thoroughly put out by the efforts of our Ambassador to NATO, Michael Alexander, and the FCO to lean on me over my presentation of the PM's speech. The media think the speech is weighty and they file their copy before we fly due east over Bornholm and Riga to a chilly Moscow.

I spend some time with the PM at the residence of our Ambassador, Rodric Braithwaite, and in the spy-proof briefing room until well after midnight Moscow time. She says I look serious. I am. This is one of the trickier visits to the USSR because of the weakened positions of both the PM and Gorbachev. The FCO are doing their best to try to get me to distance the PM from Gorbachev in case he does not survive. I have no intention of doing that, and certainly not before she has talked to him.

I get away about 1 a.m. Moscow time to the National Hotel, with a wonderful view of a floodlit St Basil's Cathedral. Judging by the drunks and ladies of the night who are hanging around or being thrown out of the hotel, this is not the most salubrious place in town. Still, I get a quiet suite on the sixth floor and Peter Bean, the travelling press officer, who is still working out media rotas for the tour, also has a suite, so we are reasonably well catered for.

On Friday, I take a car to the Embassy for a hearty breakfast with the PM around a large table. Then we are off to GEC's exhibition, designed to corner the market in communications equipment for Russia. Next is the visit to the town hall to meet Mayor Popov, a professor of Greek extraction, who turns out to be a pure Thatcherite, though moderately radical. He says the USSR is like a boy who has climbed a tree and doesn't know to get down but knows he needs to do so quickly.

After the ritual wreath laying, the PM meets Mr Gorbachev in his second-floor office in the Kremlin – a climb that nearly creases me. Afterwards, I brief myself on the talks with the PM and Charles Powell on their way to lunch in a dacha and then I return to the Embassy to brief the media. I tell them the ground is moving under the Soviets' feet and they are casting around for means of reconciling themselves to a united Germany's membership of NATO and presenting it to the people.

After lunch in the Embassy, I go in the biting cold to the PM's meeting with Prime Minister Nikolai Ryzhkov. He remains a centralist and his remarks about the need for a decisive step towards reform are couched in similar terms to those of a jet-lagged Gorbachev at his joint press conference with the PM. Gorbachev hogs the last twenty-two minutes of the press conference after being provoked by a French question on the need to sack Ryzhkov. I conclude that he is tired and rambling.

Probably the highlight of the day is the PM's meeting just before the press conference with Soviet defence chiefs, who emerge a little battered. We have dinner in a dacha in the Lenin Hills, where a general tells the PM they never thought she would seek to recover the Falklands.

Saturday is a test of endurance. An extremely assiduous floor lady in the hotel rings me at 5.10 a.m. after I have had only four hours' sleep, believing I am to leave with the press party. When I am still in bed at 6 a.m., she starts banging on the door.

I decide to walk to the Embassy through Red Square, where they are already queuing to visit Lenin's tomb. The PM has breakfast at 7.30 with a group of dissidents and refuseniks, who urge her to watch carefully any legislation introduced to extend human rights lest it contains an all-embracing excuse. They thank the PM for supporting them and she says it will continue.

We fly to Kiev by Aeroflot. It is as green and sylvan as I remember it from a holiday tour in the late 1970s when I was at the Department of Energy. We spend the morning at the British Day at Kiev's fair, with its splendid exhibition of the lifestyle of the statistically average British family, untidy teenagers and all. This astounds Russian visitors.

We have lunch with vodka in the splendid Mariyinsky Palace, official home of Ukraine's President. Then on to the war memorial overlooking the Dnieper to which newly married couples go after their wedding. We also visit Babi Yar, the memorial to one of the worst Holocaust massacres. The PM then gives a boring interview to Central TV before the major event of the day: her splendid extempore speech to the Ukrainian Parliament. I tell her she must never write a speech again.

On Sunday, we fly from a damp Kiev over the Caucasus to Leninakan in Armenia, where the runway gives us a very rough landing indeed. The area had a terrible earthquake in 1988 and much political unrest last year. The entire city turns out – tens of thousands – up trees, in earthquake-wrecked buildings, on roofs and by the side of the road. The welcome and support are overwhelming. The convoy grinds to a halt about a quarter of a mile from the school, a gift from Britain, that the PM is to open.

Andrew Turnbull, Charles Powell and I fight our way through the crowds, our briefcases banging into people, to catch up with the PM. By the time we do, we are somewhat dishevelled, with battered shoes and trouser legs. We link arms with the KGB, who are getting into a bit of a panic. We clean ourselves up at the venue for the PM's lunch with the Armenian Christian leader.

After the ceremony, we get the PM out of the school by a side door and are then double-crossed. The KGB leader prevents the PM from meeting the people. Instead, she is installed at the front of a bus to the airport so that the crowds can catch a glimpse of her. Back then to Kiev, where the PM gives a short interview to Russian TV before flying home.

WEEK 24: 11–17 JUNE

A good night's sleep for a change – 10 p.m. to 6 a.m. The trip to Armenia gets excellent coverage, especially in the broadsheets. On the whole, it was a most successful visit – as I tell the FPA in the afternoon.

The main story of the day, apart from some miraculous escapes from terrorists over the weekend, is the idea of the USSR trading a united Germany in NATO for £7 billion (or is it £12 billion?) in German aid. I don't believe it.

The PM is in good form at the week-ahead meeting. More important, she has taken the need to plan for the next election to heart – as she tells David English, editor of the *Daily Mail*, when he calls on her for a briefing. The target has to be vested interest groups in the public services – policemen, prison officers, teachers, doctors and nurses. The government has to ensure that they serve the public rather than themselves.

Worse is to follow Scotland's 1–0 defeat in the World Cup by Costa Rica: England draw 1–1 with Eire in a plodding, punting, bad-passing and mistake-ridden game.

On Tuesday, the USSR is showing signs of compromise with Lithuania and the Baltic states and casting around for a formula to get themselves off the united-Germany-in-NATO hook.

The PM slaughters Kinnock at PMQs over the position of Sir Alan Walters, whom, I have admitted, she sees from time to time. She tells Kinnock he is worse than the KGB.

I seem to brief endlessly today, both the morning and afternoon lobbies – the latter being its sometimes intolerable self – and the regional lobby. The main issues are a leak from the Treasury that the PM will agree to enter the ERM in September or October, which seems not a bad bet, and the Channel Tunnel rail link, which is thought not likely to make much progress this week.

Nancy and I have dinner with Michael Jones and his wife Sheila after they have shown us their new London base – a flat in Clifford's Inn, wonderfully central with a good view over the Inns of Court.

The USSR makes progress on Wednesday on three fronts: economic reform, the Baltic states and East–West relations. It all seems to be going the West's way.

Philip Stephens of the *FT* has an out-of-date piece – by about ten days – on the community charge to follow up his leak on the ERM yesterday. As it happens, there is a ministerial meeting today on the community charge to try to get agreement on the way forward – i.e. wider capping with provision for a local referendum if councils refuse to accept capping. In the end, the meeting reaches no decision, but things seem to be going the PM's way. Other preoccupations today are terrorism – Tory treasurer Lord McAlpine's former home is hit this time – and the likelihood that the Channel rail link will be sorted out tomorrow.

I have lunch with the PA before attending a farewell party for Hans-Ingvar Johnsson, the London correspondent for the Swedish newspaper *Dagens Nyheter*, who is returning home.

By Thursday, it is clear this has been a poor week for the government – a nineteen-point Labour lead, according to ICM; fratching over the community charge; and Sir Geoffrey Howe stirring it up again.

I tell John Wakeham before Cabinet that this is not the image the government should be presenting. Both the Chancellor and Wakeham call in to see me after Cabinet. The Chancellor is furious about the ERM leak and suspects his own department.

Kinnock walks into a trap at PMQs. He calls on the PM to

provide public money for the Channel rail link. She tosses him contemptuously aside, saying that the Labour Party has simply no idea about costs and, in pressing her to subsidise the project, would throw £2 billion at it, just like that.

I have dinner with Peter Morrison, Energy minister and soon to be the PM's parliamentary private secretary, after another lively and enjoyable party for more GIS members. I have too much to drink and get a car home.

Ina Lord and Beryl Chatburn, with whom I went to Hebden Bridge Grammar School, come down on Friday to visit me and be shown around No. 10. It proves to be a hectic day. I finish the press digest in record time – 8.30 a.m. – because the leaks seem to have dried up.

Romania is the main story – 'miners' beating everyone into submission on behalf of the government, except that they are not miners but former members of the dissolved Securitate [secret police]. At 9 a.m., I go over to the COI to talk to a GIS induction course, and return to find my visitors waiting for me at 10.20. After coffee while I prepare for the lobby, they go with Murdo Maclean to see Mr Speaker. They have a right old time with him while I am briefing the lobby (inflation is up to 9.7 per cent), followed by a briefing on the birthday honours list. I catch up with my guests on the terrace at the Commons, having drinks with the Flying Squad. At lunch at the Reform Club, it is clear that Beryl is upset by the sale of the family farm at Brearley, Mytholmroyd. My guests leave at 4.15 p.m., having had a thoroughly enjoyable day.

I am afraid I have an enormous amount of paper to plough through this weekend.

On Saturday, Nancy and I go to Glyndebourne as guests of Harold Bolter, along with Mr and Mrs David Fishlock (*FT*) and my former deputies, Neville Gaffin and his wife, Jean. Benjamin Britten's *Albert Herring* is well presented but almost tuneless.

On Sunday, I tackle our garden, which is rather out of hand, after discovering why my new car won't start. A garage mechanic tells me the battery is useless – the connection bolts are rusty after only two months. The car must have sat a long time on Dees' forecourt awaiting a buyer. And then more bad service. My wife waits in all morning for the delivery of carpet underlay. Nothing turns up from Allders and I have a severe word with the manager at 3 p.m. And to think I once told the American correspondents that service was improving in Britain.

On a warm and sunny Sunday, Charles Powell rings me at 10 a.m. to say the PM has spent thirty-five minutes on the phone with Nelson Mandela, who has been resting overnight in Kent. He wants her to soft-pedal the idea of lifting sanctions at the forthcoming EC summit in Dublin, while she tells him he should come off the armed struggle. But they both look forward to meeting for the first time in July. My deputy and I decide to keep quiet about this telephone call.

After sending the PM a press digest to Chequers, I tidy the rockery until 12.15 and then after lunch and a nap I spend the rest of the day from 2.15 p.m. wading through reading matter.

WEEK 25: 18-24 JUNE

At 10 a.m. on Monday, I brief the PM, via the press digest, for her appearance on the *Jimmy Young Programme*. We have a fast trip up Regent Street and arrive early, as usual, at 10.45 a.m. Young asks forty-four questions falling into four parts: Europe and the UK's threatened isolation; community charge; her style; and her 'confrontational' approach, which she turns neatly into the confrontations she has to confront. He is brisk and tough and the PM performs reasonably well.

There is an embarrassment of stories in the press, but, to judge from the 4 p.m. lobby, they count for nothing apart from the community charge. I brief the FPA after a farewell lunch for Donna Foote, an American journalist who is leaving London to cover the west of the USA.

I dash back from the 4 p.m. lobby for the PM's meeting with Andrew Knight, Rupert Murdoch's right-hand man. He says

Murdoch has recovered from his run-down state. Sky TV is doing better but has a long way to go. He turns out to be rather pro-German – too pro for the PM, who is trying to counter the EU's tendency to concentrate and protect itself from competition.

On being called to Robin Butler's office, I am surprised and delighted to discover he is taking an even tougher line than me on Employment Secretary Michael Howard's plan, according to the press, to appoint a £50,000-a-year 'minder' from the WPP media company.

On Tuesday, I suspect that Kinnock has made a big mistake in saying that under Labour fourteen out of fifteen people will not pay more tax. This is unrealistic, given the extent of their commitments. And, sure enough, by the end of the day shadow Chancellor John Smith is trying to explain this assertion.

I urge the PM to nail this as a matter of both substance and presentation, but no one gives her an opening at PMQs, so we are left to get out the government's line.

I find it difficult, as yesterday, to get work done, what with meetings with the PM for PMQs and others until 1 p.m. PMQs are not very eventful. I brief the 4 p.m. lobby and then the regionals lobby. In both, I try to explain how the government is trying to encourage local authorities to moderate their community charge demands.

On Wednesday, Nancy and I go to Ascot as guests of George Russell (IBA) and his wife, Dorothy. They have got together a group of pleasant people. Betting-wise, I come out just about even, but Nancy shows a 66 per cent return on capital. It is a splendid day, but I am not sure Russell understands the pressures on political and economic journalists in the hurly-burly of day-to-day reporting.

My fifty-eighth birthday on Thursday brings a lot of cards and presents. But it has a frantic start because of the many interruptions while I am preparing the press digest. I simply do not get round to reading *The Guardian, Independent, Times* or *FT*, which are digested by press officers for me.

The accumulation of reading matter is a positive deterrent to taking time off. Among the things I have to read are the Chancellor's speech on a hard ecu (the EU currency unit) and the briefing for next week's EU summit in Dublin. I have to lead the 4 p.m. lobby through all this maze.

The Chancellor gives me an excellent run-down on Cabinet, which spends a lot of time on fishing following a judgment on Spanish fishermen. John Wakeham briefs me on the decision to return the War Crimes Bill to the Lords, and before Cabinet Defence Secretary Tom King consults me on how I might view returning alleged war criminals to the USSR. I don't think it will run politically. The Leader of the Lords, Lord Belstead, also rings me because *The Times* has got hold of a tale that Trade minister Lord Trefgarne is going to resign because he has made a mess of an issue.

On Friday, I shift paper like a madman until 11.30 a.m., when Anne Nash updates me on GIS progress. Things seem to be well in hand. Ian Kydd, formerly my FCO press officer, calls on leave from Canada and hopes we can visit him there.

I throw another lively party for GIS members at lunchtime and feel a little worse for the wine. It poisons my system. I must cut it out. The Sunday lobby focus on EMU entry and I try hard not to put my foot in it. It is followed by a large number of telephone calls which leave me feeling rather harassed by 7 p.m.

On Saturday, I am industrious. After reading the papers, I spend the morning giving our wood-block floors a protective coating and laying the new tapestry carpet in the living room. After that it is gardening, watching TV sport and reading, ever reading.

The Sunday press is predictably hostile to the Calcutt Report on privacy, except, curiously, for the *Sunday Correspondent*. Kinnock gets another hammering as two polls reduce Labour's lead to four points – a reduction of eleven on the month. It looks, however, as if trouble is brewing for the Dublin summit. We are against a Franco-German plan to send financial aid to the USSR.

I watch Argentina beat Brazil against the run of play and Germany beat Holland in between reading briefs and doing domestic chores.

WEEK 26: 25 JUNE–1 JULY

To Dublin. A car takes me direct to Heathrow on a humid day. At breakfast with the PM on the plane, we wonder what surprise the French or Germans will inject into the proceedings. Our best bet is aid for the USSR.

I give briefings at 11 a.m., 1.30 p.m., 6.30 p.m. and midnight and manage to keep a reasonably even temper with those who would question the PM's motives. In the meeting, the PM has a sharp exchange with President Mitterrand, who also questions them. 'Who, me, guv?', she seems to say. 'Me, who is open, outward-looking, candid and direct?' Subtlety is not the PM's strong point.

The council seems to be going well, without much acrimony – as distinct from finger-stabbing. My final midnight briefing reveals that the opposition in London is trying to commit the UK to a £20 billion Soviet aid programme, subsequently reduced to £15 billion. To bed at 1.15 a.m.

On Tuesday, I get up at 7 a.m. and read the press digest from London before delivering it to the PM over breakfast. Then I am off to Dublin Castle, where our officials have good news: the overnight communiqué drafters have had a productive time without much trouble. Famous last words. The French and Germans row back on Soviet aid and generally behave badly. The PM fends them off and the outcome is not too bad – and much less worse, the PM maintains, than our officials thought it might be.

Her final press conference is easy to handle, notwithstanding two long replies by the PM to questions. Security demands we climb out of the castle as we went in – in a helicopter to the airport, landing in London at 3 p.m. Sarah Charman goes off with the PM to visit Lord Kaberry, a veteran former Yorkshire MP injured in the Carlton Club bombing. Paul, No. 10's tearaway driver, takes me home with my smoked salmon and vodka presents. I arrive unscathed.

The traffic is so appalling on Wednesday because of the Queen Mother's birthday parade rehearsals that I walk to lunch with Trevor Kavanagh at the RAC Club. All the floats and the champion steeplechaser, Desert Orchid, are gathered in Birdcage Walk. Bands and choirs rehearse all day, including a beautiful bagpipe and choir tribute.

The Dublin summit comes across reasonably well in the press apart from a piece by that sneering federalist Peter Jenkins.

I learn that the government has sorted out the community charge to everyone's satisfaction, thanks to the Solicitor General, Sir Nicholas Lyell. I am also told that, with a bit of luck, Michael Howard will drop the idea of importing an advertising man as his 'minder'.

Altogether a satisfactory day. But I get very shirty at the 4 p.m. lobby with its hasty response to the EU's call for British Aerospace to pay back £44 million 'sweeteners' in the BAe takeover of Rover, which the government has privatised.

At the 11 a.m. lobby on Thursday, Charles Reiss of the *Evening Standard* reports that his predecessor, Robert Carvel, has died after a second heart attack. I pay tribute to him on behalf of the PM and press office, recalling his professionalism and mischievous good humour.

The lobby is concerned about my humour. After my black mood yesterday – reflected in today's reports of No. 10's anger over how the BAe/Rover controversy has clouded a good privatisation – Robin Oakley from *The Times* rings my deputy early to see if I am still on speaking terms with the lobby.

In the morning, I see Cecil Parkinson and Malcolm Rifkind, both of whom are pilloried over nuclear power. I am robust in their defence on the lines of a letter by Energy Secretary John Wakeham to a select committee.

Nancy and I are off to Hebden Bridge in the afternoon for a repeat of last year's walking and dining weekend for No. 10 press officers and their journalist contacts to mark my tenth anniversary in No. 10. We leave No. 10 after 4 p.m. and are at the Hebden Lodge Hotel by 8.30 p.m. Good going.

I take Nancy on Friday to her sister Miriam; drop Sarah Charman off in Haworth to explore the Brontë literary shrine; and return some paintings to Donald Crossley in Mytholmroyd, together with cheques for £500 or so for his Yorkshire scenes that I have sold to discerning lobby journalists. My next stop is Calder High School, where the energetic headmaster, David Scott, shows me some splendid designs for the school's development. I have a good time talking to the sixth form, who present me with a pencil drawing of their school. After that, I give interviews to the local paper and to two sixth formers, one with rings in her nose, for their Europe newspaper, which the *Halifax Courier* is to produce.

Our weekend party has by now assembled and we go off in convoy to Far Flat Head Farm for an enjoyable dinner.

On Saturday, we trek up the Hardcastle Crags National Trust valley to Wuthering Heights. It is an unforgettable experience – as is the local paper's earlier fascination with photographing me and Charles Anson, the Queen's press secretary, by the canal.

En route, Fernand Auberjonois, the Swiss journalist who is the *Toledo Blade*'s correspondent in London, takes a keen interest in Cosy Corner, a picnic spot, which Swiss exiles who come here each year have called Grütli because it reminds them of the origins of the Swiss Federation.

All goes well amid lowering clouds until we get on the Pennine Way beside the middle of three reservoirs at Walshaw Dean as we start the last climb to the derelict farm, Top Withens (Wuthering Heights). We are caught in a thunderstorm which we could see approaching across the Pennines. It drenches the party to the skin. Chris Moncrieff from the Press Association, dogged man that he is, reaches the summit in short sleeves and pumps. Keith Renshaw from the *Sunday Express* and his wife perform an invaluable humanitarian service by ferrying the soaked party back to the hotel, where I dry out my currency notes on the mantelpiece.

On the last day of our weekend on my native heath, it rains until 11 a.m. By this time we have had coffee in the Mount Skip Inn, which affords a magnificent view of Calder Valley and looks down into Hebden Bridge. It is good of the pub to cater for the drenched party.

After a walk along Heights Road to view its Pennine panoramas, we return to Hebden Bridge via Old Town (where my brother used to farm), Sandy Gate and Birchcliffe. We have a quick lunch at the Hebden Lodge before driving home at 2 p.m. and are back in Purley for 7 p.m. I spend forty-five minutes sorting myself out for the coming week before settling down to watch England win a World Cup quarter-final 3–2 against Belgium in a harum-scarum game. I doubt whether we shall beat West Germany in the next round.

CHAPTER 19

JULY 1990: DISASTER STRIKES

First, Nicholas Ridley, Industry Secretary, is forced to resign for some intemperate remarks about the Germans in The Spectator. *Then, at the very end of the month, the IRA kills Ian Gow, the PM's former PPS, by blowing him up in his car outside his home in Eastbourne.*

The resignation of Ridley, a loyal ally of the PM's, is the first terrible blow to hit her. We are also frustrated in demonstrating decisive government in the consequential reshuffle when the machine cannot find Ridley's chosen successor, Peter Lilley, who is at a constituency dog show.

With Labour's lead down below ten points, in line with the government's aim before the recess, Ridley's departure imperils the improvement in public sentiment towards the government.

Gow's murder is a bitter blow for the PM in a month in which she played a constructive part in a successful NATO summit in London and an equally satisfying G7 economic summit in Houston, Texas.

WEEK 27: 2–8 JULY

Monday comes as a shock to the system with the return to reality. The press has had a weekend of cerebration, as I tell the lobby, dreaming up all sorts of policy stories, of which we have heard few. The main story is of Nelson Mandela putting his foot in it by urging the British government to talk to the IRA. It tends to take the gilt off the Mandela gingerbread.

I lunch at the Reform with Clive Branson (*Chartered Surveyors'*

Weekly) to repay him for his hospitality and to thank him for bringing on our son as a journalist.

I try to read accumulated papers when I get home early, but fall asleep after our weekend exertions.

Mandela gets a very firm telling-off by Tuesday's newspapers. He could probably not have done the government a better turn. I think we are right in studiously underplaying his remarks.

My main concern today is to get a speech written for Mr Speaker (Bernard Weatherill), who has asked for notes for the very first press gallery party under his presidency in Speaker's House. Michael Jones, chairman of the press gallery, comes to my aid and I draw on a speech by the PM at the gallery's centenary dinner amid the 1981 riots.

In the morning, I preside over a briefing on next weekend's economic summit in Houston, Texas, by Nigel Wicks, formerly the PM's principal private secretary and now the UK Sherpa for the summit. He is so indeterminate about the likely outcome that few are going to know how to write their previews.

I have a hilarious dinner with Brian Hitchen, editor of the *Daily Star*, who has me in tucks telling how he got the Paras' mascot horse, Pegasus, on to the Express Group's editorial floor via the lift without it misbehaving.

On Wednesday, Mandela has three hours of talks with the PM, who introduces me to him as he is leaving No. 10. Both are obviously very satisfied with the outcome. After a good briefing from Robin Renwick, our Ambassador to South Africa, and Charles Powell, I give the media a full account of the talks, which come over well on TV. Elinor Goodman, political editor of *Channel 4 News*, says this must be the first time that both sides have recorded a triumph in the rain.

I have lunch with Hans-Ingvar Johnsson, who is leaving London to cover Eastern Europe for the Swedish newspaper *Dagens Nyheter*. Britain then closes early for business, including me at 5.15 p.m. The roads are so crowded I get home only just in time to watch West Germany eliminate England in the World Cup semi-final.

Thursday brings the NATO summit in Lancaster House. I am profoundly uneasy about it. The PM, determined never to be late, leaves No. 10 with a copy of our press digest at 8.30 a.m. for a 10 a.m. start!

The press tells us how well Mandela and Maggie got on, amid much wailing and gnashing of teeth over England's World Cup defeat.

I dash over to Lancaster House at 8.45 a.m. to read myself into the summit. Manfred Wörner, Secretary General of NATO, President Mitterrand and President Bush speak before the PM, who is followed by Chancellor Kohl. The PM takes the same line as Bush, counselling caution about too much change in NATO too quickly, given the uncertainties in Eastern Europe. The meeting breaks at 4.15, leaving Foreign Ministers to battle over the text of the communiqué. They seem likely to be at it until the early hours.

The summit ends in success on Friday. This is established at 7.10 a.m. when Charles Powell rings me to report that he has the final text of the London Declaration from Foreign Ministers. Leaving aside three bits in square brackets, it is OK. After many interruptions, I finish the press digest well before the PM and George Bush conclude their breakfast upstairs at No. 10.

I travel with the PM to Lancaster House to go over the communiqué. There is only one point of concern: the Icelanders' desire to include naval power in arms control. The PM does not agree, given that, in contrast to the Soviet Union, the seas are our highway, and she makes this clear in her intervention.

The communiqué is cleared by heads of government at 10.25 a.m. I brief Chris Moncrieff by phone on behalf of the media and then, when the PM appears at 10.40, I prepare her for her press conference and seven radio and TV interviews. All goes well and the summit dominates the airwaves, with ITN more objective and less confrontational than the BBC.

I prepare for Houston tomorrow after a winding-down drink with the PM in her flat.

On Saturday, we fly out of Heathrow at 10.55 a.m. with Chancellor Major and Foreign Secretary Hurd on board. Because of the NATO summit, I have still not read all the briefing properly for this economic summit, so I concentrate on the paper in the early part of the flight. We stop for refuelling at Andrews Air Force base near Washington, where we watch most of England *v* Italy for the third place in the World Cup.

In Houston, a green city if you ignore the docks and petrochemical plant, our hotel, the Ritz Carlton, is magnificent. I brief the media at 8 p.m. local time. However slow the summit is getting under way, I fear it is going to be difficult on aid for the Soviet Union, the environment and agriculture/GATT. We dine with the PM on some superb local fish at 8.30 p.m. (2.30 London time) and I get to bed two hours later.

On Sunday, the party goes with the PM to church at the invitation of Mr and Mrs Bush – at the very well-heeled St Martin's Episcopal Church, with not a black person in sight and no hymns, only Communion. While the PM is attending a conservatives conference, I brief the media, and by the time she returns to the hotel we are immersed in the Argentina *v* West Germany World Cup final. The PM wants Argentina to win and is not best pleased with the sending-off of two Argentine players, leaving West Germany reigning supreme. After that, we go to the Astrodome rodeo with barbecue and bucking broncos.

WEEK 28: 9–15 JULY

After four hours' sleep, we breakfast with the PM in her room overlooking the railway tracks and within earshot of that peculiarly haunting sound of the American trains' siren. The PM makes a habit of breaking off to count the wagons because of the length of the trains. The record for the summit is 105, though effectively 155 because some are double-banked.

I go down to Brown's Convention Center for a media briefing at 10 a.m. and am astounded at its size. I have plenty of support, for we are mob-handed for this event: Gus O'Donnell, the Chancellor's press secretary; Brian Mower, the Foreign Secretary's press secretary; Francis Cornish, from our Washington Embassy; Mike Horne, a former No. 10 press officer with me from British Information Services in New York; and Helen Mann, FCO Houston; as well as Sarah Charman and Anne Allan from my press office. It turns out to be the happiest team I have worked with.

We have lunch with the PM at the Ritz Carlton before she leaves at 12.45 p.m. for the opening ceremony. It has become abundantly clear that if I do not discipline myself, I shall spend my time in cars racing from one venue to another. I decide to stay at the press centre and rely on Andrew Turnbull and Charles Powell to keep me closely informed about the discussions, which they do. I get an early copy of the PM's remarks and feed them to the British media around 1 p.m. for their first editions.

At the end of the day, it seems that aid for the Soviet Union is not going to produce desperate divisions.

On Tuesday, I marshal my considerable forces just before 7.30 a.m., because a political declaration has appeared overnight for release at 12.30 p.m. As soon as I get clearance – and before breakfast with the PM – I brief the British media on the substance of it for their first editions.

By now feeling as fat as a pig, I go to the press centre to give a general briefing at 10 a.m. This summit is proving far easier than I expected, with two of the three most contentious issues out of the way – i.e. aid for the USSR and the environment. Only agriculture/GATT remains. Here, Sherpa Nigel Wicks comes up with a form of words that we hope will produce agreement.

George Bush is not overworking the summiteers. He finishes the discussion early, allowing plenty of time for his guests to prepare for dinner and entertainment, leaving the Sherpas to sort things out.

The media are sceptical that the circle will be squared over agriculture/GATT, but in my bones I feel it will be in spite of fighting talk from American officials. The Sherpas are still working on it when I go to bed. On Wednesday, to my delight, they have virtually agreed a communiqué which is satisfactory to the PM. On each issue she has been an agent for change, but she does not get adequate credit from the media for her constructive contribution. They have a clichéd view of her.

I celebrate with a hearty breakfast with the PM and then trot off to tell the tale to the *ES* and others, who are grateful for my help in meeting their deadlines. But not *The Independent*. They are cut out of my briefings because they boycott my lobbies in London. Their representative, John Lichfield, does not like it. I tell him they cannot have it both ways.

The communiqué is approved before 10 a.m. It is then downhill all the way. I brief the PM over the phone and later in person for her press conference and seven radio and TV interviews and another for two Houston newspapers.

We drive to a polo field, then go by helicopter to a waiting Gulfstream at the airport – all luxurious, posh, computerised and cramped for the PM's party. We fly out over the Gulf of Mexico and over New Orleans and Birmingham, Alabama, and then on to Nova Scotia to catch the winds for home.

After two hours' sleep, we arrive at Northolt on Thursday at 6.30 a.m. and helicopter in to Wellington Barracks. To my surprise, there is a TV crew and reporter in the Downing Street pen, shouting, 'What have you to say about Ridley's remarks?' We are mystified. All is revealed twenty minutes later on the 7 a.m. news. Industry Secretary Nicholas Ridley has made some disobliging remarks about the Germans in a *Spectator* interview with Dominic Lawson, son of the ex-Chancellor. By 9.30 a.m., the PM is clear that this is the worst 'Ridleyism' yet.

In the interview, Ridley said that the proposed European economic and monetary union 'is a German racket designed to take over the whole of Europe' and that giving up sovereignty to the EU was as bad as giving it up to Adolf Hitler.

I take the view that he will have to resign, in spite of the fact that, taking my cue from the PM, I have been briefing similar views about the Germans but in much more temperate language. The PM tells Cabinet that Ridley, currently in Budapest, has withdrawn his remarks. But they have ruined the presentation of the Houston summit and they dominate PMQs and the PM's subsequent statement on Houston.

Later, I tell her of senior whip Tristan Garel-Jones's idea of smoking out Kinnock with debates led by her. His point is underlined by her early commanding performance in the Commons. But I am almost too worn out to care. Home by 7.45 p.m.

Friday the 13th – and it feels like it. I tell Paul Potts of the *Express* that over the past month we had got things under control. Public sentiment was improving and opinion polls were moving the government's way, with a poll of polls showing Labour's lead is under ten points. And then Nicholas Ridley!

This is very frustrating and no doubt some condemnatory remarks by Tory MPs are due to this. The press's near universal opinion is that Ridley will have to go. Only *The Sun*, *Express* and *Times* are ready to see him in another government post. I share the former view, although I understand the PM's desire to keep a close friend and ally. The reality is that if she did, she would be dogged by his remarks, provide ammunition for Commons taunters and generally make her life more difficult. The irony is that the *Star*, *Today* and *Express* have conducted polls of their readers showing that a majority support Ridley. The pity of it is that he did not express himself in moderate terms.

And then Dominic Lawson, lacking nothing in cheek, rings me to ask for an interview with the PM, saying he thought Ridley was speaking for the government but now it seems he was not. He therefore needs to speak to the head of the government. I tell him that I doubt he will be surprised if he does not get to see her. He doesn't.

On Saturday, a lovely day, we are into another reshuffle, though not before the PM has put me on the spot over the phone. What should she do? I explain why I think Ridley will have to resign.

She retorts, 'You are only saying that because others are.' 'Not true,' I say, as I rehearse the problems she will have if he remains in post. I then get down to some gardening amid a procession of telephone calls about the Ridley affair. I learn at about 1 p.m. that Ridley has resigned after a fifteen-minute conversation with the PM at Chequers. He and the PM need time to write the customary letters, so I hold the fort by saying there is to be a further period of contemplation.

I drive into the office after lunch, sensing an opportunity to salvage something from the mess by demonstrating decisive government – i.e. by announcing Ridley's resignation and the appointment of his chosen successor, Peter Lilley, in quick succession, if not simultaneously. But Andrew Turnbull cannot locate Lilley, nor does he succeed until about 5.30 p.m. Mr Lilley has apparently been at a dog show in his constituency. I tell Chris Moncrieff on behalf of the media in general that Ridley has resigned and that I shall give a briefing at 6.15 p.m. when all will be revealed.

The Sunday press's treatment of the Ridley affair is straightforward and it is clear from opinion polls – as distinct from reader surveys – that a majority think he should go. I can't imagine what the press would be like if he had stayed in office, even though Foreign Secretary Douglas Hurd tells the BBC's *On the Record* programme that it would not have been disastrous if he were still a member of the government.

Nancy and I then go to Coulsdon Court Hotel nearby for the retirement party of Dr Betty Bass from the practice at which Nancy works in the baby clinic. It is a very friendly affair and I meet the retired Dr Mary Wilson, who, more than anyone else, is responsible for my being here today by getting me to stop smoking and lose three stone back in 1968.

WEEK 29: 16–22 JULY

I'm a bit panicky today because I have done next to no office work over the weekend. At the PM's week-ahead meeting I have my say about events of recent weeks, but all my instincts tell me the Ridley affair is receding. I doubt whether Kinnock's visit to the USA will this time provide a little light relief, because Labour seems to have arranged his programme much better.

Kenneth Baker seems delighted that Nicholas Ridley has gone, but can he be happy about his reason for going? He takes me to one side after the PM's meeting to say he is distressed to see *The Sun* has reported his view that the PM would face a challenge this autumn if she did not sack him. He denies he has told the PM that. I know that he didn't, but I also know that he did tell Mark Lennox-Boyd that was his view.

Lunch with Peter Vey, PR officer for National Power, who is missing Walter Marshall, his chairman when he was at the CEGB, and his distance from nuclear power. I brief two lobbies and the FPA and preside over MIO. Home for 9 p.m.

The most significant thing on Tuesday is that the lobby cannot summon up a question on the Ridley affair. Roy Hattersley, standing in for Kinnock, who is in Washington, makes a forlorn attempt at PMQs to perpetuate the affair, but the PM sees him off. He ends up with egg on his face. 'Is Labour in favour of an EU currency?' the PM asks him. Answer comes there none.

I am reinforced in my view that the Ridley affair no longer has legs. Moreover, the government is coming up with some good stories this week on community care and the outcome of the community charge review.

I give the regional lobby an informative briefing before seeing a visitor from Africa at 5.30. Home early.

The PM addresses the women's 300 Group lunch on a very hot day. I am the guest of Barbara Hosking, who was in the No. 10 press office during the Wilson/Heath years. The PM gives a competent performance on the advancement of women in society and gives the media a good story: a welfare package for abandoned, single-parent children. It all comes over reasonably well on TV, allowing for their need to give airtime to opponents' knocking copy.

I have a nap after the wine at lunch before a ninety-minute meeting with GIS information staff who did not attend the weekend conference in Bath. There is little criticism of what we are trying to do for the GIS, but I am disappointed by the number who do not attend.

The PM's 300 Group speech gets a lot of press coverage on Thursday but quite a bit of grudging reaction. This is a grudging country that is finding it difficult to cope with a successful woman PM. Kinnock has not done badly out of his trip to the USA but is not returning home in triumph. He also has a renewed problem with the Militant Tendency in Liverpool. I suggest to the PM she might say at PMQs, highlighting 'entryism', that this is not surprising because the faster Militant goes out of the door, the quicker they come back in through the window. She does not get a chance to say that in the House, but she bangs on about the big increase since 1979 in spending on social care, including the elderly.

The Cabinet turns to consider public expenditure and the community charge review and we put over a suitably severe line on bids for public spending. After PMQs, the PM concentrates on her speech this evening to the Tory Party's 1922 Committee, announcing she is setting up manifesto study groups.

On Friday, a relaxed community charge regime gets a poor but not unfair reception. After all, Health Secretary Kenneth Clarke yesterday told Cabinet it is not a good use of money and there is no certainty that local authorities will spend it. On the other hand, Environment Secretary Chris Patten thinks he can extensively cap local authority spending.

I start to write an 800-word article for the new GIS journal for finishing over the weekend, and then at 11.30 a.m. go for what is called a JAR – a career interview – with Robin Butler. He speaks admiringly of the way I am doing two jobs – press secretary and head of the GIS. He gets on to Charles Powell's role and we agree he is obsessive.

I lunch with Sue Cameron, who lands me with the task of

persuading the PM to give a TV interview about televising the Commons.

Our guests for the weekend are David and Marion Illingworth from our days in Halifax. They arrive while I am on the phone with Tristan Garel-Jones, who is concerned about the publicity given in *The Times* to the Chief Whip's warning letter to Nicholas Winterton MP. I speak to the Chief Whip in Wales and suggest he gets Garel-Jones to talk to the *Sunday Telegraph* and *Sunday Times* to make it clear, as the Chief Whip's letter does, that this is not the heavy jackboot of Thatcherism.

I give my guests a tour of No. 10, followed by lunch and walks on Farthing Down and Reigate Hill in glorious weather. In the evening, we have dinner at a Sanderstead restaurant. David is unchanged from the complete chatterbox of old.

The Illingworths leave after breakfast on Sunday. I send a note to the PM at Chequers telling her that the damage of the Ridley affair is there for all to see in the unfriendly broadsheets, who are once more trying to write her off.

After a post-prandial nap, I work solidly on the terrace into the evening on a hot day tempered by a north-easterly breeze.

WEEK 30: 23–29 JULY

I do not do much else on Monday but cope with a government reshuffle of junior ministers. It begins with Tim Sainsbury MP waiting nervously in the corridor. I tell him not to worry. It ends at 5.25 p.m. when Peter Bottomley leaves without a ministerial job.

As soon as Bottomley has left No. 10, I brief MIO on the changes and then race over to the House to inform the lobby and get the news on the early evening bulletins. By then, the shuffle has begun to leak. I make sure Trevor Kavanagh is able to catch his chronically early first edition. On the whole, the changes are well received. The surprise package is the return of Sir George Young to government. The PM wrongly sacked him four years ago. This is a public repentance.

Peter Morrison, the PM's PPS, calls in to say he is delighted with the outcome – as am I.

I feel as though I am living on the edge of a volcano, because we are due to attend a garden party at Buckingham Palace on Tuesday afternoon and I feel it in my bones that something is about to happen. It is. Robin Catford, the PM's appointments secretary, tips me off that George Carey, Bishop of Bath and Wells, is to become the new Archbishop of Canterbury. He saw the PM yesterday. This will surprise everyone and not least the bookies, who are taken to the cleaners by presumably insider dealing, since in a matter of hours Carey's odds are cut from 25–1 to 2–1.

After PMQs, we all troop off to Buckingham Palace's lawns, which the baking heat has turned brown. The garden party is pure Trollope, with vast arrays of clergy (and some Obadiah Slopes) along with sea captains and mayors. I enjoy myself until our return to No. 10 and more work until 8.15 p.m.

On Wednesday, I produce a terribly long press digest of little political substance. There is a welcome for the return to the Civil List, as recommended by a select committee, but the murder of two estate agent girls takes the headlines.

John Wakeham drops in after the 11 a.m. lobby to warn me that the *Sunday Times*, which is paranoiac about any relaxation in the promotion of enterprise and share ownership, is ill disposed to the PowerGen sell-off.

I then go off to St Bride's, Fleet Street, with the PM for the memorial service for David Woods, former political editor of *The Times*. William Rees-Mogg gives a superb oration. I then go on to lunch at the *Express* with Nick Lloyd and Paul Potts.

After the 4 p.m. lobby, I start to draft a 1,000-word article for the PM for the *Sunday Express*.

The recess approaches and there is little to concern us in Thursday's press apart from opposition efforts to stir up more trouble over the British Aerospace/Rover merger. This is because in the late rush of announcements, government departments have for once got all their news of any substance out in the public domain. It is true that there remain 600 PQs, but few of them will produce even medium-weight stories.

I concentrate on getting to the bottom of my in-tray before I go over to the QEII Conference Centre to view Sue Cameron's Channel 4 interview with the PM on televising the Commons. The PM is characteristically ill-disciplined during the interview, but C4 produces a lovely programme. I am so delighted with it that I show it to Peter Morrison, who has declared his determination to make everybody in No. 10 laugh. He tells me he has sent his personal driver to Vienna to take him into Hungary on his first holiday abroad in eleven years in government.

After an afternoon nap, I revise the *Sunday Express* draft before holding another drinks party for members of the GIS. Then I go over to Speaker's House for a retirement dinner for Sir William Heseltine, the Queen's principal private secretary. It is anything but a stuffed-shirt occasion. We even have a sing-song.

On Friday, the PM is in Warrington, Liverpool and Ellesmere Port against the background of a MORI poll showing Labour is only eight points ahead. The government has thus achieved its objective of getting the lead down below double figures before the recess.

I set about the backlog of paper with a steely determination to clear it. I might have made some impression but for telephone calls, visitors and a late follow-up to the Sunday lobby. I try to put across the paucity of the PM's pension, even when raised by legislation that the Lord President foolishly announced yesterday. This earned him a fearsome rocket from the PM, who has just discovered that ministers made redundant have not got their intended golden handshakes.

I lunch at the German Embassy with three journalists and during a somewhat mundane afternoon I feed out the government's opposition to the proposed EC directive on working time. The *Sunday Times* and *Sunday Express* are especially receptive.

On Saturday, Nancy and I go to Ascot as guests of the ICI and Martin Adeney, their PR officer. I end up £15 to the good and Nancy breaks even. Before the trip, my optician tells me I shall need spectacles for driving in two years' time. The main news is an attempted Muslim coup in Trinidad.

John Wakeham rings me on Sunday morning for my advice on whether he should go on radio, given the encouraging MORI poll. I urge him to do so. In a note to the PM, I say that the most encouraging news for her is the drift back to the government of C2s and younger voters, and rising optimism about the economy.

For the rest of the day, I garden in the morning and work on the terrace afternoon and evening in bright, warm weather, with a break to watch the England v Argentina Rugby Union international. Hartley Booth, an ex-member of the PM's policy unit, rings asking me to intercede with the PM on his behalf because the PM thinks he has leaked a story about development on Rainham Marshes.

My brother tells me he hopes to finish haymaking on Tuesday if this glorious summer weather holds.

Tragedy and grief hit us on Monday (30 July). Ian Gow MP, the PM's former PPS, is killed by the IRA. A bomb under his car explodes at 8.40 a.m. The PM is told about the explosion and it becomes clear just before the Home Secretary goes in to see her that Ian is dead. The news sickens all of us. The risks come ever closer to home. I pop up twice to see the PM – first to clear a tribute to Ian for immediate release and then to sort out arrangements for her speaking to TV in Downing Street – an idea with which she agreed with remarkable ease, given her usual reluctance to face the media. At 12.30, she goes out to pay her tribute to a loyal friend and to utterly condemn the IRA, who, she says, cannot be allowed to win. There are no tears, but her face looks drained and drawn.

She leaves at 1 p.m. in the care of my deputy, bound for Eastbourne to see Ian's widow, Jane, and the security services.

We cancel an office lunch and eat over our desks, which is where we need to be. Some of the media traffic is quite emotional, according to Sarah Charman.

In the afternoon, I draft an article for the PM for the *News of the World*; see Kenneth Harris from *The Observer* about a proposed visit by President Reagan in November; review GIS progress before my holiday; and have a good chat with ITN editor David Nicholas, who seems to be having a rough time with the commercial TV companies.

Just as I am about to leave for home at 7.40 p.m., I am told there is a bomb scare on Horse Guards Parade, where my car is parked. I get away thirty minutes later.

On Tuesday (31 July), I tell the PM that there can now be no question, in view of events, about my going with her to Aspen, Colorado, tomorrow. I had intended to leave what seemed to be a 'swan' to Terry. She is grateful and says I look tired. I tell her I am shattered.

This is partly because this morning I walked nearly two miles each way in sweltering heat to take my car in for pre-holiday service and to collect it before I go into the office. I am clearly out of condition.

I go into No. 10 for the sale for charity of gifts given to the PM on tour. I buy a large canvas bag for Nancy. I've had my eye on it for some time.

CHAPTER 20

AUGUST 1990: ON A WAR FOOTING

No sooner are we in Aspen, Colorado, on what was thought to be a prime ministerial 'swan' – i.e. a speech to the Aspen Institute – than we hear rumours that Iraq has invaded Kuwait. We are instantly on a war footing. President Bush comes down from Washington for talks with the PM on the situation, held in his UK Ambassador's ranch house 8,000 ft up in the Rockies. They agree the invasion cannot be allowed to stand.

While the world ponders how Saddam Hussein can be removed from Kuwait, we are treated to a scenic tour of the Rockies to visit US environmental monitoring and security installations.

My wife and I then embark on a wonderful motoring holiday to Vienna and back. Fortunately, the press office can assure me that all is quiet on the Middle East front while I am taking the mountain air.

While my son goes with Tom King, the Defence Secretary, to the Gulf, I am in Finland with the Prime Minister, who is there to address a conservative conference. She emphasises the West's need to be ready to act out of area in its own interests.

The month ends with her talks with King Hussein of Jordan and, via the telephone, with President Bush. Thoughts are turning to war.

WEEK 31: 1–5 AUGUST

It is now 3.15 a.m. London time on Thursday. I have been in Aspen, Colorado, for three hours. During that time, I have unpacked – at the Little Nell Hotel – watched TV news, given a media briefing, been to the top of a mountain and back on a chairlift, handled media calls and had a shower. I am going to bed if events allow, even if it is only 8 p.m. Wednesday in Aspen. As I write, there are unconfirmed reports that Iraq has invaded Kuwait. The No. 10 press office have heard nothing of it but tell me of a rail crash at Reading. Confirmation or not, we are instantly on a war footing. So much for Aspen being a swan.

Our flight from London is the scene of much industry. I edit and clear with her the PM's article for the *News of the World* and give the travelling media a briefing en route to Andrews Air Force base near Washington. We then fly over the prairie to the foothills of the Rockies near Colorado Springs. We are not affected by a fierce thunderstorm to the north-west over Pikes Peak.

We then embark on a US Air Force plane for Aspen after the PM's VC10 crew have made a presentation to her on behalf of No. 10 Squadron to mark her 500,000 miles and 1,000 flying hours with the RAF. I have the privilege of sitting in the cockpit as the US plane wends its way through a gap in the mountains into Aspen Airport with its short runway. Altogether, we have been in the air for fourteen and a half hours.

On Thursday, President Bush comes down from Washington for talks with the PM, principally on the Middle East situation, but also on East–West relations after an upbeat meeting between US Secretary of State James Baker and Soviet Foreign Minister Eduard Shevardnadze in Irkutsk, Siberia. I sit in on the meeting with Marlin Fitzwater, the President's press secretary. It is held in the splendid ranch house of the US Ambassador to the UK, Henry Catto, 8,000 ft up in the Rockies.

I must confess that the talks do not take me much further – but then I have just spent ninety minutes with the PM and others preparing for the meeting in the ranch's guesthouse higher up the mountain. They agree that Saddam Hussein's behaviour cannot be allowed to stand. The question of how to get Iraq out of Kuwait is unanswered except by 'effective and collective' UN action, to quote the PM, when speaking to the media on the ranch house lawn afterwards. Just before this, Bush tells the PM he had been wondering whether to come to Aspen for the Aspen Institute conference, at which both are due to speak, but she had given him a good reason to do so. He pays her a very warm and handsome tribute in his conference speech.

They think alike, but, speaking to the media on the lawn, the contrast in styles is marked. Bush is his somewhat diffident, understated self, while she is all fired up to remove Saddam from Kuwait.

Before going up to the ranch for the meeting, I brief the media extensively on events but do not satisfy them because I do not produce the PM for radio and TV quotes. I spend the afternoon wandering around Aspen, having one too many with the press in the Aspen Lodge and ringing home to hear the glad news that our son, John, has been appointed defence and diplomatic correspondent of the *Express*.

Friday is spent flying to and fro across the Rockies for our enlightenment. We have several ports of call on US government installations. First, we go to the National Center for Atmospheric Research, giving us a distant view of downtown Denver, which Nancy and I visited last year on holiday. We have a look at atmospheric monitoring planes before going up into the mountains overlooking Colorado Springs to visit the actual centre, where we are told, 'At present it is not possible to attribute observed local atmospheric changes as the effects of observed greenhouse gas increase.'

We return to the air force base to waving crowds to board helicopters for a wonderful flight down the Rockies to the west of Denver to Falcon Air Force base near Colorado Springs. Here is the national testbed facility for the Strategic Defense Initiative (SDI). This visit is notable for two things:

1. The astonishing pace of miniaturisation, which the host general says would be even faster if only they did not suffer from budget uncertainty; and

2.   A twelve-minute check call from President Bush to the PM just as she is completing her tour.

On then by helicopter to the Cheyenne Mountain command HQ for protecting the USA from attack. In this James Bond world 1,700 ft under granite, we witness a simulated attack from Siberia. Back then to Aspen for me to brief the press on the day and then dine with the PM's party with Barbara Walters, the celebrated TV presenter, who naturally wants an interview with the Prime Minister.

The highlight of Saturday is the PM's visit to the physics group at the Aspen Institute, which gives you a feel for the excitement of discovery and exploring the meaning of life. We go from quasars to quarks and from 18 cm to ten billion light years and theories about the meaning of our existence. It is fascinating. We then meet the chairmen of various study groups on education, health, poverty, environment, the Third World and East–West relations. There is a broad consensus on how to tackle the world's problems.

I give several media briefings on Iraq/Kuwait and the PM's conference paper to be delivered tomorrow. In the evening we dine at the Cattos' ranch. The Ambassador's daughter turns out to be a student of the Brontës. I come from that part of the Pennines and we have a wonderful chat. We also meet a physics professor who has given up his university post to raise cattle and teach children.

On Sunday, the PM makes a great speech to the conference. Even the *FT* is moved to recognise its quality. I am up just after 6 a.m. to brief on it at 7.30 a.m. In the conference centre, the filmstars Robert Wagner and Jennifer Jones are seated behind us. The PM gets a great reception and much applause when she gets on to drugs, terrorism and Iraq, which overlays the PM's substance on global issues.

In the afternoon, we go to the summit of a mountain in a chairlift for the superb views which produce awe-inspiring thoughts about the kind of life led by the pioneers.

My resolve to take a nap is wrecked by a call while I am in the bath to inform me that the US government has leaked UK support for a naval blockade of Iraq. The visit ends with a barbecue at the Catto ranch.

WEEK 32: 6-12 AUGUST

En route home to a baked-brown Britain, we are whisked into Washington by helicopter from Andrews Air Force base for the second round of Bush–Thatcher talks in five days. This is an exclusive affair, with only General Brent Scowcroft and Charles Powell present. In their forty-minute meeting, they plan the reinforcement of Saudi Arabia and an oil blockade of Iraq. Vice-President Dan Quayle and Secretary of State James Baker are called in to the talks and when Manfred Wörner arrives, they break for a photocall at 3.55 p.m. I go into the meeting with Wörner, who announces his intention to call a meeting of NATO Foreign Ministers on Friday.

The PM is disinclined to give a press conference back at Andrews Air Force base. I tell her she must, especially as news has just come in of a 13–0 vote in the UN Security Council for a tough sanctions resolution. Only Cuba and the Yemen abstain. The PM's meeting with the press is uneventful, but our timetable does not allow radio and TV interviews.

We fly at 6 p.m. with Wörner and his wife on board. They will be picked up in London by an HS-125 plane to fly them on to Brussels. I get some much-needed sleep across the Atlantic while fretting about going on holiday with the Middle East in crisis.

I am home for 7 a.m. on Tuesday to find our son staying with us. He has been moved on the instant from Manchester to London on his promotion to defence and diplomatic correspondent of the *Express*. He and Christine are now looking for a new home near us. The day is spent gardening and preparing for our motoring holiday to Vienna.

I start my car somewhat hesitantly after Ian Gow's murder by the IRA, even though my locked garage looks intact. I tell John never to park his car outside our home. Nothing much doing on the news front.

On Wednesday, we are up at 5 a.m. to sail from Ramsgate to Dunkirk in glorious weather. We leave satanic mills behind at Charleroi and drive through the rolling Meuse country and eventually find a motel apparently noted for its gastronomic excellence. It deserves its accolade.

Next day, I drive 413 miles, skirting Luxembourg and then on through Saarbrücken, Kaiserslautern, Mannheim, Heidelberg and Stuttgart to Ulm. German motorways are fast but the driving disciplined and the land is heavily wooded. Never try to find a hotel in a town centre during the evening rush hour. We abandon the idea in Ulm and go south to Reutti, where we find a hotel just outside the town and dine al fresco to the tune of combine harvesters bringing in the grain. We have never been this route before.

On Friday, we drive through Bavaria to Oberammergau, where the play is just finishing, and get swallowed up in the crowds. There is a proliferation of wood-carving shops which don't seem to sell much. I am not surprised. We then go down via Seefeld and Kematen to Mutters, where we have previously stayed.

We have an afternoon run up Sellraintal to Gries and Praxmar and walk to the head of the valley, where there is a full run of water off the glacier. The panorama is magnificent. The herds of milking cows have grown noticeably since we were here last.

Saturday is a difficult day because the motorway near the German border is closed and I get lost near Bad Ischl. We eventually find, high in the hills, our hotel, the Knappenhof, recommended by Peter Weiser, a friend from my energy days when I chaired an OECD group on energy conservation in Paris. This is to be our base – Reichenau – south-west of the Austrian capital. My deputy, Terry, rings (once he knows where we are) to reassure me that all is well back in London.

We explore the area around Reichenau on Sunday. It is by far the most attractive place we encounter. Its park is idyllic and we wander around it several times. We write postcards until 6 p.m. and then somewhat apprehensively dine on the hotel terrace, because we are suffering from midge bites.

WEEK 33: 13–19 AUGUST

We spend a glorious Monday from 9 a.m. on the mountaintops reached by a mountain railway and get a splendid view of Reichenau, Payerbach and Gloggnitz villages below. The flora is abundant and is identified by wood carvings along the way to Seehütte for lunch. By now it is becoming very hot and tiring, even at this altitude, so we go down on the 2 p.m. train. Later, we hear from John to say he has got his PhD after his two-hour viva. Who says the thirteenth is an unlucky day?

I shall never forget our revisit to Eisenstadt, south-east of Vienna, and the Neusiedlersee on Tuesday. The changes in Eisenstadt from our first visit twenty years ago are remarkable: the town centre seems to have been rebuilt. We visit the Esterházys' baroque church and the Haydn mausoleum before going on to the Neusiedlersee, a resort where everybody seems to be sunbathing. This is not our scene. We then go to the Hungarian border. It looks as inhospitable as ever, with its watchtower and soldiery. We dine on Wiener schnitzel and Apfelstrudel with Peter Weiser.

Even though the clouds are down on the mountains, we decide on Wednesday to explore the Schwarza Valley. Halfway up, we find a nature park in the making with deer, mountain goats, marmots etc. After a walk in the woods and coffee, we drive up the valley into the wilds towards St Pölten. The rain stops as we get to lower ground at Mürzzuschlag. We have tea at Semmering and then back to Reichenau. Terry Perks rings to say all is OK back at the ranch as the tourniquet around Saddam tightens.

We have a lunch date with Peter Weiser on Thursday in Vienna. We get there and parked from Reichenau in seventy-five minutes and explore the open market, full of Turkish and Yugoslav traders, before searching for Peter's office opposite the Opera House. He sends us off with his assistant (who apparently knew Peter Morrison, the PM's PPS, in his youth). He takes us to the old town; the Habsburg Palace; St Stephen's Cathedral, crowded with tourists; the synagogue, ominously policed because of the threat of Muslim attack; lots of old churches and courtyards; and at noon to see the Anker clock chime and, over ten minutes, take us through twelve personalities of the city, including Haydn.

After lunch, Peter has to see the Minister of Transport, so we go off window shopping before returning to the Knappenhof for dinner. I find it much easier getting in and out of Vienna than I expected.

On Friday, we go mountain climbing behind the Knappenhof, heading for the top of a cliff 6,000 ft above the valley. After two and a half hours we are near the top on the roughest scree yet when the clouds come down so, disappointed, we deem it prudent to retrace our steps as rain sets in for the day. After lunch at the Knappenhof, we while away the afternoon reading. I am immersed in Wilkie Collins's *The Moonstone* and read 100 pages as the rain belts down.

On Saturday, we walk around Payerbach and then take the mountain road to Semmering. At the top, we have a Bratwurst lunch. On then to Mürzzuschlag, where parking is difficult, the police inclined to be fierce and roads closed. This evening we are guests of Peter Weiser and his wife, Elly, at their home with the Reginald Thomases, a former Austrian Ambassador to the UK. Driving in the dark back to Reichenau is an experience.

After church on Sunday, we walk for three hours in the forest, and the views in the clear air after the rain are wonderful. Having finished *The Moonstone*, I read 150 pages of Melvyn Bragg's *The Maid of Buttermere*, lent to me by Cynthia Crawford, who assists the PM on tour.

Sarah Charman rings after dinner to say the PM is returning to London tonight and that there is otherwise not much doing. She suggests I sound subdued. Indeed, I am. I've got a chill and Nancy a nasty cough.

WEEK 34: 20–26 AUGUST

We start the journey home by making for St Pölten and the autobahn. It is a lovely drive through the mountains to the Danube

Valley. We then embark on a long drive to the German border at Rosenheim, where there is a great deal of congestion due to road-works and lorries bullying their way into the queue. Then we take the road to Munich and come across a magnificent rural ecclesiastical scene on a hilltop: a herd of cows clustered around a church with onion domes. We see Dachau, but not the site of the atrocity, signposted.

Eventually, after a frustrating day, we find the Hotel Heimer in a farming village on the outskirts of Memmingen, where huge rabbits play freely in the yard. A soothing sight after 371 miles of hard graft.

We are sorry to leave Memmingen and our hotel on Tuesday. We drive via Ochsenhausen, dominated by a magnificent palace, on to Biberach and then ever westwards to Tuttlingen near Donaueschingen, criss-crossing the infant Danube. Crossing the Rhine into France, we hit more heavy traffic, so I head for the hills to Gérardmer, then Épinal and finally to Charmes on the Moselle, where we book into the Hotel Dancourt in the main square. It proves to be a good choice, with a splendid dinner – a large salad, sea trout and snails, all topped off with ice cream.

Wednesday sees us back home after 440 miles' driving via Laon, St Quentin and a little-used new motorway to Boulogne. Overall, we have covered 3,600 miles. My lasting impressions are of the order and cleanliness of Germany and Austria and the much more run-down nature of France and England. Folkestone is not a good advert. It shows why the PM launches drives against litter.

An entirely domesticated Thursday follows after seeing John off at 8 a.m. He is going home to Lymm for the weekend. It is a familiar pattern of digesting the newspapers, gardening and a late lunch before the arrival of four – repeat, four – boxes of paper for me to wade through. I manage to read enough to fill one of those boxes for collection by No. 10 in the evening.

It is hot and sunny for my return to the office on Friday at 2.30 p.m., just as the PM is about to visit the Gulf Support Unit. Charles Powell is moaning about having little holiday while his boss, Andrew Turnbull, is taking the month off. If only he did not try to do everyone's jobs!

On Saturday, after more gardening, I watch England's disastrous Test performance against India before blackberrying at Chipstead. I manage to collect seven pounds in ninety minutes, in spite of some jealous lads who do not seem to understand that to fill a carton with berries requires application.

The Sunday press presents a confusing picture of the political and economic effects of the Gulf crisis, and I do not waste much time on them in preparing a digest for the PM. I also write to Peregrine Worsthorne, the editor of the *Sunday Telegraph*, on the death of his wife.

In the evening, we announce that the PM is to see King Hussein of Jordan on Friday. President Bush rings her for a twenty-minute review of the Middle East situation. They are in absolute agreement. I watch a nostalgic video of the songs of World War II led by Max Bygraves. It is astonishing how well I recall the lyrics after fifty years.

WEEK 35: 27 AUGUST–2 SEPTEMBER

Not much in the bank holiday papers – so little that I am gardening by 8.30 a.m. before fitting a new carpet in the bedroom. I watch the Test match and racing in the afternoon. The PM is back in No. 10 before lunch to see Prince Saud of Saudi Arabia and then the Chancellor on ERM entry. Our son goes off with the Defence Secretary, Tom King, to the Gulf.

Back on the move on Tuesday – this time to Helsinki, flying over Clacton, Aalborg, Gothenburg, Stockholm, the Åland Islands, of which we get a superb view, and Turku. At 7 p.m., I do a rushed and poor media briefing in my dinner jacket – poor partly because there is not much to impart of substance and partly because I am not up to speed after the holiday, even though I have read the entire legacy of paper from my break. Our Ambassador, Neil Smith, and his wife give the PM a lovely dinner, including frozen cranberry in a hot, sweet sauce.

We are quartered in the very busy European Democratic Union conference, which the PM is to address on Thursday. I have a late check with the No. 10 press office and fill them in on the PM's day.

After breakfast at the Embassy on Wednesday, the PM inspects new offices next door. This gives me a chance to get abreast of the Gulf situation. It is always uncomfortable on tour trying to keep up with a crisis elsewhere. In the quayside market, the PM has the best-organised walkabout I have experienced, followed by talks with the President and Prime Minister. We lunch in the presidential palace and I am seated next to the Finance minister, who used to be in the energy business and was deeply impressed by a visit to a Nottinghamshire coal mine about ten years ago.

On a sunny afternoon, we visit an oil refinery by helicopter and learn of the environmental disaster that is the Kola Peninsula in the north and the problems they are having in the Baltic because it is becoming less salty the less it is flushed by the North Sea. We return by boat and I get a wonderful photo of the PM splicing the mainbrace. The PM has an informal dinner at the Embassy.

We leave for home on Thursday after the PM has spoken to the conference. After breakfast at the Embassy at 7.45, I give the press the text of the PM's speech and send it to London. Since the PM is speaking at a party political conference, I go shopping for gifts in Stockmann's with Det. Supt Trevor Butler, the PM's senior bodyguard.

Back at the Finlandia Halls, I brief the media on the government aspects of the PM's powerful speech, emphasising the West's need to be ready to act out of the NATO area if it is serious about defending its interests. After a desultory press conference, we leave Finland at noon for the PM's meeting with the Foreign Secretary, Douglas Hurd; the Energy Secretary, John Wakeham; the Lord Privy Seal, Lord Belstead; and the Chief Whip, Tim Renton, about a recall of Parliament because of the Middle East situation. I work out with the PM the announcement of the recall and assemble a briefing on the justification for the move, for release at 7 p.m. The Defence Secretary returns from the Gulf with John.

In between her meetings on Friday with King Hussein and John Sununu, White House chief of staff, I try to brief the PM for her interview with David Frost tomorrow. Her speech in Helsinki gets a remarkably good press, but only the *FT* focuses on the real point: the need for NATO countries to face up to their out-of-area security.

I process the backlog of paper as fast as I can until the police arrive at noon to satisfy themselves that I am fully aware of the risks I am running during the IRA campaign as a long-time servant of the PM. I arrange for them to visit my home to inspect its safety arrangements on Tuesday.

I get a fast run-down from the PM and Charles Powell on her meeting with King Hussein as she steps inside after seeing him off in Downing Street. Just before that meeting, President Bush has a word with her. Thoughts are turning to war.

David Frost's interview with the PM takes seven hours of my time on Saturday, including travelling time and checking the newspapers. Two main stories are running: the release of Lebanese hostages and the impending formal announcement of a Bush–Gorbachev summit in Helsinki on 9 September. John rings to say he has to cover the Finland talks.

Frost spends ninety minutes asking sixty-four questions for a 55-minute programme. In the end, he decides to split it and use one half next week.

On Sunday, with little or nothing in the press, I gather four and a half pounds of blackberries, making a total of around fifteen pounds so far. Then we have over five hours of noise from our awful neighbours, the Cripps, who are holding a party. I work away at the paper and watch our two regular foxes call for their dinner on the terrace.

CHAPTER 21

SEPTEMBER 1990:
ARE THINGS BEGINNING
TO COME RIGHT?

This is the question in a largely humdrum month. It follows a somewhat triumphant tour of central Europe – the Czech Republic, Slovakia (as it is to become), Hungary and Switzerland, with crowds all the way through the former Communist countries. Alexander Dubček, the leader of the Prague Spring in the 1960s, tells me the PM is 'not the Iron Lady but the Kind Lady'.

Inflation at home is still in double figures – 10.6 per cent – but the opinion polls narrow, MORI giving Labour a seven-point lead while a BBC poll halves it to five points. And a confident PM tells Newsweek *that Thatcherism is 'not just for the '80s but for centuries'. This explains why, as late as this in the year, we in No. 10 doubt whether there will be another challenge to her leadership.*

WEEK 36: 3–9 SEPTEMBER

It rains at last on Monday (3 September), the day war broke out. On the whole, it is more gentle than this day fifty-one years ago, reading and admin. In between lunch with Mike Brunson from ITN, I make it clear to the PM's private office that if I am excluded from ministerial meetings on the Gulf, I shall leave at the first good offer. I mean it. After the Falklands, I have had enough of being excluded from subjects I have to brief on.

I find not much progress is being made with the public expenditure round, leaving aside those departments – e.g. Energy – that have decided to settle. And the Gulf and inflation have eaten away the room for extra spending. Life is going to be difficult.

Tuesday is police inspection day at home. Three officers arrive just before 9 a.m. to advise us on what needs to be done to protect us. It all leaves me feeling terribly vulnerable after they have crawled over the garage and bungalow. Nancy thinks it is all overkill. I lunch with Michael Hoffman, formerly with Babcock and now with Thames Water.

I have a long talk with John Wakeham on Wednesday about a presentational strategy for the autumn and he commissions a paper from me.

I brief the American correspondents under the handicap of not being at a ministerial meeting. Consequently, I tell John Wakeham, in charge of government presentation, of my resolve to leave No. 10. He says he has decided to retire at the next election because of the effect on his legs of the IRA bomb at the Brighton Tory Party conference in 1984. I need a change.

George Russell calls to inform me of his plans for commercial TV in the regions and I have a talk with Professor Graham Ashworth, head of the Tidy Britain Group.

The recalled Parliament meets on Thursday. The PM does a competent job in the House, and Kinnock makes one of his better speeches until he equivocates over legal cover for the use of force in the Gulf. The PM, who has always been meticulous about legal cover – e.g. the Falklands and President Reagan's raid on Libya – is the only one willing to take action without further recourse to the UN. Kinnock wouldn't. Nor would Paddy Ashdown.

In the evening, I give a group of Eastern European journalists a seventy-minute Q&A session on how a free press operates in Western democracies. I then have to cancel dinner with George Bull because of a plan to move Michael Forsyth, chairman of the Scottish Tory Party, into government as Minister of State at the Scottish Office. The snag is that Forsyth is refusing to budge. When I call on him in his room before leaving for home at 9 p.m., Peter Morrison is trying without much success to get him on board.

Next day the argument is still raging, and when I get back from a meeting on honours I find Peter Morrison and my deputy trying to decide how to play it. I tell them that it seems to me we shall be lucky to get a draw. Imagine my surprise when the Sunday lobby declare that Forsyth has won and that Scottish Secretary Malcolm Rifkind, who is alleged to have been rubbishing Forsyth publicly, has gone north with his tail between his legs. (Forsyth eventually rejoins the government and gives up the party chairmanship.)

I communicate all this to the PM in Scotland for her annual stay with the Queen. I am also able to sweeten the pill with news of a Gallup poll showing a surge in respect for her as PM.

Another typical Saturday follows: reading newspapers, shopping, gardening, processing paper and watching sport on TV. The Sunday press is vastly empty, so I am out picking blackberries (for my next-door neighbours, the Bromleys) by 10 a.m.

Today is John's big day in Finland with the conclusion of the summit. The story seems pretty simple and immensely welcome to the PM because of the degree of 'superpower' agreement on the Gulf.

I tell the police that a car has been driven up my rear drive to the garage. A policeman duly arrives and asks if it was a blue Astra. It was. Oh dear, it was driven by the very policeman I have called out. At least it proves we are both taking security seriously.

WEEK 37: 10–16 SEPTEMBER

I don't see much of this lovely day because press officers are thin on the ground. Terry Perks and Philip Aylett are with the PM in Newcastle upon Tyne and at the Gateshead Flower Festival while Sarah Charman is in Rome doing a recce for an EC summit. On top of the usual work, I have to write a brief for Robin Butler for his lunch with the PA news agency and for the PM for her meeting on Wednesday with William Randolph Hearst Jr.

After lunch at White's with a PR contact, I brief a heavily attended FPA where I have to run the gauntlet of Swiss journalists who are upset because the PM is giving an interview only to a Zurich newspaper. On then to preside at MIO before I beard Colin Webb, editor of the PA, in his den for not sending a reporter to cover the PM's recent visits to Aspen, Colorado and Helsinki. He admits it was an error of judgement and clears the way for their representation (in the interest of all media outlets) on future trips. John is back from covering the Bush–Gorbachev Helsinki summit.

On Tuesday, I fly to Newcastle upon Tyne by Dan-Air to put some flesh on the bones of my visiting fellowship in the politics department of the university. I meet Professor Hugh Berrington, Rod Hague and Richard Wylie to plan:

1. My talk at the university next month;
2. A programme of three seminars and a course over the next nine months;
3. Research and publicity.

They clearly mean business, and it is encouraging that a scour of the literature has produced no evidence of research into communication between government and industry – our chosen field – as distinct from relations between the two.

I tell my friend from Halifax days, David Illingworth, that I shall not now be taking up a post with his former firm in Yorkshire when I retire, because they have made him redundant at fifty-nine. Back home at the unearthly early hour of 6.45 p.m.

During Wednesday it seems that the idea of sending a tank brigade to the Gulf is hardening. Earlier, Charles Powell told me what he refused to tell my deputy yesterday after a meeting of ministers but which is now in the press about the options for sending a ground force there.

The PM gives a serious interview to the *Zürcher Zeitung* and has a farcical meeting with William Randolph Hearst Jr. He has been injured in a fall at the US Embassy and when he is not fiddling with his hearing he is irascible, not to say lecherous. He is an appalling caricature, accompanied by two sycophants. I lunch with IRN/LBC.

John Wakeham, as the minister responsible for government presentation, visits the IOMU and COI. First, I give him an enthusiastic account of what we are trying to do for the GIS, and he seems to appreciate this. We then go to the COI, who put on a very professional presentation of their capabilities. I stress to the minister the sheer variety of GIS work, which is attractive to recruits. From his remarks relating back to his managerial experience, I think we have established with him a clear understanding of what we can do and how we do it.

On Thursday morning, I ring Ivor Manley, a senior civil servant, to say what a cross he has to bear with William Davis, head of the British Tourist Authority, who was all over the show, incoherent and insensitive at a recent meeting. He thanks me for my support against 'the conmen of the tourist world'.

After lunch with Philip Johnston and Nick Assinder (political correspondents), I give a media briefing on the PM's visit next week to Czechoslovakia, Hungary and Switzerland.

Friday is a military day, with the government deciding to send the Desert Rats to the Gulf and my lunch with Guy Wilson, Director of the Royal Armouries.

The government is to dispatch the 7th Armoured Brigade to the Gulf. I learn they are the successors to the Desert Rats of World War II, and my mere mention of the term takes the heat out of higher than expected inflation of 10.6 per cent. Officials think the inflation rate has little impact because the markets expect us to go into the ERM, possibly next week, and so keep interest rates fairly high.

At the Tower of London lunch, Guy Wilson presents me with a magnificent plan to take the bulk of the Royal Armouries collection to a new site at Sheffield's Meadowhall to make more space available in the Tower. Unfortunately, he says he is being blocked by Department of the Environment officials. My advice is for him to get the blockers blasted out by a high-powered politician with a background in defence – Michael Heseltine, George Younger or Willie Whitelaw.

Saturday brings a lovely day for a Battle of Britain fly-past. I am occupied on gardening, watching the St Leger and preparing for next week's tour.

I weigh my Sunday newspapers on the bathroom scales – eight and a half pounds – and marvel at the desecration of forests that this entails. It is certainly not justified by their news content. The most worrying thing in them is the way the word 'recession' has become fashionable in journalism.

Just before 1 p.m., I leave for Heathrow for the PM's European tour. The first stop is Prague, where we arrive at 5.30 p.m. Crowds – more than Embassy staff say they have ever seen in the city – turn out for the PM all her way in and in the Old Square just as the sun goes down. The only nonsense is from some juvenile Bristol students shouting, 'Maggie, out, out, out'. The day ends with an interminable reception in the Embassy and dinner with dissidents.

WEEK 38: 17–23 SEPTEMBER

I breakfast at the Hotel Praha, former home of the Czech Communist Party hierarchy. They did themselves proud. My suite is measured in acres. The view from my room of the cathedral through the dawn mists is magnificent and the view of Prague's bridges from the PM's balcony superb. We are told her room is the only place in the city that you can see all its bridges.

Now the action. We start the day with the most ludicrous car journey I have ever made with the PM – all of fifty yards from the Embassy to the Czech Parliament to meet Mrs Dagmar Burešová, the Speaker, and PM Petr Pithart. They say they are learning about a parliamentary democracy and what better example to follow than the Mother of Parliaments. They give the impression of working hard and enthusiastically at it but being overawed by the task and a little exasperated that democrats can be so cussed.

Highlights of the day:

1. A visit to Cardinal František Tomášek, ninety-one, venerable, fresh-faced but ageing. His only remark to the PM is: 'This is an important visit.'
2. The old Jewish cemetery – a higgledy-piggledy amble through the most extraordinary lopsided collection of gravestones.
3. The Commonwealth War Graves cemetery, through ranks of poor, ill-postured conscripts, which is beautifully kept as ever. The PM walks to the graves flanked by aged Czech RAF officers – a great day in their lives, for now their contribution to winning the war can be recognised. Some of them, we are told, went to prison on returning home in victory.
4. The huge presidential palace – the opulence of the rooms and the sheer vastness of the ballroom, now being restored.
5. President Václav Havel's inability to look you – and the PM – in the eye during their ninety-minute meeting is remarked upon. Perhaps this brave dissident developed this as a defence mechanism during his imprisonment. The talks, through a fog of Havel cigarette smoke, are fairly inconsequential apart from his declared determination to rid Czechoslovakia of the Warsaw Pact.

The day ends with another interminable Embassy reception before a very acceptable duck dinner. How the Czechs smoke! I conclude that the function of Embassy staff is to patrol the room with ashtrays to prevent the place burning down. I have a nightcap with the media.

Tuesday dawns wet and miserable, but it is fine by 11 a.m. The PM goes to the federal Parliament near Wenceslas Square and comes out glowing to much applause. She even got a standing ovation in mid-speech. It all goes down extremely well, but her tribute to Mr

Gorbachev is heard in silence. She presents a copy of the Magna Carta to President Havel. Alexander Dubček, the celebrated leader of the Prague Spring in the late 1960s, with whom I had a long talk last night, says the PM is not the Iron Lady but the Kind Lady. She is much loved in Czechoslovakia – as is obvious in Parliament and at the wreath laying in Wenceslas Square and paying homage to the memory of Jan Palach, who immolated himself when the Prague Spring was crushed. There are crowds everywhere, including at her visit to a vintage bit of the city – the Lucerna entertainment complex of café, theatre and ballroom – built by Havel's grandpa. This is the first time I have seen the PM sitting on a bar stool sipping coffee while Havel downs a pint and Denis Thatcher a herbal liquor.

On we go to Bratislava – industry and tower flats overlooking the Danube, but very welcoming. PM Vladimír Mečiar of Slovakia entertains the PM to lunch. In Bratislava Castle, Speaker František Mikloško receives the PM with good humour and reveals his secessionist tendencies. The Tatars, Turks and Commies have all invaded us and retired hurt, he says, while Slovaks live on.

We then take a short flight to Budapest to be received by PM József Antall, the only conservative so far elected east of the Iron Curtain, who met the PM recently in Helsinki. He gives us a quick run-down on the perils of privatisation in his barn of an office. 'How can you morally give ex-Communists privatisation pickings when they benefited from the old regime?' he asks. We have a high-cholesterol dinner near Heroes' Square.

There is an autumnal chill in the air in Budapest on Wednesday. I take some sunrise shots of Pest from my room in the Hyatt Atrium. The PM spends the first part of the morning laying wreaths at the memorial to Raoul Wallenberg, the Swedish diplomat who saved tens of thousands of Jews from the Holocaust – a rather accusatory statue in Heroes' Square of a man of an age he probably never attained.

The PM gets a bit shirty when she is waylaid for a comment on the shooting of Air Chief Marshal Sir Peter Terry and Lady Terry, he the retired governor of Gibraltar, where the SAS shot three IRA terrorists a few years ago. A bit of a spat follows. I tell her life would be simpler if she cut out on-the-hoof stuff. She says we should protect her. I say there would be no need if she ignored the media. In fact, she knows she has made a bloomer by calling the IRA thugs and guerrillas, thereby conferring on them a spurious legitimacy. We soon get over it.

The PM spends an hour with PM Antall before a plenary session of Parliament – a truly splendid building on the banks of the Danube. She also has talks with President Árpád Göncz, just back from a visit to the USA, before calling in on the stock exchange at work. It is clearly a young person's game. We have a 'light' lunch with enthusiastic entrepreneurs before the PM calls on a china exhibition where the management is keen on a board/worker buy-out. My general impression is that Hungarian business wishes change would come faster.

A walkabout to the Embassy is as enthusiastic as ever. The evening reception at the Ambassador's residence is notable for my meeting with a Hungarian journalist formerly stationed in London.

On Thursday, we take off for Switzerland before the sun is up at 8.15 a.m. I am distressed to find graffiti in Berne. What is the world coming to when tidy Switzerland is affected by graffiti? I later learn that there is a drug problem in the capital and that the police look on benignly as addicts inject themselves in a park near Parliament.

In the Maison de Watteville, President of the Confederation Arnold Koller reveals the Swiss interest in getting closer to the EC but concern about any transition. He has a similar view to us of a wider EC and quotes extensively on this and the Gulf from the PM's recent speech in Aspen. It seems that Switzerland is coming out of its shell and readdressing its definition of neutrality. The PM pledges support in the EC–EFTA negotiations, which are going too slowly for the Swiss, and Swiss membership of the EC if they want it.

The media clearly do not like the Swiss and try to get the PM to criticise them for not spending more of their riches on helping the Middle East operation to drive Saddam out of Kuwait. The PM will have nothing to do with their mischief-making at the press conference.

At dinner with the President, I have a good time with a man from the Jura Mountains, where we have spent several holidays, and a Swiss civil servant who knows Hebden Bridge.

On Friday, we breakfast in a train's restaurant, taking us from Berne to Basel, to a Ciba-Geigy plant. Its chairman opens up with an over-long and cliché-ridden prepared welcome, which the PM unaccountably praises to the skies, though there were admittedly some good points in it. We are dogged during the day by trouble with sterling after the *Mail*'s misinterpretation of the PM's remarks on the ERM.

The PM then goes to some humdrum meetings with the cantonal president and the Swiss equivalent of the CBI and to a textile factory before we return to Zurich. The PM is staying on for a break with friends. We are back in Heathrow by 8.15 p.m.

Saturday's press does what it threatened to do with my briefing on the PM hoping to win a fourth term and not intending to be Leader of the Opposition again. The *FT* and *Sun* ignore the story, such as it is. The *Star*, *Independent* and *Guardian* don't count because they have not travelled and have relied on Chris Moncrieff's straightforward reporting on the PA. But *Today* and the *Mail* are sensationalist and the *Mirror* licentious. According to Charles Powell in Zug, the PM is up in arms about the *Mail*'s misreporting of her press conference remarks and wants me to write to its editor, David English. There is also some interest in the economy and a security review due next week.

I shift an enormous amount of paper at home before we take John and Christine to a restaurant to celebrate their wedding anniversary and John's PhD.

On Sunday, I prepare a digest of the press for the PM in Zug. The main issue is concern about a recession and a forecast that we shall be in the ERM by Christmas. The CBI tries to make our blood run cold with talk of a recession, bankruptcy and unemployment. I tell Gus O'Donnell, Treasury press secretary, that if I get the chance I will say that the CBI would carry more conviction if it did not give in so easily in wage negotiations and grossly overpay themselves as directors.

For the rest, I go (unsuccessfully) house hunting with John and Christine in Hartley Down, Purley.

WEEK 39: 24–30 SEPTEMBER

A late start because of a visit to the dentist. It turns out to be an easy day which ends with the PM, with her usual show of reluctance, giving an excellent interview to *Newsweek*. 'The dash for democracy' (in Central and Eastern Europe) and 'Thatcherism is not just for the '80s but for centuries' are just two of her quotes.

Earlier, I wrote a brief for the PM's visit to the Newspaper Press Fund's reception tomorrow. This year's appeal chairman, Ray Tindle, has raised £140,000 – a tremendous achievement for the owner of a chain of weekly newspapers.

I also clear the way for the conduct of my fellowship at Newcastle University with Professor Berrington. In preparation, Jean Caines from the DTI briefs me on the subject of government/industry communications. I have lunch with Chris Davidson of Guinness.

On Tuesday, it is so cold that I am shivering in my office even in a jumper by 11 a.m. Exceptionally, I put on the electric fan fire. I write a paper on communications strategy for John Wakeham for his talks with ministerial colleagues. He is gearing them up for an election. But Kenneth Baker calls in to discuss his suggestion that the election might be put off until 1992. Do I know what he is up to, he asks. Well, I think so, say I. You are making sure that, if a slow economic recovery causes the election to be put off, the government cannot be seen to be running scared since 1992 has always been part of your strategy.

I lunch with Adrian Lithgow from the *Mail on Sunday*, a well-spoken young man with more to him than meets the eye. In the afternoon, I prepare for a meeting with departmental heads of information tomorrow. Then I'm off with the PM to the NPF reception – her ninth consecutive visit – where she makes a rousing electioneering speech.

By the end of Wednesday I feel exceedingly plump after lunch at the Guildhall and dinner with Lord (Dick) Marsh at the Savoy. I feel better for having sorted out briefing for John Wakeham and worked on my impending speech to the Guild of British Newspaper editors' conference. But I do not feel better for reading the reception to the government's Environment White Paper. *Today*, the *Express*, *Mail*, and *Telegraph* are reasonable, but *The Independent* and *Guardian* are sour. The reality is that there is no satisfying some on this subject.

Lunch at the Guildhall with Peter Rigby. He has been trying to get me to one of their series since the PM was made an honorary freeman and I helped him with his anti-drugs campaign. He brings together an interesting collection of guests, including Sir Alan Bailey, Permanent Secretary at the Department of Transport.

My dinner with Lord Marsh and a number of PR practitioners is interesting, but I sometimes feel that Lord Marsh and I are the only two on song.

On Thursday, the press gives reasonable coverage to speeches by the PM and Chancellor in Washington. Their message comes through loud and clear: the government is utterly brassed off with the CBI clamouring for cuts in interest rates while raising their own costs by giving excessive pay increases to both themselves and their employees regardless of their ability to afford them.

Cabinet has a desultory discussion of the economy on the basis of a report by the Chancellor, just back from Washington. They are keen to align our retail price index with similar indices on the Continent when we join the ERM, probably in November. The Home Secretary has to report a bomb under the Speaker's chair at an anti-terrorism conference. How embarrassing! The police do not seem to have a lead on the IRA operating on the mainland. It is very worrying.

My lunch with David Frost is a jolly affair. He is a good host. A busy afternoon follows, answering calls about the Cabinet, a Cabinet committee meeting on the Gulf and an ad hoc meeting of ministers on security.

Crime, petrol prices and the economy are the main concerns in Friday's press. I do a press digest for the PM before I leave for Northampton to address another in the series of lunches given around the country by the Yorkshire building firm Shepherd's. I suppose I ought to be disturbed by their gloom. They say things are 'tight'; Shepherd's seem to be OK for now but are worried about six months down the track because people with building plans are shelving them.

Back in the office at 5.45 p.m. I hear from Michael Jones of the best MORI poll for a long time: a seven-point Labour lead. Later, a BBC poll finds Labour's lead has halved to five points. Are things beginning to come right for the government? At 6.30 p.m., Stella Speak (née Moss), who went to Hebden Bridge Grammar School with me and is over from Canada, comes in for a chat. She has a pronounced Canadian accent, quite unlike the one she was born with. It is good to hear from her and news of Jim Gibson, another schoolmate, who also lives in Mississauga, Ontario.

As we leave for New York and the UN at 10.15 a.m. on Saturday, I feel somewhat resentful about another lost weekend. I miss home. On the plane, the time passes quickly as I prepare for the visit, write a note for the PM on a speech she is to make in November and clear my briefcase.

We drive in from the airport to a sunny New York and install ourselves in the UN Plaza Hotel with the slow lifts. Mike Horne, now with British Information Services, New York, and a former No. 10 press officer, had hoped that I would go out for dinner with him, but our new Ambassador to the UN, David Hannay, collars me. When we get back to the hotel at 2.30 a.m. London time, I find that the PM has already met thirty heads of government at receptions.

We have superb views of the East River from the No. 10 office in the hotel. I cut out the PM's visit to a small church near the Waldorf with President and Mrs Bush. Instead, I go over to the UN for the opening of the session and see Peter Ustinov and Audrey Hepburn, a special UN Ambassador.

The PM gets applause in the middle of her contribution to the debate for emphasising the role and responsibility of parents for bringing up their children. She has two bilateral meetings during the afternoon with President Turgut Özal (Turkey) and PM Toshiki Kaifu (Japan). This gives me a new angle for an appreciative media – the PM's determination to insist that Iraq pays reparations for the systematic sacking of Kuwait. I brief again at 10.45 p.m. after extracting a great deal of information from the PM about the two and a half hours she has spent with President Bush. On the Gulf, the USA and the UK remain very close, with both moving towards a UN resolution on the use of force.

CHAPTER 22

OCTOBER 1990: THE TORY PARTY ON ITS WORST BEHAVIOUR

Things go from bad to worse, with inflation at 10.9 per cent, the Tories losing the late Ian Gow's Eastbourne seat to the Liberal Democrats just before his memorial service and some polls putting Labour fifteen points ahead – roughly double the lead last month.

If the month ends curiously on a high note because of the PM's performance in the House after an appalling EC summit in Rome, nobody kids themselves that things will get better with Sir Geoffrey Howe, Nigel Lawson and Michael Heseltine rumbling in the background, the Tory Party on its worst behaviour and some sections of the press arguing the PM is on her way out.

All this in spite of the government at last entering the ERM, bringing a 1 per cent fall in interest rates as evidence, we say, of the efficacy of the government's policies. But entry does not do the PM much good in media terms. The outlook is very unsettled.

Peter Morrison, the PM's PPS, tells me the PM has lost sleep over my tough minute on the government's plight. He tells her it is only because I love her that I wrote it. If this is Morrison's way of getting No. 10 laughing – his avowed intent – he may well succeed in spite of it all.

WEEK 40: 1–7 OCTOBER

A crowded day starting at 6 a.m. local time and ending 4 a.m. London time. I start early to brief the PM for her interviews with the four US breakfast TV networks. The brisk and workmanlike interviews give the British press an early story – notably the PM's firmness over Iraq and reparations and her manifest lukewarmness to German reunification, which is going to cause us trouble.

Afterwards, we breakfast with the PM in her room before bilaterals with Brian Mulroney (Canadian PM) and the Emir of Kuwait. The Emir has some appalling tales of Iraqis shooting Kuwaitis before their families.

At the UN, President Bush, looking tired after his dash back to Washington to try to settle the US Budget, gives a firm speech full of good phrases. The PM then has a chat with Foreign Secretary Hurd, who has been travelling endlessly, before her meeting with the UN Secretary General, Pérez de Cuéllar. The UNSG tries the PM's patience by bemoaning the lack of room for diplomacy in the Gulf. She then zaps the *Wall Street Journal* at an afternoon briefing for their 'misguided' attitudes to the UK's Hong Kong and Vietnamese boat people policies.

Back in chilly London on Tuesday at 8.30 a.m. after being lifted in from the airport by helicopter to Wellington Barracks. The helicopter sends the autumn leaves swirling. There is surprisingly little backlog and I go off to the Savoy for lunch with Kenneth Harris from *The Observer* with good conscience. He first offers the PM more money for a charity from ARCO through its UK head, Lod Cook, and then shows great interest in the PM's Aspen speech.

He follows with a frank briefing on Tiny Rowland's paranoia about his reputation and the trials of the sinking *Observer* under Rowland. He is clearly frustrated as a director of the Observer Trust at its lack of power to get rid of the editor, Donald Trelford, and doubts whether anyone else would take over as long as Lonrho owns it.

On the way home, I give Paul, a No. 10 driver, my 200 duty-free cigarettes. He says he is thinking of changing jobs – to become a platelayer on the Docklands Light Railway. I feel so tired on reaching home that I wonder why I am killing myself like this. I must have a medical check-up.

Our main interest on Wednesday is how Neil Kinnock's Labour Party conference speech is received. So far, he has had a poor conference, but I thought his speech yesterday would be treated better, given that the press has always been kinder about his performances than they strictly warranted. I am wrong. His words are badly received – except, of course, by the *Mirror* and to some extent *Today*. Even *The Guardian* and especially *The Independent* have serious reservations about its lack of substance. *The Times* is fascinating: it says that Labour is still the party of the public sector and vested interests – i.e. the unions.

I am worried that the arrest of three Irish people in connection with Ian Gow's murder may not stick. The police look to have made a bog of it. I brief Robin Butler for his lunch with the BBC and then I have lunch with Ken Cooper, chief executive of the British Library, who has great stories to tell. He is a former colleague at the Department of Employment.

The outstanding event of Thursday is positive news of the ERM and interest rates. At 6.30 p.m., Andrew Turnbull calls in to tell me the PM and Chancellor have decided to seek membership of the ERM and to cut interest rates by 1 per cent on Monday. We propose to enter at 2.95 DM, with 6 per cent either side, and to present it as an opportunity to cut interest rates created by the efficacy of government policy in slowing down the economy and taking the heat out of inflation.

I got a hint of this at 12.15 p.m. from the Chancellor, briefing me on the Cabinet. I asked him if we are likely to go in before November. He said yes but I would have to wait until he and the PM met later.

This news will put the Labour Party in limbo, cutting its economic policy from under its feet. I thought it would be far too gimmicky for the PM to announce it during next week's Tory Party conference.

During lunch at the Garrick, Eric Jacobs, my predecessor at both *The Guardian* and the Prices and Incomes Board, propositions me about working for his executive search firm when I retire. I have dinner with Brian Hill of Higgs and Hill, the construction firm, at the Node course reunion. His firm is going through a sticky patch.

We announce our ERM entry at 4 p.m. on Friday and I organise for the PM to go on the doorstep at 5.15 p.m. to catch the early evening radio and TV news bulletins. Earlier there was a bit of scare because of overnight news from Washington that the US Congress had rejected a Budget compromise. Andrew Turnbull assures me that we are not going to hesitate over ERM entry because of this and, as it turns out, there is no reason why we should have done in exchange rate terms.

For the rest, I see Anne Nash to keep abreast of GIS developments, brief a group from the Colgate University and lunch with the PA at Rules, where, to their embarrassment, the service is appalling.

At 3.10 p.m., the Chancellor rings me, and fifteen minutes later Gus O'Donnell briefs me and No. 10 press office on the impending announcement. I brief the PA, Reuters and AP at 4 p.m. on agreed lines. The PM does not like the line when she comes down to see me at 5.10 p.m., so we have another spat. I'm afraid we keep quarrelling these days. The announcement goes well.

Saturday's press welcomes entry on the whole except for *The Times*, which sees it as a triumph of politics over economics. The tabloids concentrate on the mortgage rate and the political effects of entry. The *FT* acts as apologist for ex-Chancellor Nigel Lawson, who claims inflation would be lower had the UK entered in 1985. The important point is that the government has seized the political initiative and signalled that the race is on for a fourth general election victory.

In the afternoon, I watch racing on TV and the Barbarians just beat Wales in an excellent game.

Considering that the press reception of entry has been negative for the PM, the Sunday press is just about as good as it could be. John Major is the hero of the hour and the impression is that he and Foreign Secretary Hurd have been more successful in persuading the PM to go in than Howe and Lawson, the latter having behaved rather badly over it. Editors are disgraceful. Having spent years arguing for entry, they now discover that the ERM is not a panacea and could be tough on us. What a shower!

I discover that Professor Berrington at Newcastle University has organised the police to protect me while I am up there.

This year is very prolific in conkers. Our horse chestnut tree is exceptionally fecund. You need a tin hat on walking under it. As a matter of interest I have decided to count them. So far the total is 6,636!

WEEK 41: 8–14 OCTOBER

It is the Tory Party conference, so Nancy and I are off to Hebden Bridge on a cold and frosty morning. We leave at 5.45 a.m. and are in Halifax by 9.15 a.m. We spend the morning with Nancy's sister and her husband, Ted. Drugs seem to be keeping Miriam's Parkinson's disease at bay. After a fish-and-chip lunch, I go to help my brother concrete the floor of a new cowshed. We lay 2.5 cubic metres in 2.5 hours. The cattle will rest on sand and straw, not the bare concrete. Another first-class dinner at the Hebden Lodge Hotel.

We go to Haworth on a drizzly Tuesday with the cloud down over Cockhill between Hebden Bridge and Haworth. We look around the village before lunch at the Black Bull, calling in at the Parsonage and The Apothecary, where Branwell Brontë is reputed to have bought his opium, and in the afternoon visit the Information Centre, the Brontë Gift Shop and the Weaving Shed, which is outrageously Scottish and where we buy a Brontë tweed. In the evening, I put the final touches to my talk in Newcastle upon Tyne tomorrow.

On Wednesday, we drive through the Yorkshire Dales, lost in mist, to Newcastle. By Leyburn it is fine and remains so. We have a good look round the Eldon Centre and then find the Special Branch awaiting our arrival at the Hospitality Inn opposite the

Northumbria, from which the police have moved us on security grounds. After being interviewed by the local paper, I give my lecture. Professor Berrington judges it to be a great success because of the way the audience filled in the allotted hour with questions.

The drive back home on Thursday is uneventful to Harrogate. We then get caught up in horrendous traffic problems around Wetherby. Still, we are home for 3 p.m. I ask No. 10 to send down to me the accumulated paper and I have virtually cleared it by 10 p.m. when John and Christine arrive to continue house hunting.

Back to work on Friday. The PM's party conference speech is longer on political knockabout and shorter on vision than usual. I then have to cope with an inflation rate of 10.9 per cent, which sets the pace for the next pensions and social security uplift. The PM announces the uplift in her speech, which is not helped by the activities of her deputy, Sir Geoffrey Howe, on Europe. He can only have intended to be creating difficulty for her with his reference to the need for the UK to be in the driving seat. Ted Heath's on-off trip to Iraq is also sent to try us. This government and Parliamentary Tory Party have a propensity for doing themselves damage. In spite of all this, Geoffrey Tucker (PR consultant and formerly the Tory Party's director of communications) is in good form at lunch in the Savoy. He offers to help when I retire and advises me to leave at the next election.

We have a useful meeting on handling the media in relation to the Gulf crisis – in short, how the media war is to be fought. I leave for home about 6 p.m.

Saturday is devoted to house hunting with John and Christine. They settle on a substantial semi in Riddlesdown Road, Purley. I believe they have got a bargain. We have dinner as a family at a Chinese restaurant in Croydon.

I dictate a digest of the Sunday press to the PM at Chequers. It is frankly very negative at the end of the Bournemouth party conference. It takes me a long time to compile because the papers are full of fables – as foreshadowed by Cecil Parkinson last night: Parkinson's dinner with Julia Langdon and Geoffrey Parkhouse; Foreign Secretary Hurd allegedly encouraging Ted Heath to go to Iraq; and the PM supposedly at loggerheads with Education Secretary John MacGregor over education.

WEEK 42: 15–21 OCTOBER

Just as the PM's week-ahead meeting is ending comes news that Mr Gorbachev has won the Nobel Peace Prize. I wander back into the Cabinet Room to hear the PM tell us, 'Terrific news. Richly deserved. Delighted.'

We are back into the old routine – two lobbies, the FPA briefing and the MIO meeting. John Chartres OBE TD, who covered the north for *The Times* when I was working there, and his wife come in for a chat on the eve of his investiture at Buckingham Palace.

I find myself on top of work. I lunch with Elinor Goodman (C4) and Philip Webster (*The Times*) at Simply Nico's, where the price is daylight robbery, though for admittedly good food. I have little to tell them, but I make the tactical point about the public expenditure round: no one can expect to get more from the Star Chamber than the Treasury, though there will be one or two who try. Employment Secretary Michael Howard, for example, is reported to be relishing the opportunity to make his case. That is the trouble with barristers.

PMQs on Tuesday – the first after the long recess – is not a raging success for the government. Dominic Morris, the PM's parliamentary affairs private secretary, thinks the PM was over-rehearsed. We certainly spent forty-five minutes with her on the ERM, on which Kinnock focuses, and it became clear that she does not take it too seriously. In rehearsal, she actually proposes to say that she would cheerfully set interest rates according to economic requirements rather than those of the currency. I tell her that there will be a lot of trouble if she does.

Several other things try us:

1.   Education Secretary John MacGregor cuts short a visit to Nottingham, causing speculation as to whether he has been recalled to be sacked, to settle his department's budget, or what? It turns out he returns to do some work.

2.   The Secondary Education Advisory Council leaks the postponement of a press conference on educational testing.

3.   Jim Coe, one of my former No. 10 deputies and now at the Department of Education, rings to say the Treasury is demanding a leak inquiry into his department's handling of the pay round; I suggest it is a blatant bit of pressure and to tell the Treasury to get stuffed, but I also urge them to settle their budget.

4.   Finally, *The Times* tells us it knows John MacGregor is coming in to see the PM tomorrow on educational testing; all this suggests that someone is not out to help MacGregor.

Wednesday brings disturbing news that Michael Jones, political editor of the *Sunday Times*, is in intensive care after a presumed heart attack. There but for the grace of God go I.

The American correspondents make for a lively briefing, mostly on the Gulf. They spend a lot of time probing Allied resolve. They are much worse in this respect than the lobby. Then off to the City Club, where I am received by two peers – Robert Carr, my former Secretary of State at the Department of Employment, and Tom Boardman. Cranley Onslow MP, chairman of the Tory 1922 Committee, presides and uses my wearing a Yorkshire tie as an excuse for calling me to open the batting. It is a daunting task. I take the opportunity to present my perspective on the next six months and sell the PM as the architect of the EC's revival and growing importance. I think I make some headway.

I have dinner with Neville Chamberlain and Harold Bolter (both BNFL), who offer me work when I retire. I have no hesitation in accepting.

The PM is supercharged at Thursday's PMQs. The press wonder what she had for lunch (soup and a sandwich). I blame myself for this because I have been feeding her indignation over Labour's cheek in assuming the high ground on education. She really goes for Kinnock and in the end calls him a crypto-Communist, which is predictably seen by the media as evidence that she is rattled. She is quite overcome by Labour's 'monstrous' posture as the pupils' friend when it is in hock to the teachers' unions and when so many Labour councils are against choice.

I have another drinks party in the evening for GIS as I steadily work through the roll call of 1,300 or so. This bunch is the most mature I have met in a long time. They wish there had been more time for questions and discussion at the preceding seminar.

We awake to news on Friday that the Tories have lost Ian Gow's seat in Eastbourne to the Liberal Democrats. It is a severe blow to the PM. On the other hand, a return to three-party politics could be a good thing for the Tories – or might be if they did not continue to behave self-destructively.

The Chief Whip is worried about the PM's crypto-Communist view of Kinnock. I tell him there is no point in trying to get her to apologise. In any case, Kinnock's handling of his party is almost Stalinist in getting rid of freely chosen candidates who do not suit his book. I send the PM a note of this conversation and the line I propose to take. Crypto-Communism tends to go away after Mr Speaker rules that it is not parliamentarily unacceptable.

I have lunch with a Polish journalist and a member of the Polish Foreign Service with Sarah Charman at the Polish Club in Princes Gate. My host, in the manner of a wise old owl, says that in the absence for centuries of the rule of law in Eastern Europe, proportional representation is probably unavoidable. Nancy and I have an enjoyable dinner with Fernand Auberjonois, European correspondent of the *Toledo Blade*, and his wife in their flat.

Saturday's press continues to be awful, with more inquests on the Eastbourne by-election and the threat (once more) of UK isolation in Europe. It is also a busy day for the duty press officer, with calls on the PM by Giulio Andreotti (Italian PM), preparing for a future

EC summit, and Yevgeny Primakov, Mr Gorbachev's envoy. Gardening takes up most of my time. The conker count is now 8,187.

The Sunday press is an appalling mess. The inquest on Eastbourne blames the Conservative Central Office and its chairman, Kenneth Baker; *The Observer* and *Independent* say the PM should go; and some think Ted Heath is bound to succeed in his mission to Iraq etc. I dispatch a highly distasteful press digest to the PM and then talk to Terry Perks and John Wakeham about the press before going to lunch with Ken Dodd, a journalist colleague from my Halifax and *Guardian* days, and his wife. I have to confess I am somewhat distracted over the meal by the government's predicament.

Michael Jones's wife, Sheila, rings me to say he is coming on well.

WEEK 43: 22–28 OCTOBER

It is a lovely autumn day for Ian Gow's memorial service, but frustratingly I find I cannot attend because it is an all-ticket affair. I use the time to write a tough, 'colloquial' minute to the PM on the government's declining fortunes and the need for more fire in its belly – a phrase I get from Paul Potts. I am trying to set up a meeting with the PM, John Wakeham, Peter Morrison, Andrew Turnbull and myself.

In the afternoon, I am called over to the Department of Energy because of a (non-existent) crisis over the Cullen Report on the Piper Alpha North Sea rig disaster. I resolve this and then preside over a short meeting of MIO.

Then I have to deal with a leak of a meeting on child benefit. It is amazing how these discussions get into the press.

On Tuesday, I find that my minute of yesterday to the PM, which I copied to Messrs Wakeham, Morrison and Turnbull, kept her awake. Things are not going right and the evidence is there for all to see in the treatment of the child benefit leak. I tell the lobby that they are only too willing to bring down tablets of invention from the mountain of ignorance. It is nonetheless damaging.

Social Security Secretary Tony Newton comes forward with a

mitigatory statement, but no sooner has he delivered it than another idiot leaks that child benefit will be frozen except for the first child. I begin to wonder whether the government party really wishes to win the next election, especially when ex-Chancellor Nigel Lawson, in a debate on ERM, seeks to justify himself in the worst possible way (for the government). I am very downcast. Even the PM tells me to cheer up. But all sorts of things are crowding in and I need to break free and do my own thing. Over the past few weeks life has got difficult.

We have three parliamentary statements on Wednesday: on the Gulf (Douglas Hurd); the social security uprating (Tony Newton); and IRA terrorism (Northern Ireland Secretary Peter Brooke). Brooke reports a devastating new approach to terror by the IRA – forcing hostages to drive at border posts with car bombs under them, killing six and injuring many more. A new depth to IRA depravity. I learned about it on the radio driving in to the office.

At 10.30 a.m. I go into the Cabinet Room to rehearse a line on all this. Child benefit has been so comprehensively leaked that it does not cause Newton too much trouble.

The American correspondents at 11.45 a.m. are incorrigible, spending much of the time probing for weakness in the PM's resolve. They do not find it. I remain concerned, however, about the EC Council in Rome at the weekend. The PM seems to be getting more belligerent the more adverse things become. I suppose she will calm down by Saturday.

Ted Heath comes home from Iraq with some forty hostages. I refuse to criticise him under media pressure. It does seem that he has honoured the humanitarian nature of his visit, though I am bound to say that I think his presence in Baghdad will have brought comfort to the Iraqi regime.

An outraged press on Thursday goes for the IRA, with the tabloids showing a more reliable sense of public opinion than the so-called qualities.

Peter Morrison tells me the PM is deeply hurt 'after all these years' with my minute on the government's position. He says he told her it is only because I love her that I wrote it. Steady on, Peter. We are supposed to discuss my minute with her after Cabinet, but this has to be postponed because she has a meeting on security and I have to give a briefing at the FCO on the weekend EC summit. The Metropolitan Police Commissioner, Sir Peter Imbert, rather advertises the security meeting by walking straight into No. 10 before the cameras. Eventually, a discussion of my paper is arranged for tomorrow at 9 a.m.

My FCO briefing goes well, only for later in the day Karl Otto Pöhl, chairman of the Bundesbank, to talk in a BBC broadcast about a two-speed Europe developing in Rome. Michael Heseltine also attacks the PM without naming her over her continuing refusal to get with it on Europe. Obviously Heseltine senses the PM is in trouble. We have got to get her out of it. I discuss how with the Chancellor, briefing me after Cabinet, and he agrees with my analysis. He wants to stabilise public spending at 40 per cent of GDP.

I spend the late afternoon on GIS succession planning.

Friday is a hard day as pressure builds in advance of the dreaded Rome summit. It starts with a meeting in my room with John Wakeham, Peter Morrison and Andrew Turnbull to agree a way ahead with the PM – namely, a supper with her after the forthcoming Queen's Speech.

Anne Nash seems to be very much on top of GIS management at a meeting before a lunchtime seminar and drinks for more members of the GIS.

In the afternoon, I brief myself for Rome and then the Sunday lobby. The main story to emerge is the PM's determination to see that when Saddam Hussein has been removed from Kuwait he is divested of chemical and biological weapons and prevented from acquiring nuclear arms.

Michael Jones rings me to say he is in pretty good shape after overdoing it in the garden yesterday. I tell him to take it easy. Murdo Maclean, private secretary to the Chief Whip, then comes in for a drink and repeats the idea of my becoming John Wakeham's assistant in the Lords.

Off on Saturday to a wet Rome for this wholly unnecessary summit. What a way to spend a weekend! We arrive in a thunderstorm for a meeting with President Mitterrand, who gets an ear-bashing for blocking a GATT mandate on agricultural products. (Some years ago, he told the PM over lunch in Rome, 'Ma cherie, but ze purpose of ze CAP is protectionist.') We do not make much headway, but the PM and I on her behalf work quite a bit of indignation out of our systems. In fact, the GATT issue has clothed the PM in white raiment, which may make her passage on the issue of political and economic union easier. I do three briefings in the course of the day – one late at night before I go to bed at 2 a.m.

I suppose I have no more than two hours' sleep overnight before today's summit wind-up session, but the press digest from London, shoved under my hotel room door, eases the pain. It gives the PM excellent coverage on the GATT issue. But we all know what will happen today when she is isolated 11–1 on political and economic union. The PM gives a Sunday lunchtime press conference in an appalling building and does an effective job in pouring contempt on all their Euro-pride for running away from a decision on GATT.

Back home to early darkened London – the clocks went back last night – after an appalling summit. The Italians are the worst kind of hosts, abusing the PM all weekend in a petty, disobliging way.

The best news of the day is Great Britain's Rugby League triumph over Australia. The worst is opinion polling putting Labour into a 15–16-point lead – roughly double that in September. The PM is depressed. I fear that the EC is going to haunt and trouble the government. Another difficult week lies ahead.

I feel much better on Monday (29 October) for eight hours' sleep, and the press is better than we expected. This is because the PM had a highly principled cause on the GATT mandate. Of course, some commentators, notably in the *Mirror* and *Guardian*, see the

PM as on her way out. But there are a number who express a great deal of sympathy and *The Times*'s leader is truly magnificent.

It is a fiercely busy day: the week-ahead meeting at 10 a.m.; the PM's meeting with Rupert Murdoch at noon; lunch with journalist Ronald Spark, who discloses that he is attacking Geoffrey Howe for his rebellious approach to the EC; then the FPA briefing, where I enjoy myself at the expense of the Italians, Germans and French – Count Paolo Filo della Torre, correspondent for *La Repubblica*, apologises for the Italians' behaviour in Rome, and I tell him that the Italian government has done itself great harm. Then a lobby at 4 p.m. followed by MIO at 5, and then meetings with journalist Chris Buckland and my Austrian friend Peter Weiser. The day ends with Nancy joining me at the PM's general reception at 7.30.

Europe has not gone away and I am appalled by the delusions of the Tory Party.

The PM lays on a superb performance at Tuesday's PMQs and statement on the Rome summit. It is another vintage, commanding performance which puts Kinnock in the shade. It is at times like this that all my doubts about continuing as press secretary disappear. I feel convinced it is right to be where I am.

My problem is that after thirty-one consecutive European summits I have no respect whatsoever left for the EC. It is one thing coping with international organisations that do not come within spitting distance of reality, but it is entirely another having to put up with the biggest band of brigands masquerading as idealists hell bent on 'union'.

I have a lively day of briefings and on the whole relish them even though I tell the PM at her 9 a.m. meeting that I am a bit worn by the exertions of the weekend. Dinner with David Illingworth, who is bearing up well after his redundancy.

The month ends with a superb press on Wednesday for the PM's performance in the House the day before. Even the opposition grudgingly admits that she was on top form. But even her strongest supporters wonder whether she is securing Britain's best long-term interests by her intransigent opposition to a single currency and central bank.

It would be nice to think that this morale-booster of a press at the end of a rough month signals an end to a bad period in the government's fortunes, but I doubt it. Geoffrey Howe, the marginalised, is widely reported as being on his way out because of the PM's approach to Europe.

The 11 a.m. lobby is boring, but I let the American correspondents have my – i.e. the PM's – views on Europe at full rip. I have an enjoyable and valuable talk with the Country Landowners Association over lunch. They present themselves as a reasonable body. I make suggestions as to how to pursue the development of the rural economy. The day ends with our hosting another party in my room for the Buckingham Palace press office.

CHAPTER 23

NOVEMBER 1990:
A GIANT BROUGHT
DOWN BY PYGMIES

The denouement: nothing becomes her more than the manner of her going; a giant brought down by pygmies. The month begins with Sir Geoffrey Howe's resignation and ends with John Major as the new PM.

In between, Michael Heseltine takes a fortnight to decide whether to challenge Mrs Thatcher and only throws his hat in the ring when Howe leaves him with no alternative with a devastating resignation speech. Up to then, opinion is divided as to whether the PM will be challenged.

Political opinion as to whether she will win is also divided, while we are all run off our feet with visits to a UN environmental conference in Geneva before the Queen's Speech and the Chancellor's Autumn Statement, then to Northern Ireland and finally to Paris for a CSCE conference to end the Cold War where she learns her fate. She fails to secure the necessary super-majority over Heseltine by a mere four votes.

The Cabinet says it will back her but thinks she will lose. She feels deserted and resigns on 22 November amid tears in Cabinet. But she recovers to make the speech of her life in a confidence debate and actually says she is enjoying it. I miss her departure from No. 10 because of a family funeral in Halifax.

She leaves No. 10 knowing that she is undefeated in the country and the Commons – only by her own side. I retire with the satisfaction of knowing that the trio principally involved in the long, slow assassination

– Heseltine, Lawson and Howe – discover, as Heseltine later puts it, that 'he who wields the knife never wears the crown'.

WEEK 44: 1–4 NOVEMBER

Geoffrey Howe, Lord President of the Council, Leader of the House and formally deputy Prime Minister, resigns. Nothing else matters.

Thursday starts quietly. Parliament is prorogued after a Lords revolt over dog registration ends in a whimper. Cabinet meets and Howe gets a handbagging because so few major Bills are ready for the Lords in the new session of Parliament. But no one gets any inkling of his intentions, even though it seems he has been brooding for days – or at least since Tuesday.

Then Murdo Maclean marches into my office just after 5 p.m. to tip me off not to go home early. Howe, he says, is with the PM in a very determined mood. Just how determined is revealed at 5.50 p.m. when he hands in his letter of resignation. I announce this at 6 p.m., and then issue the customary exchange of letters at 8.35 p.m., briefing Chris Moncrieff, the BBC and Sky TV. We work late into the night briefing the media. It is clear the PM is beleaguered by lesser people. The government is seen to be disintegrating before our very eyes. Kenneth Baker does well in rallying opinion through TV.

Friday's press sees the PM–Howe divorce as inevitable and there are suggestions that Norman Tebbit will be offered an opportunity to return to government after his departure to look after his wife, crippled by the 1984 IRA bombing of the Brighton conference hotel.

My day begins closeted with the PM, Andrew Turnbull, Charles Powell and, later, the Chief Whip in the PPS's room next to the Cabinet Room, debating her proposed reshuffle. She is determined to bring back Tebbit against the advice of the Chief Whip, who says it would make it all the harder to unite the party on Europe. Tebbit comes in via the Horse Guards' garden gate at 10.45 and turns down the opportunity of rejoining the Cabinet in order to care for his wife. The PM reverts to Plan B, which is well under way by the time I get to the Commons to speak at an Institute of Public Relations lunch. I run back after an enjoyable occasion to find the machine is two hours away from any announcement of the reshuffle, though C4 breaks the main changes at 4 p.m.

I go over to the House at 5 p.m. for what turns out to be an easy press conference, apart from the Tebbit issue. The working day ends with me, Terry Perks and Sarah Charman chatting to the PM for half an hour until 8.15 p.m., when we see her off to Chequers for the weekend. We try to encourage her, but the truth is that I am distressed.

Saturday is our wedding anniversary and I am delayed in rushing out to buy a card, chocolates and flowers for Nancy – such has been the past week – by telephone traffic on three main issues:

1. The Chancellor tips me off about a letter sent by Michael Heseltine to his constituency chairman in Henley. I tell Chris Moncrieff, who had not heard of it. Michael Jones, back at work, gives me the details of the letter, which I relay to the PM and Chancellor.
2. The mixed media reactions to Howe's resignation and a welcome for the PM's reshuffle, which I set out for her in a press digest along with calls by the *Mirror, Guardian, Independent* and the *FT* (more or less) for her to be gone.
3. Later, when asked, I describe Heseltine's letter to Moncrieff and Jones as typical of his operations when he is in trouble – he lights the blue touchpaper and retires to a safe distance – to Amman in Jordan in this case – to see what happens.

The going will be tough tomorrow and during the week ahead.

By the end of Sunday, I think we have deflected the venom from the PM to Heseltine. My quote about lighting the blue touchpaper comes over strongly. I carry on with a tough line after talking to the PM, who, notwithstanding a bad press and poor opinion polls, is robust and ebullient. During the day, I learn that junior ministers led by Michael Portillo and Francis Maude are active on behalf of the PM.

After giving Chris Moncrieff a line on the PM's conversation during the day with President Bush, I get to work on Kenneth Baker, the Chancellor and John Wakeham to move in hard behind the PM. John Wakeham is particularly effective with the media in his use of language. By 6 p.m. the bulletins are full of ministers rallying to the PM and defending her stance on Europe.

WEEK 45: 5–11 NOVEMBER

Monday's press reflects my hard work yesterday – the late rally of Cabinet ministers to the PM; the tough, defiant stance adopted by the PM; and my blue touchpaper remark. On the face of it, it looks as if Heseltine has made a serious error of judgement.

I continue the tough line in briefings during the day and at lunch with Nick Wood (*Times*), David Bradshaw (*Today*) and Peter Hooley (*Express*). Later in the afternoon, I learn that Heseltine's Henley constituency has moved against him. I tip off the press before we leave at 5 p.m. for an international environmental conference in Geneva, with Westminster in ferment and my having my little joke with them – the PM talking to Willie Whitelaw about the next ten years.

We dine on the plane from Northolt and have drinks with the Ambassador and Environment Secretary Chris Patten. I find only Simon Walters and Andy McSmith waiting for my briefing in the suite of the travelling No. 10 press officer, Philip Aylett. To bed at midnight, satisfied with my day's work.

I awake on Tuesday to snow on the Jura Mountains to read an enormously satisfying press digest from London. The PM thinks I have probably done enough, if not gone slightly over the top. I promise to cool it a bit.

The PM sees King Hussein of Jordan in the Palais des Nations. His fifty minutes with her are rather gloomy as he worries about the plight of Jordan's economy. He turns discussion of the environment into a prediction of ecological disaster if the balloon goes up in the Middle East and oilfields are put to the torch.

The PM's speech to the conference is the most profound and scientifically the most learned, but I cannot really say the journey is worthwhile, though she would have been castigated had she not turned up.

The flight home over the Jura, with distant views of Alpine peaks, is terrific. Back in No. 10, I learn that Heseltine's constituency chairman has told him to cool it.

The Queen's Speech on Wednesday makes for a testing day. By the time we open for business the PM has a good speech for the ensuing debate in the House; she worked on it on the plane last night. As expected, the American correspondents are interested only in the PM's personal position. I then go to the Commons for the PM's last-minute briefing before the debate. I tell her she has a good speech and that she should go for it. She wonders why so many ministers appear relaxed. Kinnock's speech is a disaster, partly because Tory MPs gossip while he is speaking. The PM wins hands down.

Later I get terribly shirty with John Harrison from the BBC, whom I suspect has briefed Tony Bevins of *The Independent* on my lobbies, which Bevins boycotts. This is against lobby rules.

Kenneth Baker turns out to be less sanguine about a challenge to the PM. He believes Heseltine will stand. Chris Moncrieff tells me he is in the doghouse with Heseltine for reporting his being rebuked by his constituency.

The PM gets a good Thursday press and Kinnock a bad one, but the main question is still whether Heseltine will or won't stand. David Frost rings from TV-am to say that they are about to put out a press notice recording that Heseltine has demanded not to be asked in any interview about the reaction of his constituency, Geoffrey Howe's resignation and the current political situation. Not surprisingly, they have rejected his terms.

The PM begins to appear even more statesmanlike when Tony Benn announces he is going to Baghdad for political as well as humanitarian reasons. The Labour Party is appalled.

I go over to the House to hear the Chancellor's Autumn Statement, which is well crafted and presented. Then I have visits from the Chancellor, Kenneth Baker and Chief Secretary Norman Lamont on the publication of the PM's renomination as party leader this evening. This puts me in a more difficult situation. As a member of the GIS, I can act only for the government and the PM, not the party in office or its leader. But the PM's nomination is for leadership of her party. She is still the PM and I must act for her in that capacity but keep out of any party matters. That does not stop the media from asking awkward questions.

The day ends with my having an excellent chat with Angela Rumbold, Home Office minister, in the House and Marshall Stewart, ex-BBC, repeating his offer of a lucrative job when I retire.

Friday is fraught. All the speculation about a challenge to the PM by Heseltine – Geoffrey Howe apparently having said he won't stand – is exhausting. So is the prospect of the PM's lunch with the BBC hierarchy – John Birt, John Cole, Jenny Abramsky etc. When I see her at 10 a.m., the PM works out her frustrations with the media on me. I tell her not to have a go at the BBC – or, if she feels so inclined, to keep it terse. In fact, she does not let them have it and on the whole the occasion is helpful.

The Sunday lobby is preoccupied with testing me on the PM's resolve and policy – is she a consolidator or a radical? – on Europe and then on a possible successor. I turn them away.

The Independent, via Tony Bevins, plays me false on Saturday. He twists a tale from yesterday's Sunday lobby into the PM endorsing Douglas Hurd as her favoured successor. I told the Sunday lobby, who threw names at me, that if she were run over by a bus – and to quote Lord Carrington the bus wouldn't dare – then Hurd, as a senior minister, would be among the favourites to succeed. I ring several members of the Sunday lobby to let them know of my outrage at this breaking of rules. They generally sympathise, so who leaked? I alert the Foreign Secretary, Chancellor and PM, and the PM regrets that I 'have to put up with all this'.

For the rest of Saturday I concentrate on domestic jobs, watch Australia's last-minute win over Great Britain in the Rugby League Test and go with Nancy for dinner with John and Jackie Shepherd, both fellow former pupils at Hebden Bridge Grammar School, at the RAC Club in Epsom.

Fortunately, the Sunday papers are delivered at 7 a.m., so I am clear of them by 9.30 and ring the PM at Chequers (in my pyjamas) to give her my impressions. I tell her I get the feeling that Heseltine will not stand, reporting that *The Observer* and its well-informed commentator, Alan Watkins, are of that view. I don't think she shares it. She is gearing herself up for a fight. She vouchsafes that if it runs to a second ballot, all is lost. Charles Powell seems to think Heseltine will not stand and relates to me the PM's concern about Willie Whitelaw and others coming out strongly on her side. I ring John Wakeham, who agrees that nothing more should be done today and that we will regroup tomorrow.

In the evening, I work on a GIS speech I am due to give in Leeds on 22 November.

WEEK 46: 12–18 NOVEMBER

I am now in a minority of one in believing that Heseltine will not stand, though sometimes so does Peter Morrison. John Wakeham sees the point of my argument – namely, that if Heseltine wants to be PM, he won't blow it now when he knows he cannot win without a contest. ITN concludes at 10 p.m. that the vast majority of Tory MPs don't want a contest and says the PM is not going to comment beyond that she is ready to take on all comers and win. She underlines this in her speech to the Lord Mayor's banquet, which is full of cricketing metaphors, hitting everyone and everything for six to all four corners of the table.

The PM's week-ahead meeting at 12.15 p.m. is far more relaxed than I ever expected. She clearly has good nerves. I lunch with lobby members Christopher Bell and Nick Assinder. Charles Lewington, who was also supposed to attend, has been dispatched to Hamburg to keep an eye on Heseltine.

My FPA briefing is notable for their rejection of the UK's EC credentials. I tell them to be careful about questioning our community spirit when we are one of the largest contributors to its funds.

The fateful day: Geoffrey Howe delivers his resignation speech on Tuesday. My emotions listening to his well-constructed statement are mixed. While I recognise that it will damage the PM – at least in the short term – I am equally sure that it reveals him as bitter, twisted and malevolent. How sad, bearing in mind how much he bore the heat and burden of the day in the early Thatcher years as Chancellor. I'd say the PM is sad, too.

As to substance, I ask myself whether Howe believes in the EC at any price while the PM looks after the UK's interests?

I lunch with ITN and feel bound to tell David Nicholas and Alastair Burnet that I have been told they will both be out by Christmas. They seem very relaxed since they have contracts until 1992–93. More important, they believe that the prime mover against them, Greg Dyke (LWT), has only 6 per cent of its stock and that other companies want to talk up their shares instead of having an upheaval.

I retell this to the PM, who says she will not help ITN if Nicholas and Burnet go. I tell her that is not the point: ITN is the BBC's only competitor.

By Wednesday, it is clear that Howe has made sure Heseltine contests the leadership. I still doubt whether he would have done so had Howe held his peace. The fact remains that the fat is in the fire and the PM needs to make the best of it. Heseltine announces his candidacy and the media get to work either to handicap him or to breeze him to victory.

I am greeted on my arrival for lunch at the *Mail*'s sumptuous new offices in Kensington High Street with news that Heseltine shrewdly wants to modify the community charge and possibly to remove education from local government to the taxpayer. There is nothing new in this, but it excites my hosts. Willie Whitelaw issues a statement in support of the PM after talking to me by phone in the *Mail*'s kitchen.

Everyone seems to enjoy lunch and one of the party suggests I would make a good successor to columnist George Gale! On my return to No. 10, I learn that Neil Kinnock has rung David English, editor of the *Mail*, inquiring whether I had been to pray for the PM.

In the evening, I give an interview to the *Yorkshire Post* while dancing to the tunes of several masters. I do hope my interviewer has not been put off.

Cabinet on Thursday turns out to be a happy affair at which all the normal conventions break down. The PM thanks the Cabinet for its support. The Chancellor, briefing me on the meeting, says he is preparing for a nasty wisdom tooth extraction which will keep him out of action at this crucial time. I commiserate with him. He hopes the PM will make it and feels strongly that she deserves to succeed, but he is clearly not bubbling over with confidence that she will. I thank him for standing by her as Howe addressed the House and tell him that No. 10 admires him for that.

The PM handles PMQs competently, after which I give a briefing at the FCO at 4.45 p.m. on this weekend's Conference on Security and Cooperation in Europe under the Helsinki Final Act in Paris to end the Cold War. David Nicholas tips me off that Bob Phillis of Carlton Communications is to join ITN as chief executive at some cost in salary. I then get caught up with the PM and do not get away until 9 p.m. She is concerned but not down.

John, back from defence correspondent duties in the Gulf, is waiting up for me.

On Friday we are off to Northern Ireland, without so much as a hint in the day's press that the PM is going there. After landing at a wet Aldergrove, we fly close to the ground to Enniskillen.

Charles Powell says this is the first time he has flown underground. Fermanagh looks to be under water. We have a dangerous trip in a vehicle to a border checkpoint and then to one of the most dangerous police stations in the province, at Kinawley, on the border south of Enniskillen.

These missions follow the PM's opening of an electronics factory, visiting the Spirit of Enniskillen Trust at a lovely theatre on the shores of Lough Erne and inspecting the Erneside shopping centre. After lunch at the barracks in Enniskillen, we embark on the fifth of eight helicopter flights during the day: to Holywood on Belfast's Golden Mile, to Lisburn to open a fire station and to Hillsborough, the seat of the provincial government, for a reception. The PM speaks as well at the end of the tour as at the beginning, but she is worn out and worried. I try to ease her fears that Foreign Secretary Hurd will stand against her.

Altogether, this has been the easiest and friendliest of many prime ministerial visits to the province – and certainly the wettest.

Saturday's papers are full of the possibility of Hurd standing if the PM falls. Peter Morrison organises a counter to all this in the form of a statement by the Foreign Secretary and Chancellor. The *Sunday Times* goes bad on the PM and *The Independent*, from its usual massive ignorance, tries to stir up the old idea of a referendum on the single currency. After noting all this, I record with some pleasure the coverage of the visit to Northern Ireland.

John rings me from Empingham, near Stamford, where Christine is on a course, to say that they have a keen prospective buyer for their house in Lymm.

I begin to have doubts whether the PM will win, even though Peter Morrison remains confident and ebullient. The press office has a difficult time handling the media when we are effectively hors de combat in a party election.

A most extraordinary week in British politics ends with the PM flying to Paris for the CSCE summit, which is being attended by President Bush and Mr Gorbachev. I organise a photocall in

Downing Street before we leave at 5.35 for Northolt. On arrival in Paris with the Foreign Secretary, we go to the Ambassador's residence to a warm welcome from Ewen and Sarah Fergusson. The PM relaxes over a scotch while Brian Mower, Hurd's spokesman, and I go next door to brief the media. They are interested only in the leadership election and its effect on the CSCE summit – or summits, for there is talk of EC/US/Canada and G7 leading economic nations meetings to put pressure on France and Germany over GATT and agricultural products.

The media are civil but determined to explore what the PM is going to do and how she is going to play the leadership election. It is fierce but friendly and all we can say is that she is the head of a team and confident of victory.

WEEK 47: 19–25 NOVEMBER

Monday is a curious day of waiting and hoping. It is also a nice day for the signing of an agreement in the Elysée Palace. We assemble in a room normally used for press conferences, and I find it interesting that the French, Germans, Americans and Russians are on the top table and the PM well down below the salt. I am assured that this is in the order they sit around the negotiating table. When the signing is over, it is fascinating to watch Mr Gorbachev work the room like a Western politician.

The PM talks to him and Ruud Lubbers (PM of the Netherlands); Michel Rocard (the French PM), Cardinal Casaroli (the Vatican's Secretary of State), and Brian Mulroney (PM of Canada). She attracts a lot of media attention. We lunch and dine well at the Embassy, and in between I do a lot of briefing, partly because I am asked to react to events in London. What will tomorrow bring?

Tuesday begins well enough, with the PM having a friendly, workmanlike, spirited and mutually understanding talk with Mr Gorbachev at the Russian Embassy's residence. The PM also sees President Mitterrand, who, like Gorbachev, will go along with a UN resolution on the use of force re. Kuwait. But Mitterrand draws a distinction between a UN resolution and a national decision in principle to commit troops.

The PM lunches with Mr Lubbers and his Foreign Minister, Hans van den Broek, and meets President Turgut Özal of Turkey. All this keeps her mind off events in London. She returns to the Embassy about 4.45 p.m. and we sit around over tea until she leaves for her room at 5.20 to prepare for the leadership election result.

We assemble in Peter Morrison's room at 6.10 p.m. He sits chatting to Alastair Goodlad, senior whip, on an open line to London while Charles Powell mans a reserve open line. The PM sits at a dressing table sipping a drink. The Ambassador presides and I prowl.

Suddenly Peter Morrison scribbles the result – Thatcher 204 (54.8 per cent), Heseltine 152 (40.9 per cent), leaving the PM four votes short of the required 15 per cent super-majority – saying, 'Not as good as we hoped.' His canvass gave the PM a solid victory, but he said she would be in trouble if his allowance of a 15 per cent lie factor was anywhere near accurate. It seems that the lot of them lied.

The PM has an elaborate graph, prepared last week, showing what she should say according to the vote. Failure to get the necessary majority requires her to say, 'I fight on. I fight to win,' to stop support haemorrhaging in London. Accordingly, she gets up, smooths her suit down and walks purposefully down a long, slippery staircase and across the reception hall to a door leading down to the assembled media pool – i.e. the selected few representing the media posse on the other side of the courtyard – to whom she will speak. Instead of waiting for me to give the all-clear, she marches through the door and down the steps to the pool, interrupting John Sergeant making a BBC broadcast.

As Brian Mower reminds me later, warning me of possible trouble, I have no status in these party political events. He does so after I rush down the steps after the PM because I see that a central microphone placed in the pool by the COI for the benefit of the vast mass of media on the other side of the courtyard has gone missing. Every journalist present, up against deadlines, needs to hear what is said. So I go in search of the mislaid mike and when it is restored the PM delivers her 'fight on to win' message.

Afterwards, I tell Brian Mower I had no place in the event but I do have a responsibility for the reputation of the government and the Embassy. Such is the media's sense of entitlement that there would have been a riot had the COI microphone not been in a position to relay the PM's remarks to the bulk of the media across the courtyard. Nonetheless, I expect I shall get hammered for helping them.

After this, the PM goes off to the CSCE conference dinner, where her host, President Mitterrand, and fellow guests are concerned about her position.

During the final session of the CSCE conference on Wednesday, Brian Mulroney comes up to me beside himself with anger and anxiety about the PM. He says repeatedly that anyone in Canada who loses three elections will get a statue erected in their memory, yet in Britain you can win three elections and be discarded. What is going on? I can think of only one answer: politics.

Mulroney's bewilderment is shared by other leaders. Lubbers shows a great deal of concern and affection for the PM. President Bush and Brian Mulroney are very supportive of her on TV.

As soon as the signing ceremony is over, the PM and her party leave for Orly Airport. Charles Powell and I are allocated the ambassadorial Rolls-Royce – the last Rolls, we say, we shall ride in for a long time. I tell Ambassador Fergusson on the tarmac that we shall not be coming back (with the PM).

Over lunch in No. 10 with John Wakeham, Norman Tebbit, John Moore, John MacGregor, Chief Whip Tim Renton and Cranley Onslow MP, the advice to the PM is inconclusive. No one has a better idea when Wakeham forces the issue of her fighting on than for her to say she will. Accordingly, I urge her to say just that as she leaves No. 10 for the House to report on the CSCE meeting.

Things then begin to unravel as she sees Cabinet ministers one by one. They say they will vote for her if she fights on but most of them fear she will lose. They urge her to open up the competition. Around 8.45 p.m., when she is starting to write her speech for tomorrow's confidence debate, she says with tears in her eyes that they are all deserting her. I am not sure I help by saying, 'We aren't.' I know all is up. Late at night I am chased at home by journalists – and persistently by *The Sun* – claiming they have it on good authority that the PM is resigning. I tell them that they may well be right but the formal and actual position is that she is sleeping on it.

Having done so, she announces her intention to resign on Thursday 22 November. She does so at 7.30 a.m. to Andrew Turnbull and Peter Morrison, and I am told immediately. I go up to her flat to see her at 8.05. She is very tearful but grateful for our support. Her mind is not on Cabinet papers she is supposed to be studying. Charles Powell and I reiterate our support, but in return she worries about what is going to happen to us. We tell her we'll be all right and to start thinking about herself for a change.

We find Denis Thatcher in good spirits over breakfast. Life may be returning to normal for him. He is dressed in black for the memorial service for Lady Home.

At 8.30 we meet the PM to brief her for PMQs prior to Cabinet at 9 a.m. What is normally a lively throng in the Cabinet ante-room is silent, full of foreboding or expectation. The PM breaks down reading the text of a press notice announcing her resignation but recovers in time to hold a reasonable Cabinet discussion in all the circumstances. It decides to reinforce the UK's Gulf contingent.

At about 11.30 the PM goes to see the Queen to tender her resignation. Sarah Charman ushers her into No. 10 and both break down. This is the repeated effect on each other during a long day. We all wonder after what Caroline Slocock, a private secretary to the PM, says was an awful Cabinet how the PM is going to get through PMQs and the confidence debate. But, displaying amazing powers of recovery, she succeeds with a mastery, courage and inner strength that makes it all the more distinguished a performance. She even says at one stage, 'I am enjoying this.' Nothing becomes her more than the manner of her going.

In view of this tragic turn of events, I clearly cannot go, as planned, to Leeds to give a lecture on behalf of the GIS. The COI, who are the formal hosts in Leeds, quickly arrange to film me reading my speech at a lectern – as I would in delivering a lecture – in my room. They then rush the film up to Leeds to screen at the event. This is the first and only time I have given a speech in absentia.

By Friday, all life has flushed out of No. 10 as letters and flowers flow in – flowers in such profusion that I get hay fever. There is a vast anger around that a giant, as Jim Wightman, the *Telegraph's* political editor, puts it in a letter to me, 'has been brought down by pygmies'. A reaction sets in against those who supported Heseltine, and Howe, I am glad to say, is identified as the real assassin.

I begin to work out my future, resolving to walk out immediately if Heseltine wins but possibly to stay on for a little longer to help either Gus O'Donnell or Brian Mower settle in if John Major or Douglas Hurd succeeds.

I meet the Sunday lobby for what I resolve to be the last time. They are all pretty decent and shake me by the hand as they file out of my room. It is a slightly emotional time. The PM decides to stay in London until tomorrow to plan her departure. It is highly therapeutic, deciding what goes where.

In the midst of all this, Nancy goes to Halifax to be with her sister Miriam, following the death of her husband, Ted O'Hara. I am at a loose end and dine in an Italian restaurant.

On Saturday I am drained and find it hard to get going. *The Independent* has an astonishing profile of me with a cartoon – astonishing for its kindness and the admission that they failed to break the lobby system. Do I qualify for plaudits now I am about to go?

In the morning, I pop next door to give Margaret Bromley more flowers from No. 10, which has become just like a florist's shop. In the afternoon, I talk to the Chancellor, who is confident of victory, and Gus O'Donnell and watch Australia deservedly retain the Rugby League Ashes against Great Britain.

The Sunday press suggests that John Major is doing well. I take a lot of calls – from Charles Powell; Lord Harris of High Cross, who wants academics in the Bruges Group to be elevated to the Lords in the resignation honours list; Philip Webster (*Times*); Ronald Spark (*Sun*); and the *Star* and *Express*, after a nauseating *World at One* interview with Heseltine which is shot through with hypocrisy and lying.

I discuss with Alan Frame of the *Express* another alliterative description of Heseltine in my Tonsorial, Technocrat and Toff summary of the candidates. He suggests 'TURD', which is rather unkind on Douglas Hurd.

I drive into No. 10 in the afternoon for the PM's farewell meetings or telephone chats with editors – Simon Jenkins (*The Times*), Kelvin MacKenzie (*Sun*) and Brian Hitchen (*Daily Star*). She is in good form and cheerfully signs two photos for Hitchen.

WEEK 48: 26 NOVEMBER–2 DECEMBER

All my efforts to get on top of the accumulated paper are set at nought by people kindly ringing me up to wish me well. I see Gus O'Donnell at 9 a.m. and Brian Mower at 11 to tell them how I propose to play the succession if either of their principals succeed. Both seem rather diffident about taking the job while hoping they will get the chance. The Chancellor clearly has Peter Riddell of *The Times* in mind as his chief press secretary.

I give the American correspondents what I think is a scintillating briefing before going off with three of their veterans – Don Cook, Frank Melville and Bill Tuohy – to the Garrick for lunch, where I meet Ian Aitken from *The Guardian* and Robin Day, who says I am 'yesterday's man' – as, indeed, I am. I then give a lively final briefing to the FPA, followed by a lobby briefing at which the chairman, Trevor Kavanagh (*Sun*), says he is hoping to arrange a lobby lunch for me next week. At 6 p.m., I brief MIO on my future and get a warm round of applause.

In the evening, I go to the PM's farewell party before conveying a message from her to ITN editors over dinner.

Tuesday is a heavy day. The Major camp seems very ebullient, but so was the PM's last week. There seems little doubt that Douglas Hurd is a poor third, but who is in the lead? After Mrs Thatcher's 15 per cent lie factor, who knows? It is against this background that the day's business is conducted. The PM decides this should be my last press digest before her final PMQs. She says she does not intend to be the Dame Nellie Melba of politics. It turns out to be an easy PMQs for her and she goes out in a dominating way.

I do both the morning and the afternoon lobbies and then have a splendid meeting with the regional lobby, who show their gratitude for my help over the years. News then comes through that Major has failed to get an overall majority by only two votes, but this is quickly followed by news of the withdrawal of both Heseltine and Hurd. We all pour into 11 Downing Street to congratulate Major, and the PM embraces him by the front door. I want the PM to go outside to say a few words of congratulation and support for her successor, but the idea pains the Major camp. This shows you how fearful they are that she will speak her mind.

On Wednesday, we go to Halifax for Ted's funeral and so miss Mrs Thatcher's departure from No. 10. The office awakens me at 5 a.m. and we are on the road by 5.30 and in Halifax by 9.45. By then, the Thatchers have gone to the Palace to take their leave of the Queen. I am told that her leaving of No. 10 was a traumatic event, but Terry Perks seems to have handled it admirably.

Ted's funeral is attended by a large number of parishioners and the service is deeply impressive. The priest is such a serious and sincere character that we have a largely tearless funeral. Ted is buried in the beautifully kept Luddenden Parish Church graveyard, literally beside a babbling brook.

Back in the office on Thursday, it is decided I should retire on 6 December after Andrew Turnbull suggests I play Gus O'Donnell in for a week. This is not before the director of establishments in the

Cabinet Office has his little game with me. He telephones to say he thinks my retiring is a bad idea. I say that, bad idea or not, I am resolved. I have had enough. He says I have got the wrong end of the stick: he wants to sack me. I protest that I have spent forty-odd years trying to avoid the sack. He says OK but what would I say if he was able to give me around £12,000 tax-free? I demand to be sacked immediately.

At 2 p.m., I see Robin Butler, who is extremely generous in his praise for the job I have done and says he will defend me in public. He hopes Mike Devereau, the putative new head of the GIS, and Brian Mower will organise a GIS lunch for me, which he would attend. I am already to have two GIS parties – one next week with departmental heads of information and another in January.

Michael Jones then rings me in an emotional state to say that the *Sunday Times* is planning a two-page feature based on an unauthorised biography of me – entitled *Good and Faithful Servant* – by Robert Harris. I let it be known that Harris should stick to fiction.

In among all this, I answer a myriad of telephone calls from well-wishers and others seeking interviews and start weeding files ruthlessly. The press office seems to be rather overwhelmed by the changeover. I leave early and take Christine to view their new home in Purley.

The *Mail on Sunday*, *Sunday Express* and *Times* pursue me on Friday about the Harris book, as do the *Washington Post*. I give them a dismissive quote and refuse *The Times*'s offer to review it. I do not intend to waste my powder and shot on Harris.

John Major and Richard Ryder, Mrs Thatcher's former political secretary, say they want to see me. When I see the new PM, I tell him of my resolve to retire. I would not want to taint him with my reputation and association with Mrs Thatcher.

I spend much of the day in between telephone calls replying to the mass of supportive letters. I also have the pleasure – my last – of showing John Round and his wife, Ruth, around No. 10. They are former fellow pupils in Hebden Bridge. We have lunch at the Reform.

On Saturday, I learn that Michael Jones has written a letter of resignation over the *Sunday Times*'s use of Robert Harris's book to denigrate me. I plead with him not to resign on my account. Then on his way into the office he collapses in the car park with another spasm. He is taken to hospital and ends up in his Lincoln's Inn flat, where I ring him while he is having a bath. Fortunately, his staff have suppressed his letter.

After this trauma, I help John and Christine to tidy up their garden at their new house and then watch Widnes beat Hull in the Rugby League Cup. In the evening, we pick up Nancy from church and go out for a Chinese dinner.

The *Sunday Times* does its worst to me – 'The hard man of No. 10' leads their news feature section. They also have an adulatory review of the book (not me) and a front-page piece by their executive editor, Brian MacArthur, a former *Yorkshire Post* colleague in Leeds, about my contribution to the Labour Party's *Leeds Weekly Citizen* in the 1960s under the pen name of Albion. I brush it all off. Michael Jones describes the MacArthur piece as 'McCarthyite'.

For the rest, it is gardening, watching sport on TV and dealing with forms associated with my retirement. I also receive solicitous calls from my friends Mohsin Ali in Washington and Peter Weiser in Vienna.

CHAPTER 24

DECEMBER 1990: WITHDRAWAL SYMPTOMS

Withdrawal symptoms afflict both Mrs Thatcher and myself. She regularly wonders when I go to see her how she could have led such a Tory Party. I formally retire on 6 December and then become absorbed in writing my memoirs on 19 December. By the New Year I have completed four chapters, but I am daunted by the task of delivering 120,000 words by 1 April 1991, as offers of jobs pour in.

On 14 December, I learn the PM has recommended me for a knighthood – a Knight Bachelor. Sir Bernard and Lady Ingham. What would our parents have said?

Mrs Thatcher discovers within a week – worryingly, for she cannot do much about it – that under the palsied hand of Hans-Dietrich Genscher, German Foreign Minister, sentiment against Iraq is softening. She is not giving up office easily.

WEEK 49: 3–9 DECEMBER

The Harris book does not carry through into Monday's press, apart from *The Times* and the provincials. Robin Oakley does a reasonable piece for *The Times* about 'Rasputin', as I am described. Thanks to Chris Moncrieff, the provincials give my side of the story.

There is a smell of appeasement in the Gulf within a week of Mrs Thatcher's departure and she is concerned about it when I see her at her Great College Street office after lunch at the Garrick with David Chipp and two Reuters colleagues. I there cut Ian Aitken for his piece in a C4 film, and he knows he has been cut.

Mrs Thatcher tells me she does not want to stay on in the Commons after the next election and does not wish to return to the Chamber, though she will vote. She wants to get her new office and affairs sorted out before she spends Christmas with friends in Zug. She will then join the lecture circuit to earn some money. Meanwhile, her son, Mark, has gone to Hong Kong to raise money for the Thatcher Foundation. She says I might care to work for it. I tell her that if I do, I don't need paying to help her.

Tuesday is an eventful day that leaves me contemplating a successful retirement. After weeding files at great speed – I find it depressing throwing away much of the past eleven years – I take a car to the *Express*, where Nick Lloyd, editor, and Paul Potts, deputy editor, offer me a Friday column. I tell them I would also like to write for the *Yorkshire Post* and see my future as a columnist if the civil service will permit it.

I lunch with Tony Cowgill, director of the British Management Data Foundation, who says he will put the word around member companies that I am available for hire. On then to Giles Gordon, my literary agent, who offers me a minimum of £20,000 for my first book about the job of chief press secretary. On top of this, Peter Morrison asks me to manage Mrs Thatcher's office.

On Wednesday, Giles Gordon rings me with a six-figure offer from HarperCollins and the *Sunday Times* if I can deliver a book of 120,000 words by 1 April. Nancy does not believe it – and neither do I. I start to work out how I can meet the deadline with my limited resources.

At 11.30, I go to see Geoffrey Tucker at his office near the Carlton Club. He offers me the use of his lawyer and accountant as well as his office and a loose arrangement by which he will steer three PR accounts my way. I reckon I can safeguard my current income, leaving aside the *Express* offer.

I get to the Gran Paradiso a little late for lunch with Ian Gillis, former head of information at the Department of Energy. He is his usual jolly self but very concerned about my future. On then to the COI to fill Mike Devereau in about high-flyers in the GIS before the announcement of his succeeding me as GIS head. He and his section heads generously set me up with drinks for the ACPO dinner at which Mrs Thatcher reintroduces me to Ronald Reagan, who is, I fear, beginning to fail.

Thursday is my last day in No. 10. I don't feel any regret. Instead, perhaps a sense of relief, though with a lingering nostalgia for the years gone by. Everyone is incredibly kind to me. I clear all my files and set up the arrangements for Mrs Thatcher's resignation honours briefing before going to the Reform for an interview with Tony Smith of the *Sunday Express*. I may be in trouble with the club's authorities because Smith tried to take notes of our conversation in public view.

Maureen Johnson presides at the Association of American Correspondents lunch for me at Brown's Hotel. It is a lively, warm, intimate occasion attended by some retired old-stagers, to whom I pay tribute. The association gives me two signed photos and an armada dish engraved with 'Bunkum and Balderdash'.

On then to an IOMU meeting, followed by a gathering of heads of information, which Mrs Thatcher joins. They shower me with gifts, and Robin Butler's handsome tribute unsettles me so much that I wonder whether I can get through my reply without breaking down. Somehow I manage it. One of the saddest things about leaving No. 10 is to remove my four paintings of my native heath by Donald Crossley from the walls of my office. They have adorned the office for almost as long as I have been there.

On Friday, Nancy and I drive to Durham via Halifax to visit Nancy's sister Miriam. We are going north for John's award of a history PhD. We leave at 5.45 a.m. and are in Halifax for 9.30. We stay with Miriam for ninety minutes before continuing our journey up through the Yorkshire Dales. The rain turns to sleet after lunch in the Devonshire Arms at Cracoe and had we lingered for coffee we might not have made it over and out of Wharfedale into Wensleydale, because the snow is intensifying at the top. We find John and Christine have been visiting old haunts in Durham all afternoon. We have dinner at Collingwood College as guests of Don Ratcliffe, John's tutor, and his wife.

John's graduations are guaranteed to bring bad weather. It hailed so heavily in midsummer when he got his BA that College Green in Durham was for a time ankle-deep in slush. Then his MA graduation in Ohio was marked by a fierce thunderstorm which drove us all inside. Now we have a northerly wind with rain, sleet and snow.

John looks magnificent in his scarlet robes and Tudor cap. He shakes the hand of Doris Lessing, the South African writer and later Nobel laureate for literature. We have a celebratory dinner at the Ramside.

WEEK 50: 10–16 DECEMBER

Before my seminar on government–industry communications at Newcastle University, we explore the Metrocentre at Gateshead, a more lavish affair than the Eldon Centre across the river. Again the university has sent Special Branch to protect us. I am not on top form – withdrawal symptoms, I suppose – but the seminar goes better than expected. Everyone contributes – many of them backers of my research. I am not sure what we learn except that government–industry communication is a problem from many angles. In the evening, I brief the politics department about Mrs Thatcher's demise. This leads to a lively exchange, especially between ardent Conservatives – Tony Cowgill (BMDF), David Kelly, a local busi-nessman who was with me on a course in 1978, and Geoffrey Tucker.

On Tuesday, we are back home in five and a half hours in spite of a jackknifed lorry on the A1 north of Darlington and other hold-ups on the A1 in Yorkshire. Just before we get home, Nancy tells me that the sale of John's house in Lymm has fallen through. She has been bottling this up since last night. Later, John and Christine say they intend to move to Purley next month whether their house has sold or not. Christine is keen to run my newly formed company – Bernard Ingham Communications.

Wednesday is an awful day. Retirement hits me. The central heating doesn't work, with a northerly gale blowing that kills six Scottish fishermen. A *Croydon Advertiser* journalist is late for an interview with me and goes to the wrong house in the bargain, and then when I drive into London I find I cannot park centrally and have to go up to Park Lane. I am twenty minutes late for a meeting with Mrs Thatcher, who looks pale and seems to be suffering from withdrawal symptoms. She says the enormity of the coup is beginning to hit her and wonders how she could have led such a party.

The COI asks me to organise a seminar for Eastern European politicians, who are having terrible trouble with their press. I go to the Reform Club with the intention of writing a synopsis for my proposed book. Instead, I am collared by Geoffrey Smith of *The Times* and Barbara Hosking, a former member of the GIS. I resolve never to drive into London again and never to go to the Reform to do some work.

I leave my car at home on Thursday and by evening I feel tired and my legs ache with all the walking I have done. At this rate I shall soon be extremely fit. Stuart Holland (*Glasgow Herald*) sees me on the train and helpfully points out that I can use my railway ticket on the Tube. You live and learn in retirement.

I deliver my synopsis to my agent, Giles Gordon. At lunch with the *Express*, Robin Morgan and Tony Smith offer me an interview feature slot every week. It is rather an attractive proposition but how on earth am I going to do all the work I am being offered? I then endure a two and a half-hour grilling by Sharon Boyle of the *Halifax Courier* in the Horseguards Hotel.

On Friday, I am informed I shall get a knighthood in Mrs Thatcher's resignation honours list. I get a call over lunch with Ian Gillis, asking me to collect a letter in connection with the honours. After picking it up, I run the gauntlet of some unpleasant politicians, civil servants and Commons staff who board the Tube for Victoria at Westminster. On the train, I open the letter and on arrival home tell Nancy she will be a Lady by Christmas.

In the evening, I write an article for the *Yorkshire Evening Post* (fee £75) and another labour of love – a 400-word valedictory to the GIS. And I still have a lot of Christmas cards to send.

Saturday starts badly with a call from Sarah Charman, on EU summit duty in Rome, to say that my former deputy and now Foreign Office spokesman Brian Mower has bowel cancer. I try all day to speak to his wife, Margaret, but do not manage to get through until 8 p.m. She is calm and collected but obviously distressed.

According to the *Sunday Telegraph*, journalists felt deprived of my presence in Rome. They were not deprived of Jacques Delors, who threatens a political crisis if the UK does not go along with his ideas for a single European currency. So much for a democratic Europe. Autocratic, more like. The *Sunday Telegraph* is critical of John Major for wanting to be liked and falling into the hands of PR chappies.

I begin to sort out my affairs and in the evening watch the film *The Mission*, starring Jeremy Irons and Robert de Niro – a haunting, cruel but beautiful film which, with its soundtrack, affects me greatly.

WEEK 51: 17–22 DECEMBER

If this is retirement, I have no time to stand and stare. Part of the morning is spent marshalling paper and my collection of press digests to help me with writing the book. I take the train to deliver my article to the *Sunday Express*. They like especially the ending, in which I record telling General Jaruzelski's spokesman, Jerzy Urban, who complains that Poles are very difficult to govern: 'If you think you have problems, try running Yorkshire County Cricket Club.' Back home, I write Christmas cards, reply to letters and organise my work schedule.

I take the train into London in persistent snow for a meeting with Neville Chamberlain, chief executive of BNFL, who offers me an attractive consultancy for two days a week. I settle there and then. On then to Mrs Thatcher's office, where she is having a meeting with Brian Griffiths, head of her former policy unit, and John Whittingdale, her political secretary. My discussion with her on her media programme is postponed until Friday.

After lunch with No. 10 press officers, I go to Hammersmith for a meeting with the top brass of HarperCollins about my proposed book. They are very enthusiastic about it and I fascinate them with tales of the good life with Mrs Thatcher.

On Wednesday, I start to write my book and complete the first chapter by 9 p.m. But I still see the task of finishing it by 1 April as a tall order in view of my limited research resources. I keep in touch with No. 10 press office for the gossip. I am suffering from withdrawal symptoms. John is having a very productive time reporting from the Gulf this week.

In between taking my car in for a service – and collecting it – as well as checking on John's new house, I make good progress on Thursday with Chapter 2 on my life in the Hebden Bridge that formed me. It is both a painful and a pleasurable task. Soon the calls start coming after No. 10 has announced the resignation honours list, on which Terry Perks fills me in fully. Its virtue is that it recognises the wonderful service given by No. 10 staff – messengers, cleaners, telephonists, typists etc.

The Independent, with a sarcastic edge to their voice, want to photograph me. I refuse. They cannot have it both ways – boycotting my briefings and then wanting my cooperation. I do, however, give the *Telegraph* a picture. *The Independent* nonetheless turn up – a reporter and a photographer – and try – and fail – to get a snatch picture. It is then warm congratulations on my knighthood all the way. I write a sentence of Chapter 2 and then another call comes in. It is some recompense for all my hard work and the sacrifices of my family, though I did not go to No. 10 for a bauble.

Sir Bernard and Lady Ingham. What would my lifelong Labour parents think? I doubt whether they would have objected to my working for Mrs Thatcher. After all, I worked for Tory governments in the 1970s. On the whole, the announcement goes down well in the press apart from one or two Tories grumbling about my inclusion. I drive into No. 10 to collect all my belongings, and the police have a great deal of fun calling me Sir Bernard. It is rather embarrassing.

I drop in on the IOMU party, complete with Mother Christmases in full rig. I then take my No. 10 secretary, Anne Allan, for a farewell lunch to the Howard before visiting Brian Mower in St Thomas's Hospital with two of his former Home Office staff. I find him in remarkably good form less than a week after the removal of a tumour, with chemotherapy to follow.

Nancy and I go to dinner on Saturday at the Monty Meths' in Oakwood, north London, with Geoffrey and Margit Goodman and Michael and Sheila Jones. The Meths and Goodmans are glad Mrs Thatcher has gone, but they have no confidence in Neil Kinnock. I feel rather drained over dinner because for the second night running I have not slept well, worrying about completing my book.

On Sunday, John brings me an Amstrad computer/word processor and teaches me how to use it. I feel much restored by late afternoon, having made excellent progress in getting Chapters 1 and 2 in type. Christine helps by sorting out my papers. In the evening, we all have dinner with Clive Branson, who has played an important part in John's development as a journalist, to discuss his idea of launching a European property publication. He wants me to be chairman. I reserve my position until I see the prospectus.

WEEK 52: 24–31 DECEMBER

Christmas Eve and Nancy's birthday. After reading the papers – I must keep up with the news – I rush out to collect birthday flowers for Nancy and we toast the milestone with champagne at lunchtime. Otherwise, it is a working day – in many ways enjoyable as I wander through my life in Hebden Bridge for Chapter 2. I write until 10 p.m. and later we go to midnight mass at John's former school, John Fisher, nearby. Father Fawcett takes the mass at such a measured pace that we do not get home until 1.30 a.m.

One of the worst Christmas Days I can remember – wild, wet and windy. I am so absorbed in writing Chapter 3 that I have to be reminded just before lunch that it is time to open presents. Christmas lunch is a great success and then I have a nap. Thereafter, I plough on with my writing, worrying from time to time how on earth I shall finish it in three months. Michael Jones tells me that Ted Heath has launched a severe attack on me in a *Sunday Telegraph* interview.

I write 1,000 words on Wednesday – wild, wet and windy again – before I decide to join John and my next-door neighbour, Ken Bromley, to watch Crystal Palace play Sunderland. We get soaked on the Holmesdale terrace but go home happy when Palace scrape home 2–1. We go with John and Christine for our usual Boxing Day tea at the Redhill home of Nancy's brother and his wife.

I finish Chapter 3 on Thursday, having written nearly 3,000 words during the day. It covers my early years in journalism and is designed to show how I was formed. I am cramming in a great deal, but there is much more I could write if I did not discipline myself. John's Amstrad is a boon. I would not have made this progress without it. Already I have 10,000 words in type, though I am still not yet up to the schedule required by 120,000 words by 1 April. But I am in business with Christine's help.

Because the newspapers arrive late on Friday, I write thirty letters of thanks to well-wishers. I do not start Chapter 4 – my life in Halifax – until after lunch. I spend the next eight hours reminiscing through the 1950s, which I spent there.

On Saturday, I venture out only to take Nancy to church. I hope to finish Chapter 4 by New Year's Eve. War in the Gulf looks ever more likely.

It is nose to the grindstone on Sunday and by the end of the day

Chapter 4 is in type. I am now poised to write about my days in Leeds with the *Yorkshire Post* and *The Guardian*. On the whole, I am satisfied with my progress, but there is so much more to write – the writing of which will be more difficult – that I remain haunted. I have a break at 3 p.m. to watch Crystal Palace beat Liverpool.

New Year's Eve takes my book up to 1960. I would have made more progress had I not become fascinated reading my newspaper cuttings from the late 1950s. It has been quite a year and I never expected to be writing my memoirs so soon. But here I am, battling on with the rough stuff to write still to come. I ring Brian Mower, who, I judge, is a little depressed because of his failure to put on weight.

Nothing much else seems to be happening except that the EC under German Foreign Secretary Hans-Dietrich Genscher's palsied hand looks to be going soft on Iraq.

EPILOGUE

It is now virtually thirty years since the events set out in this book. During that time, I have been as busy as ever, until a lifetime's asthma caught up with me in 2012. Since then, shortness of breath has much restricted my activities and mobility.

Before I was forced to retire, I entered the third stage of my life in the communications business. I wrote six books – four on Yorkshire and two on official communications, entitled *Kill the Messenger* and *The Wages of Spin*. After twenty-five years, I returned to Fleet Street, writing columns for the *Daily Express* and also for *PR Week* and the *Hebden Bridge Times*, on which I started my career in 1948. I still write a weekly political column for the *Yorkshire Post*.

I formed my own communications company, was a director of McDonald's UK and the media company Hill and Knowlton and became a consultant to British Nuclear Fuels Ltd. Later, I was secretary of Supporters of Nuclear Energy for ten years.

Among all this, I ran a media course for Queen Mary and Westfield College in London and was in heavy demand as a speaker and broadcaster. For twenty years, I travelled the world with my late wife, working as a speaker on cruise liners on the Thatcher years.

In academia, I held honorary posts at Newcastle upon Tyne, Huddersfield and Middlesex Universities and honorary doctorates were conferred on me by Middlesex, Bradford and Buckingham Universities – the last by Lady Thatcher when she was Buckingham's Chancellor.

At the same time, I kept a critical eye on government communications, and my book *The Wages of Spin* is a critique of the approach by the Blair and Brown governments to communication. It is sometimes ignorantly said that I was the first spin doctor. In fact, I regard 'spin doctor' as a term of abuse. Its practice – guided entirely by tactical advantage regardless of longer-term consequences – has done much to damage the credibility of politicians. They have still to recover it.

Looking back over three decades, I am struck by how only the technology seems to have changed. I did my press secretary job without a mobile phone or the tyranny of the computer. We were issued with word processors in No. 10 during the latter half of Margaret Thatcher's tenure, but, as one never at home with technology, I quickly ditched it. I found I could write or dictate far faster.

Now I sometimes wonder whether government communications are more governed by the continuous chatter of the internet than by the needs of the print and broadcast media, which are, as a consequence, in alarming decline. The implications of this for newspapers – and certainly for the local and provincial press – are grim. And, for the same reason, democracy is in danger at the hands of unelected pressure groups and all those who would try to subvert the will of the people.

Worse still, dialogue – if it can be described as such – is routinely conducted with a coarseness and foul language that underlines the decline in standards. Why, Tory MP Jacob Rees-Mogg is mocked for his courtesy as a political opponent as well as for his sartorial elegance of another age.

It has all been a very bad bargain for the taxpayer. Never let it be said that technology destroys jobs on the evidence of the past thirty years. Whereas No. 10 managed throughout the 1980s with a press office of eight, including two secretaries and an office manager, my last count of media-based jobs associated with No. 10 was fifty-three. It may not be a strictly accurate figure but it is not far out and it underlines the preoccupation these days with what I have already described as the tyranny of the net.

Whatever the cackle and cacophony of social media, what matters is what the government of the day is doing and the public's perception of its works. It is up to government to find a way of explaining itself to the world in a manner that carries conviction. It still has the opportunity, unrivalled in other eras, of getting out its message.

In short, I am thoroughly disgruntled with the defensive response to the internet and social media. My friends say I am an old fogey – and in that they are undoubtedly right – but surely governments should pay closer attention to what and how they are presenting their works than to their paranoia about rebutting social media gossip.

Labour leader Jeremy Corbyn and his Momentum machine certainly present the greatest threat to our economy and freedom than we have encountered since World War II. But you would not know it from the cavalier behaviour of the Parliamentary Tory Party over Brexit.

In this – and what it says about their self-confidence – nothing seems to have changed since 1990. As you will have read here, I often told Mrs Thatcher that her parliamentary party was her worst enemy. I think she came to accept this when it ditched her after winning three consecutive elections.

But didn't Winston Churchill tell a bright young MP who espied the enemy opposite in the Commons that they were the opposition; the enemy was behind him? And what about the treatment of John Major by those he called 'bastards'?

The Parliamentary Tory Party has probably never had the once-claimed loyalty and discipline of the Brigade of Guards. But its capacity for treachery against its Prime Minister in extremis seems to be unbounded. I am not asking for blind obedience. Policies should be subject to vigorous examination and debate. But issues are best settled in official meetings, not played out publicly by protagonists.

Moreover, everything now seems to leak. In my day there was perhaps a limit to ministerial incontinence. Now I cannot remember when I last heard of a leak inquiry, probably for the very good reason that the government machine would do little else but inquire into breaches of collective responsibility.

But perhaps my greatest concern is the continued lack of national confidence in Westminster and Whitehall. Soon after Mrs Thatcher entered No. 10, she told me that she was fed up with people telling her, 'Oh, Prime Minister, you can't do that, they [whoever they may be] won't allow it.'

By 1979, very few people thought Britain was governable any more. During the 1970s there were nearly 26,000 strikes, costing 128 million working days. We were going downhill fast and employers were tyrannised into conceding pay increases they could not afford in order to avoid another stoppage. It was said that the establishment was so comprehensively defeated that the only thing it was good for was managing national decline.

Mrs Thatcher set out to defeat the establishment's defeatism, and let it be said the nation perked up after the successful campaign to recover the Falklands and ending the abuse of power by trade union barons.

But she was up against one undeniable handicap: the European Community, as it then was. Leaving aside the false prospectus presented by Edward Heath, we entered the common market because it was believed we needed to be inside a relatively more successful bloc. We had lost confidence in our ability to secure economic success unaided.

The conduct of the Brexit debate has demonstrated all too clearly that the elite's loss of confidence, which assailed Mrs Thatcher in 1979, is still with us. The majority of our parliamentarians – Labour as well as Tory – seem bereft of any belief that British might, just might, recover their nerve and verve outside the EU.

This is a bleak conclusion to reach after a privileged life in which the hard work in No. 10 was tempered by much enjoyment and support from a loyal staff. But then, as you have seen, politicians were sent to try to condemn me.

I now revel in their calling me 'a rough-spoken Yorkshire Rasputin' (John Biffen), 'the sewer but not the sewerage' (Biffen again) and 'a menace to the constitution' (Edward Heath). They added to the gaiety of the nation, if not its welfare.

INDEX

Notes are denoted by the use of 'n' after the page number. Margaret Thatcher is PM throughout and Bernard Ingham is BI.